S0-DRF-156

# TABLE OF CONTENTS

# LIST OF TABLES

# TABLE OF FIGURES

# PREFACE

Effective managers in sport, tourism, and leisure service organizations are required to have a wide variety of skills and a good understanding of all of the resources that they manage. Not only should they be competent as personnel managers, but they also need to know how to manage their physical facilities. In addition, they need to be effective in their management of time, for time is one resource that cannot be renewed. Good managers also need to know how to use their financial resources effectively.

Throughout the history of our profession, there have never been times of such great prosperity that decisions could be made or practices maintained without consideration of their financial implications. Certainly, there have been situations where financial constraints have been minimal, but even then, some measure of financial accountability has been required of those who receive and spend an organization's money.

Similarly, there has never been a time of such flexibility that some degree of planning was not required of resource managers. In fact, experience has shown that a lack of planning reduces flexibility, as choices are replaced by externally controlled consequences. Budgeting and long-term financial planning are areas of understanding and skill that every sport, tourism, and leisure service manager must develop and magnify.

This book has been written with the needs of the sport, tourism, and leisure service manager in mind. It has been written by two people who have worked in a variety of sport, tourism, and leisure settings in several different parts of the United States and Canada and who have discovered that there is no place to hide from the opportunity or responsibility to know about budgets, finance, and fiscal management. It has been written for the mathematically challenged, for the pre-professional, for the professional who received on-the-job training, and for the professional who is keenly interested in and dedicated to continuous improvement.

Readers will learn important principles of economics and finance. They will also learn the skills necessary to prepare, present, and manage budgets, as well as generate revenues for capital development and day-to-day operations. Discussions include examples from the "real world" and offer illustrations to facilitate the learning of some of the more complex or technical points.

# SECTION A

# Financial Management
# in Context

The first four chapters present a discussion and comparison of the types and settings of organizations that most need the principles and practices explored in this book. After an introductory examination of the general differences between sport, tourism, and leisure service organizations that operate in public, private, not-for-profit, and commercial environments, complete chapters are dedicated to special financial management concerns in public and private not-for-profit recreation and sport organizations, and in tourism and commercial recreation enterprises.

# CHAPTER 1

# Financial Management in
# Public, Private Not-for-Profit, and Commercial Sport,
# Tourism, and Leisure Service Organizations

## Introduction

Approaches to the management of financial resources in sport, tourism, and leisure service organizations vary greatly, depending on the mandate and goals of the organizations, as well as the political environments in which they operate. However, almost every sport, tourism, or leisure service organization can be classified as either a *public, private not-for-profit,* or *commercial* enterprise, and each type of organization has unique and uniquely common features that relate directly to financial management and budgeting.

This brief chapter examines the finance-related differences between the three types of sport, tourism, and leisure enterprises and explores related legislative/legal parameters, social roles/expectations, market management techniques, indicators of success, and particular financial management opportunities and challenges. A concluding discussion focuses

on competition and cooperation between sport, tourism, and leisure service organizations of different types. In devoting this discussion to the unique characteristics and differences among public, private not-for-profit, and commercial sport, tourism, and leisure service organizations, there is a danger that their many important similarities will be ignored. Such is not the intent of this chapter. Although it is important to understand the differences, it is just as important to acknowledge the common principles, practices, structures, and competencies associated with financial management. Those similarities will receive ample attention in subsequent chapters.

## Public Enterprises

A sport, tourism, and leisure service enterprise operating in the public sector generally has a broad mandate to provide services that directly or indirectly benefit an entire community. The organization is usually an arm of government (e.g., a municipal recreation department, a public educational institution, or a convention and visitors bureau) that is charged with enhancing the quality of life of its patrons by providing enriching experiences and remedying social problems. The "public" nature of the organization is not only emphasized in its nondiscriminatory offering and delivery of services, but also in the nondiscriminatory way by which its operating funds are expropriated. Public sport, tourism, and leisure service organizations receive their base financial resources from the public through taxation. They may also charge fees and receive gratuitous income from private sources; but the foundation of their support is the ability of government to meet its operational goals by taxing its constituents or those who fall within its taxation jurisdiction.

### Legislative/Legal Parameters

In order for the governing body of a public sport, tourism, or leisure service organization to compel its constituents to contribute funds to support the operation of that organization, it must first win a legal right to levy taxes and to use those taxes for such purposes. The U.S. Constitution sets the legal parameters for the federal government to collect and use public funds for sport, tourism, and leisure services. The federal system also provides for the establishment and public funding of state and local governments and government programs. State governments must have their own constitutional provisions for taxation and public funding of sport, tourism, and leisure services. Local (i.e., municipal) governments, on the other hand, may extend public financial support to sport, tourism, and leisure services only if the state government already has enacted appropriate enabling legislation.

### Social Roles/Expectations

Public sport, tourism, and leisure service organizations exist for the purpose of meeting social needs. The taxpaying public expects sport, tourism, and leisure service organizations to be engaged in enterprises and programs that use public funds for the common good and for community betterment. Within the community, there is general acceptance and tolerance of certain services receiving tax subsidies, and many low-cost or free (i.e., completely subsidized) services (e.g., neighborhood parks) are expected, demanded, and even required as basic elements of social order and as important tools in social engineering.

### Market Management Techniques

Modern practices of sport, tourism, and leisure service organizations include market segmentation and target marketing. Public organizations use "need" rather than "profit potential" as the primary segmentation criterion in their marketing efforts. Products, prices, and promotional strategies are established in consideration of the desire to appeal to as many as possible in the community who need the service. Distribution considerations also reflect the priority of the public sector organization to ensure service delivery to as broad a market as possible. For example, when faced with a new private or commercial sector competitor, a public agency may choose to withdraw from the marketplace—not because it is unable to compete, but because the competitor has demonstrated that it can meet the same needs without tax support and, perhaps, with greater efficiency. The marketing objective of the public sport, tourism, or leisure service organization is either to provide the benefit or to accommodate its provision by another appropriate supplier.

## Indicators of Success

Financial managers in the public sector measure their success by comparing their achievements to their goals. That is also true of financial managers in the private not-for-profit and commercial sectors, but the goals of the latter organizations are more precisely associated with financial returns on financial investments. Public financial managers focus on achieving targeted levels of revenue and expenditure and on the social and economic benefits realized by those expenditures.

## Financial Management Opportunities and Challenges

Public sport, tourism, and leisure service organizations enjoy several opportunities that are unique to their sector. One opportunity is that of tax exemption. By convention, no government may charge taxes to a government at another level, which means that the local public agency has greater purchasing power due to being exempt from state or federal sales taxes. Another opportunity lies in the ability of the public institution to borrow money for capital projects. The government is a low-risk borrower, primarily because it can use its taxing power and its access to the taxable wealth of the community as collateral. A third opportunity enjoyed by the public sector is the goodwill and altruistic behavior of people in the community. Actively encouraged and supported volunteer programs provide human resources without the loss of the sport, tourism, and leisure service organization's financial resources.

A challenge experienced by financial managers in the public sector is the scrutiny of and accountability to the public and to other legislative/regulatory bodies. True to the democratic ideal, citizens voice their views about how their taxes are being used, and there is always someone who was not elected who is certain that he or she could do a better job. The close scrutiny of financial management also comes from other formal organizations or agencies whose job it is to ensure that the public treasury is being properly managed. This close scrutiny is usually facilitated by seemingly countless forms and reports which the financial manager must take time to complete. A second challenge comes in the form of changing political winds. Financial management in the public sector requires sensitivity to the political environment, and changes in political priorities may require readjustment of financial plans or management structures.

## Other

Two other aspects of financial management in the public sector require a brief mention before looking at financial management in the private not-for-profit sector. One aspect concerns the advantage that comes to the public sport, tourism, or leisure service organization by virtue of its taxing authority—an advantage over competitors or would-be competitors that cannot compete because they must raise capital funds at market prices *and* pay taxes to their competitor, the public agency. In many cases, the charge of unfair competition leveled at the public sector may be well deserved. The second aspect concerns the belief in the private sector that, because of the seemingly unchecked taxing power of government, the public sport, tourism, and leisure service organization has "deep pockets." Therefore, the reasoning goes, only public agencies can or should be expected to raise the capital necessary to build and maintain such major facilities as a 100,000-seat sports stadium or domed arena. Financial managers in the public sector are, however, quite aware of the limitations of public tolerance for taxation and have shortened their reach into the taxpayers' pockets. Sometimes this restraint has been self-imposed, and sometimes it has resulted from public pressure and sentiment, such as that expressed in several landmark propositions passed by voters in recent years.

## Private Not-for-Profit Enterprises

The private not-for-profit sector is composed of organizations that provide sport, tourism, and leisure services without the direct support of public funds and without the requirement to generate increased personal wealth for any owners or investors. These organizations are private in the sense that they are not owned or directed by government. They are not-for-profit in the sense that they must generate income to at least cover their expenses, yet do not generate profits for the purpose of making anybody richer. They may make a profit from certain enterprises, but overall profit is not the goal, and any profits that are realized are used to maintain or enhance the viability of the organization. Private not-for-profit sport and leisure service organizations exist to meet the service needs of selected consumers in situations where the public sector is either unwilling or unable to function, and where commercial organizations are also either unwilling or unable to conduct business. Well-known examples of private not-for-profit sport, tourism, and leisure service organizations include the YMCA, local church groups, community sport and athletic

associations, recreation clubs, Boys and Girls Clubs, Boy Scouts of America, Girl Scouts, Chambers of Commerce, Historical Societies, and Destination Marketing Organizations.

Private not-for-profit organizations receive financial resources from membership fees, fundraising projects, donations, grants, and user fees. Their need for money from such sources is reduced considerably by the ability of private not-for-profit organizations to attract and keep committed volunteers. After religious organizations (which also offer many recreational programs), community sport and leisure organizations receive the greatest share of volunteer support in the United States and Canada.

### Legislative/Legal Parameters

Private not-for-profit organizations are permitted to operate because of several important laws that free them from some of the restrictive controls that otherwise encumber public and commercial operations. For example, most private not-for-profit sport, tourism, and leisure service organizations enjoy a tax-free status. Additionally, the U.S. Postal Service and most commercial retailers and service suppliers offer specially reduced rates for recognized not-for-profit organizations. Federal and state income tax laws also encourage individuals and corporations to donate to charitable not-for-profit organizations by recognizing tax deductions or offering tax credits according to the amounts donated. In order for a donor to apply for such a tax benefit, the donation must go to an organization that is registered with the Internal Revenue Service as a 501(c3) Charitable Organization. Other state and federal tax law provisions also exist to support the valued work of private not-for-profit organizations.

In addition to filing with the IRS, all private not-for-profit sport, tourism, and leisure service organizations need to be properly constituted and registered as corporate entities. This registration may need to be with local, state, and/or federal agencies that regulate the operations of commercial and not-for-profit organizations.

### Social Roles/Expectations

Like public agencies, private not-for-profit sport, tourism, and leisure service organizations exist to meet social needs. However, they are more selective in the needs that they try to meet. Usually, a private not-for-profit organization is identified with a single "cause" or specific interest, such as helping at-risk youth, strengthening families, promoting mass involvement in camping, developing coaching skills for basketball, promoting literacy, encouraging historic preservation and interpretation, or promoting visitation.

### Market Management Techniques

The relatively narrow focus of the not-for-profit organization tends to restrict the scope of its market and dictate the techniques it must use to effectively and appropriately manage the consumption process. The identity of the client base is readily established by the needs or the shared interactions of the people with the target needs. Pricing decisions reflect the requirement to break even or generate modest profits when additional money is needed for other service activities of the organization. Service allocation for private not-for-profit sport, tourism, and leisure service organizations is based primarily on need, with little regard for merit or profit potential.

### Indicators of Success

Financial managers in the private not-for-profit sector measure their success by comparing their achievements to their goals. That is also true of financial managers in the public and commercial sectors; however, the goals of the public organizations are not at all associated with financial returns on financial investments, while the overarching goal of commercial sector organizations is to make as much money as possible for the owner(s). Private not-for-profit financial managers focus on achieving social benefits while generating enough revenue and other resources (e.g., volunteers) to stay in operation and continue benefiting their specialized markets.

### Financial Management Opportunities and Challenges

Public sympathy and affection are two important advantages enjoyed by organizations in the private not-for-profit sector. This factor is particularly helpful both in fundraising efforts and the recruitment of volunteers. Tax breaks and discounts also provide opportunities for private not-for-profit sport, tourism, and leisure service organizations to get the most out of their financial resources.

One challenge that smaller private not-for-profit organizations have is the lack of staff (or at least highly qualified staff) that can manage the financial resources in a consistent, accurate, and timely manner. Reliance on volunteers for financial management functions can, occasionally, have disastrous results for the organization. Another challenge is the relative risk associated with extending credit to an enterprise that depends so much on the popularity of its cause and the generosity of its supporters. Credit is based on confidence, and confidence is something that most small nonprofit organizations enjoy from conservative lenders. A third significant financial management challenge is that of protecting the financial resources of the organization from short-term governing bodies that do not always act with long-term wisdom. Many nonprofit sport and leisure service organizations have failed or struggled because a new board of directors decided to use their carefully developed cash reserves for an immediate program expansion or initiative that did not result in sustained or enhanced financial strength.

### Other

Financial management in the private not-for-profit sector requires many of the same skills and involves many of the same activities as those in the public sector. Sports, tourism, and leisure in the private not-for-profit sector is likely to continue as a strong and viable part of community life. It will, however, need more sophistication in the management of its financial resources as every aspect of operating in a modern society becomes more complex.

## Commercial Enterprises

Sport, tourism, and leisure service enterprises operating in the commercial sector are distinguished from the others previously discussed by their profit motivation. It is important to note that "profit motivation," rather than "profit generation," is given as the defining characteristic. Commercial sport, tourism, and leisure enterprises may not always produce profits (especially in the early stages of development or during off-seasons), but the commercial enterprise will only stay in business if, over a reasonable period of time, an expected return on the investment is eventually realized. These

organizations do not exist out of a need for a particular type of service. They exist because satisfying the need for a particular type of service is profitable. Commercial sector organizations do not receive tax revenues—they pay taxes. Commercial sector organizations do not typically receive operating grants or other forms of gratuitous income—they are called upon to make donations. Commercial sector organizations do not use volunteers—they support them. Because the commercial sector exists to benefit certain individuals (investors), it does not have access to the major revenue sources utilized by public and private not-for-profit agencies. Commercial sport, tourism, and leisure businesses must cover most or all of their costs of operating by charging fees, selling goods and services, and making other types of investments. Examples of commercial sector sport, tourism, and leisure service organizations include professional sports teams, resorts, amusement parks, meeting management companies, bowling centers, movie theaters, outdoor outfitters, and travel managers.

### Legislative/Legal Parameters

There are many laws aimed at supporting and regulating commercial activity. Profit-motivated sport and leisure service organizations are subject to those laws that apply to their particular situations. The application of some laws will vary depending upon whether the sport or leisure business is set up as a corporation, syndicate, or partnership, or is individually owned.

### Social Roles/Expectations

The primary social role or social expectation of the commercial sport, tourism, and leisure enterprise is to contribute to the economic well-being of the community. Proposals for new commercial enterprises often highlight community benefits such as diversity in leisure options, opportunities for social interaction, promotion of health, development of community pride, and educational enrichment, but the benefit that is most eagerly sought is described in terms of jobs created, household income produced, sales activity, and tax revenue generated. Of course, there is the basic expectation that the enterprise will be consistent with community social standards, but the economic impact of the venture is regarded with the most interest and concern.

### Market Management Techniques

Market management in commercial sport and leisure services is designed to do one thing: tap consumer spending power. Therefore, the only market that is of interest is the market that can pay enough and is willing to pay enough to help the organization realize its financial goals.

Responsiveness to market conditions is a key to success in commercial enterprises, and this responsiveness is often reflected in pricing strategies and in the use of advertising as a major promotional tool. Pricing strategies in the commercial sector focus on the total bottom line. That is, variation in pricing is frequently used to attract consumers by responding to price sensitivity on certain elements of the total service package. In a movie theater, for example, the admission price may be reduced to a point where it barely covers the costs of providing the cinematic opportunity, and yet, the price of the popcorn may be kept at a level that consumers can accept and that make the whole movie-going event (movie + snacks) profitable for the theater operator. The commercial sector is usually more responsive and more flex-

ible in pricing than organizations in the public and private not-for-profit sectors. For similar reasons, the commercial sector is also more inclined than other types of organizations to use advertising (both institutional and product) to promote desired consumer responses.

### Indicators of Success

Financial managers in the commercial sector measure their success by comparing their achievements to their goals. Unlike their counterparts in the public and private not-for-profit sectors, managers of commercial enterprises set goals that focus on the financial growth of the enterprise and on the return on the investment made therein. The balance sheet and the income statement serve as the primary evaluation documents rather than participant evaluation surveys. There is concern for the quality of consumers' experience, but only so far as it affects the financial bottom line. The commercial sport and leisure service organization also measures its success by comparing its financial ratios with standards established for the industry. Financial ratios are discussed further in Chapter 19.

### Financial Management Opportunities and Challenges

Commercial sport, tourism, and leisure service organizations enjoy several opportunities that are somewhat unique to this sector. Because they are profit motivated, they are not required to prop up socially beneficial but financially ineffective programs and services and can, as a result, concentrate on maximizing the utility of their assets. They can more easily identify and avoid products that do not meet their standards of success. The entrepreneurial spirit has free rein in the commercial sport, tourism, and leisure business environment, and managers find excitement in the many opportunities to move resources from areas of low productivity to initiatives that offer greater results.

Challenges associated with financial management in the commercial sport, tourism, and leisure service organization include developing the knowledge and skill competencies required in order to be effective. Foremost among the skill requirements are investment management, bookkeeping, and financial forecasting. Effective financial managers continually add to their store of management abilities by reading and studying, attending conferences and workshops, and furthering their formal education in this discipline.

Although public, private not-for-profit, and commercial sport and leisure service organizations are alike in many ways, there are important differences among the three sectors with respect to financial management goals and practices. The foregoing discussion of differences is summarized in Table 1.1.

## Competition and Cooperation

Although there are important differences among sport, tourism, and leisure service organizations operating in the public, private not-for-profit, and commercial sectors, this does not mean that these sectors never relate to each other. In one respect, they may be competitors trying to serve the same markets, provide the same kinds of services, or compete in other ways. In another respect, they may be cooperating in enterprises and activities that provide mutual benefits. It would not be unusual, for example, to see similar aquatics programs offered to a community by the YMCA, the local college, and the city recreation department. In this case, the three agencies (representing public and private not-for-profit sectors)

are competing directly for customers. On the other hand, the city and the YMCA may also have an agreement that youth soccer leagues will be offered exclusively by the YMCA, while the city recreation department will offer all softball and baseball programs in the community. Furthermore, a commercial local sport management firm might be contracted by both agencies to train and manage the officials and the umpires for both the soccer and baseball leagues, or cooperate with public and not-for-profit organizations in hosting a tourism-generating regional or national tournament.

Competition among public, private not-for-profit, and commercial agencies provides a number of benefits. They include the following:

- Greater choice for consumers (e.g., variety in program features, scheduling, location, price)
- Greater attention to high-quality service (necessary for maintaining competitive advantage)
- Greater ability to respond to increasing demand
- Greater opportunity to focus on specific market segments (i.e., establish a market niche)

Cooperation among public, private not-for-profit, and commercial sport and leisure service agencies also provides some benefits. They include the following:

- Operational efficiency (by reducing duplication of physical and human resources)
- Synergism (i.e., the total benefit of agencies working together can be greater than the sum of the benefits provided by each alone)
- A coordinated approach to the de-

**Table 1.1**
**A summary of finance-related similarities and differences among public, private not-for-profit, and commercial sport, tourism, and leisure service organizations**

| Area of Contrast | Public | Private Not-for-Profit | Commercial |
| --- | --- | --- | --- |
| Ownership | Usually government. | Private organization. | Private corporation. |
| Legal Authority | Through enabling legislation. | Through enabling legislation and designation of tax status. | Through incorporation (state and federal government recognition, regulation, and protection). |
| Mandate | Serve social welfare and commonwealth needs of all citizens. | Serve specific social welfare needs or leisure interests of a specific population. | Realize maximum return on investment through service to most profitable market. |
| Source of Funds | Taxes, grants, donations, earned income. | Grants, memberships, donations, fundraising activities, earned income. | Investors, creditors, earned income. |
| Market Management | Market limited to geographic/political constituency. Market segmented on basis of need. Might not compete. | Market defined by particular need. | Market composed of those who can pay. Defined by merit. |
| Success indicators | Social change. | Social change. Financial viability. | Profitability. Growth. Return on investment. |
| Opportunities | Tax exemption. Volunteers. Bulk purchasing and discounts. | Tax exemption. Volunteers. Public concern. | Entrepreneurship. Support for eliminating financially unsuccessful products. |
| Challenges | Public accountability and scrutiny. Changing political directions. | Relative uncertainty. Reliance on gratuitous income and volunteers. Limited qualified staff. Inconsistent leadership. | Developing and maintaining skills. |

livery of sport, tourism, and leisure services in the community (ensuring that a full range of needs and interests are considered)

- Conversion of competitive energy to service energy

## Summary

The delivery of sport, tourism, and leisure service in the community is achieved through a system that includes organizations operating in the public, private not-for-profit, and commercial sectors. Public agencies have a clear social mandate and are supported by public funds, especially tax revenues. Private not-for-profit agencies do not receive tax dollars to fund their operations, but rather seek funding through donations and enterprise activities. They may, through service fees and other fundraising activities, generate profits; but those profits are used to maintain the organization and sustain other non-profitable activities or services. Commercial sport, tourism, and leisure service organizations are motivated by profit and an expected return on investment. All business activities in the commercial sport, tourism, and leisure organization are ultimately expected to generate a profit. Although the three sectors differ in other ways, those differences do not deny them the opportunities for direct competition and cooperation in service delivery.

# NOTES

# CHAPTER 2

# Financial Management in Public and Not-for-Profit Leisure Service Organizations

## Introduction

This chapter discusses the unique characteristics of public and not-for-profit leisure service organizations with respect to financial management processes. Financial management in sport organizations and in tourism and commercial recreation enterprises is discussed in subsequent chapters. As an introduction, Table 2.1 provides an overview of types of organizations, sources of funding, and measures of success for public and not-for-profit organizations.

## Public Leisure Service Enterprises

### Organizational Structure

There is no single organizational structure that is required of public leisure service entities. The most common struc-

ture is a combined parks and recreation department or division under municipal, county, or regional government administration. Separate, autonomous park or recreation organizations are declining in number. In a few states, park districts are organized with separate taxing power and, in some areas, the park districts have an elected board. In other cases an appointed board provides the policy direction for the public leisure service organization. The park board typically has decision-making authority for organizational structure. State park organizations exist in all 50 states and are structured in a variety of ways. They may appear under a tourism umbrella or, more commonly, a natural resource structure.

It is unusual to find sport organizations as a part of the public leisure service structure. More often they operate as not-for-profit organizations that have formal and informal links to public en-

**Table 2.1**
**Public and not-for-profit organizations compared on structure,
revenue, and measures of success**

| Sector | Public | Nonprofit |
|---|---|---|
| Examples of Organizations | State park systems, county park systems, community park and recreation agencies | Boys and Girls Clubs, YMCA YWCA, swim club, scouting organizations, conservation organizations, support groups for public agencies |
| Sources of Revenue | Primarily taxes (property tax), dedicated taxes, fees and charges | Grants, membership fees, fundraising, donors, fees and charges, government grants |
| Financial Measures of Success | Fees and charges generated, financial accountability | Achievement of goals, objectives, and outcomes |

tities. The Indiana Sports Corporation, for example, is a not-for-profit organization dedicated to bringing national and international sport championships to Indianapolis and Indiana. When putting a bid package together, they work closely with the city government and the local and regional tourism office. The sporting events they try to attract may use professional sport areas (e.g., FIFA World Basketball Championship), privately owned sport facilities (e.g., a professional golf tournament), public facilities (e.g., NCAA Swimming and Diving Championships), or a combination of the three (e.g., World Police Games). Sport organizations are discussed further in Chapter 3.

Tourism and commercial recreation enterprises do include some public organizations, such as city or state tourism development offices and local destination marketing organizations. However, these public organizations typically operate as if they are commercial entities and are discussed further in Chapter 4.

### Operational and Fiscal Authority

Almost all public leisure service en-

tities report to policy or advisory boards. Policy boards typically carry decision-making authority and advisory boards provide input into operations and make endorsements, suggestions, and recommendations to the decision-making authority. Public entities are authorized to expend money only after the legislative body has formally approved a budget. Oversight authority for budget operations remains with the legislative body, and day-to-day fiscal operations and management is delegated to the leisure service organization.

Mandates or expectations of services and programs are articulated in the organization's enabling legislation at both the state and/or local level, the legislative body's vision and mission statements, and the leisure service organization's long-range plans. Fiscal operations are codified in state and local legislation and the public entity is reviewed, at a minimum, by a state auditing body on a regular basis. Organizations must operate within appropriate state and local codes that apply to fiscal operations.

## Financial Objectives

The purpose of public leisure service organizations such as park and recreation departments is to improve the quality of life for residents, enhance the beauty of the community, and provide recreation and fitness based activities and programs for individuals and groups. In some communities, public park and recreation entities are seen as social welfare agencies working in consort with other social welfare enterprises to improve individual opportunities for personal growth. The Boulder, Colorado Parks and Recreation Department mission statement is typical of many public entities and reflects the ideal of "public good."

> *"The mission of the City of Boulder Parks and Recreation Department is to provide safe, clean, and beautiful parks and facilities and high-quality leisure activities for the community. These services shall enhance residents' health and well-being and promote economic vitality for long-term community sustainability. We will accomplish this through creative leadership, environmentally sustainable practices, and the responsible use of available resources." (City of Boulder Parks and Recreation Department Vision Statement. http://www.bouldercolorado. gov).*

Public entities serving the public good traditionally were not expected to generate a profit or even large amounts of revenue. They operated as public agencies with some or all of their funding coming from tax revenue. Contemporary public park and recreation departments, however, do actively generate revenue as part

of their mandate. Public leisure service organizations, once almost wholly subsidized by compulsory income (see Chapter 8), now generate 15 to 100 percent of their operational funds through fees, charges, and entrepreneurial activities. Capital improvement funds for buildings and structures typically come from other sources (see Chapters 8 and 10).

Major capital investments such as parks, recreation centers, or specialized facilities are viewed as public commodities. Parks are typically not expected to generate revenue; however, recreation centers and specialized facilities within parks may be expected to produce varying levels of revenue (including profit) and are viewed as *investment decisions*. The decision to build a new facility is based on its revenue potential and the public good that it represents. For example, most public agencies that might construct a family aquatic center would expect the facility's revenue to cover its operations, partially or wholly contribute to the long-term debt incurred from construction, and provide additional funds to agency operations. By contrast, a skate park is seen as an opportunity to provide youths with a safer public outlet for their activities and may only be expected to recover part of its operating costs and none of its long-term debt.

## Debt Management

Simply stated, the two main goals of the public leisure service organization are to serve the public and to maintain a sound financial foundation. Public agencies are dependent upon tax revenues, fees and charges, and enterprise operations for their operating revenue. They are not allowed to engage in deficit spending. Long-term debt is controlled by state and local legislation, and public organizations may not engage in debt creating activities outside of those specifically permitted. For example, state financial codes typically limit the amount and type of debt that a city or an independent park district may incur. Public entities will engage in activities and types of activities that commercial enterprises often will not, especially when it is justified as a public benefit. Parks, recreation centers, recreation programs, and similar activities frequently fit within the public benefit rationale. Louisville, Kentucky Metro Parks operates 17 recreation centers, many of them in lower socioeconomic neighborhoods where expectations of cost recovery are low. The recreation centers are seen as meeting a public good (benefit).

### Accounting Management

Accounting management in public entities is similar to that of the commercial enterprise, with some important differences. Public entities operate under generally accepted accounting practices (GAAP) but, unlike in the commercial sector, the use of the revenue may be restricted according to the source of the revenue. For example, a special tax may be restricted for a single use, such as reduction of long-term debt. Different than for commercial enterprises, revenue generated from a public program or a facility may go into the government general fund and be made available for use anywhere within the government, or it may go to a restricted fund that limits where the funds are used.

Pricing in the public sector is becoming more sophisticated, yet it is frequently based on a mix of intuition and cursory analysis of limited measures of demand and willingness to pay. In the public sector, pricing is more often seen as a tool to recover partial rather than full costs. The need to provide for the public good and to maintain sound financial practices

drives decision-making in the public sector. It is frequently seen as a conundrum for policy makers as they strive to provide for the public good and simultaneously ensure sufficient funds are available for the public enterprise.

### Reporting

Public park and recreation entities are strongly affected by seasonal variations. Outdoor aquatic facilities typically have a 90-120-day season. Indoor sport, recreation, and fitness facilities are affected by seasonal shifts in sport, individual preferences for being outdoors or indoors, inclement weather periods, and public school calendars. For example, when public leisure service organizations prepare for summer operations they may spend up to 75 percent of their annual operating budget between May 1 and September 30.

Financial reporting usually occurs on a monthly basis and is supplemented by seasonal reports. Policy boards and advisory boards are trained to understand seasonal influences on revenues and expenditures, and historical reports are frequently provided to aid in that understanding. In addition, program reports are provided for each activity at the end of the season. The task of the chief executive officer and chief financial officer is to interpret financial data, generate reports, and educate staff, legislative officials, and lay board members about fiscal operations.

### Performance Evaluation

Serving the public good is the primary goal of public park and recreation entities. From a financial perspective, auditors require assurance and proof that standard accounting practices have been followed. Policy makers require proof that funds expended have contributed to the public good. Park and recreation entities may respond to the two different reporting needs by providing data from performance goals and objectives, attendance reports, outcome measures, and other forms of data. Application of measures of effectiveness and efficiency are becoming more common, and it is generally believed that measuring outputs (such as the number of people served) is no longer an adequate substitute for measuring how people benefited from participation in programs and use of facilities or services. Performance measurement is becoming more sophisticated and it is more important than ever that public leisure service organizations provide effective evaluations.

## Not-For-Profit Leisure Service Enterprises

### Organizational Structure

Not-for-profit organizations typically operate with a board of directors providing policy oversight to the organization. An executive director may be hired, especially in a larger organization, but in the absence of full-time staff, the president of the board and executive committee may provide day-to-day operational direction. Not-for-profit enterprises come in all sizes, from the large National Parks Foundation with tens of thousand of members, to the small local swim club with 30 or less members. Not-for-profit organizations typically have a narrow focus or purpose. For example, the Appalachian Mountain Club focuses on conservation, education, and outdoor recreation, with further concern for maintaining regional chapters, conservation activities, and lodging (all focused in the Appalachian mountains). As another example, a local youth swim club may provide a coach and the facili-

ties in which members may swim, train, and learn about nutrition. All not-for-profit organizations have a purpose and a focus that are stated in their articles of incorporation.

### Financial Objectives

The financial objectives of a not-for-profit organization are linked to its stated purpose. All not-for-profit organizations strive to generate sufficient revenue to pay for their annual operations. They are not expected nor encouraged to generate a profit. The Internal Revenue Service provides guidelines for how not-for-profit organizations might use their funds. For example, there are restrictions on the amount of money allowed for political lobbying. In moving beyond the Internal Revenue Service guidelines, not-for-profit organizations jeopardize their not-for-profit tax status.

The vast majority of not-for-profit organizations do not have major capital investments, but those that do must manage them as efficient enterprises. Not-for-profit organizations might also have unique cash-flow circumstances, such as would a Boy Scout camp that generates 85 percent of its camping revenue in the three month summer period but has year-round expenses. Not-for-profit organizations are frequently dependent upon the good will of members or donors to provide funds for ongoing operations. A Boys and Girls Club, operating in the inner city probably cannot charge sufficient revenue to cover the operating costs of the programs and facilities, so donors, the United Way, and revenue from programs are used to cover the costs.

### Debt and Account Management

Not-for-profit organizations work to maintain sufficient funds for operations. Sources of income include programs, special events, donors, bequests, government grants and contracts, private grants, and the United Way. The United Way provides support to a limited number of not-for-profit organizations that meet their minimum guidelines and are selected by a lay community-based board for inclusion in their funding model. Some self-reliance is required, as the United Way almost never provides 100-percent support to a not-for-profit organization.

Not-for-profit organizations have a wide range of financial solvency. The small, narrowly focused not-for-profit organization may struggle from month to month to generate sufficient funds for operations. A larger not-for-profit organization, such as the Appalachian Mountain Club, might have a budget in excess of $15 million with multiple sources of revenue and a strong endowment. In 2005, the Appalachian Mountain Club's operating budget was $15.6 million and they maintained an endowment of $36 million (Appalachian Mountain Club, 2005 Annual Report, http://www.outdoors.org). The solvency contrast among not-for-profit organizations is dramatic. Financial operations and debt management principles are consistent, but management of each will vary based on the size, solvency, and management competency of the not-for-profit organization. In the absence of an ongoing income revenue stream, many not-for-profit organizations adjust their operating budget on a monthly or seasonal basis to deal with operating revenue availability.

### Reporting

Not-for-profit organizations report on a monthly, quarterly, and annual basis. They often utilize more than one of the standard financial reporting formats that are discussed later in this book. Regardless, there should be a monthly reporting process, sometimes as a treasurer's report, and there should be an annual report, ideally certified by the not-for-profit organization's account manager or an independent auditing body. The variety of not-for-profit organizations, their size, scope of services, and management skills frequently determine the type and effectiveness of reporting. Not-for-profit organizations with external funding sources require standardized reporting consistent with the expectations of the funding organizations. The United Way, for example, usually requires monthly reports and an annual external audit. In addition, they may conduct their own audit on a regular cycle, such as once every three years. Financial reports should be consistent with the principles presented in Chapter 18.

### Performance Evaluation

For not-for-profit organizations, the level of performance evaluation is dependent upon the expectations of the board of directors, leadership, and outside funding entities. Annual reports are commonly required and are primarily concerned with reporting on progress made toward achievement of goals and objectives. A United Way-supported entity frequently is required to measure outcome for funded programs, and continued United Way funding may be based on progress achieved toward intended outcomes. Foundations may also require specific evaluation products or performance indicators from an organization, such as completion of a project, publishing of a report or monograph, completion of a capital improvement project, or a formal assessment report.

Larger not-for-profit organizations issue annual reports reflecting progress toward their vision, mission, goals, and objectives. The Appalachian Mountain

Club's annual report identifies goals and annual progress toward those goals. Their goals pertain to the number of acres protected, the management of miles of trails, the number of outdoor experiences provided, the provision of outdoor education experiences, and the amount of literature about the environment distributed. The annual report also identifies income sources, expenditure categories, levels of income and expenditures, and the impact of the expenditures upon individuals, regions, and the goals of the organization.

From a financial standpoint, a common measure of efficiency is the percent of the operating budget spent for administration. Not-for-profit organizations desire to maintain a low administrative cost, striving to spend the bulk of their operating budget on programs and services. The Appalachian Mountain Club, for example, spent 9.6 percent of its operating budget on administration in 2005.

## Summary

The purpose of financial management in public and not-for-profit entities is to enhance programs, service, facili-

ties, and areas for the public good, to improve the quality of life of community members or people in general, and to meet the goals of the organization in an effective and efficient manner. Public entities, while conforming to some commercial business practices, are not-for-profit enterprises and generally are not expected to generate excess revenue. There are a few exceptions to this rule. The organizations operate within legislatively mandated guidelines, reporting to elected or appointed lay and professional individuals. Not-for-profit organizations have an internal structure for reporting with the Internal Revenue Service which, in turn, provides some external review for financial accountability. Financial success is defined in terms of solvency while impacting positive perceptions of the community, meeting social needs, providing opportunities for recreation involvement, and perception of value in the public or not-for-profit leisure service.

## NOTES

# CHAPTER 3

# Financial Management in Sport Organizations

## Introduction

The business of sport has a tremendous financial and cultural impact on contemporary society, and that impact appears to be expanding. Today, jobs in sports are not limited to intercollegiate athletics and the four major professional leagues. Opportunities for a career in sports cross over into other entertainment-related industries, from video gaming and fantasy leagues, to sport tourism and event hospitality (Gangemi, 2006). The growth of the sport industry in recent years can be attributed to: (a) increased interest in sport from diverse market segments such as women, minorities, and aging individuals, (b) increased offerings of new and different forms of sports (e.g., ESPN's X-games, (c) growth in corporate sponsorship, (d) increased coverage of sporting events and matters on television,

Internet, and the radio (e.g. pay-per-view events, sport-specific channels like the Golf Channel, NBA channel, etc.), (e) the influence of technology on sport-related goods, services, and training, and (f) increased numbers and variety of magazines, newspapers, journals, and blogs related to sports (Pitts & Stotlar, 2002). Scholars agree that this growth has definitely influenced local job creation and entrepreneurial activity, but there is no consensus on the broader economic impact of the sport industry as a whole. The lack of consensus results, in part, from the fact that "sport" is not classified as an industry in the North American Classification System (NAICS – a system devised by the U.S. Census Bureau to identify industries based on the similarities of firms in economic activities). Without that classification, statistics are not collected nor analyzed in a way that readily permits independent examination of the economic contribution of sports and sport-related activities.

## Sport as an Industry

An industry is a collection of businesses and consumers that have similar products and markets, and that engage in similar economic activities. NAICS uses the similarity of economic activity to classify businesses in North America into 20 distinct sectors, including *Arts, Entertainment, and Recreation.*

NAICS industries are identified by a six-digit code in order to be placed in the hierarchical structure of the classification system. The first two digits refer to the industry sector, the third digit identifies the industry sub-sector, the fourth designates the industry group, the fifth refers to the NAICS industry, and the sixth digit designates the national industry (U.S., Canadian, or Mexican). Take, for example, the six-digit code for U.S. sports teams and clubs (711211):

| | |
|---|---|
| 71 | Industry Sector (Arts, Entertainment, & Recreation ) |
| 711 | Industry Sub-sector |
| 7112 | Industry Group (Spectator Sports) |
| 71121 | Industry (Spectator Sports) |
| 711211 | U.S. specific (Sports Teams and Clubs) |

The definitions that NAICS provides for the North American Industry of Spectator Sports (71121), and the U.S. -specific Industry of Sport Teams and Clubs (711211) are:

71121 Spectator Sports

This industry comprises (1) sports teams or clubs primarily participating in live sporting events before a paying audience; (2) establishments primarily engaged in operating racetracks; (3) independent athletes engaged in participating in live sporting or racing events before a paying audience; (4) owners of racing participants, such as cars, dogs, and horses, primarily engaged in entering them in racing events or other spectator sports events; and (5) establishments, such as sports trainers, primarily engaged in providing specialized services to support participants in sports events or competitions. The sports teams and clubs included in this industry may or may not operate their own arena, stadium, or other facility for presenting their games or other spectator sports events.

711211 Sports Teams and Clubs

This U.S. industry comprises professional or semiprofessional sports teams or clubs primarily engaged in participating in live sporting events, such as baseball, basketball, football, hockey, or soccer, before a paying audience. These establishments may or may not operate their own arena, stadium, or other facility for presenting these events.

NAICS does not consider *Sport* as a major economic activity, "and, therefore, does not treat the sport industry as a stand-alone industrial sector or industry" (Li, Hofacre, & Mahony, 2001). The wide range of sport-related activities is scattered across several of the 20 industry sectors, such as *construction, manufacturing, wholesale and retail trade, real estate, rental and leasing, education services, arts, entertainment and recreation,* and *other services.* This dispersion makes it difficult to reconcile sales or financial data (attributed to sport activities) from each of these sectors and, therefore, next to impossible to accurately estimate the economic magnitude of the sport industry. Since the government has no system in place to estimate the annual impact of sport on the U.S. economy, several analysts and scholars have tried to develop a reliable measurement for the sport industry. There is still no consensus, but most experts believe that the industry has an annual economic impact of anywhere from $213 to $560 billion (Howard & Crompton, 2005).

The importance of the sport industry and the unique aspects of financial management in sport organizations are highlighted in the following discussions of (a) public subsidy of sport facilities, (b) television ratings and broadcasting fees, (c) players' salaries, (d) sport franchise values, and (e) costs associated with attending a sporting event.

## Public Subsidization of Sport Facilities

The significance of modern spectator sports is evident in the number of cities entering the race to build expensive new sport facilities (using, to a great extent, public monetary resources) for the purpose of attracting professional sport franchises. Proponents of such endeavors argue that professional sports provide increased community visibility, enhance community image, stimulate development, and generate high levels of psychic income (emotional and psychological benefits of sports) for the residents of that community (Howard & Crompton, 2005). As a result, local and state governments work closely together to either attract professional teams, or to prevent their existing professional sports teams from going elsewhere. In the 20 years since 1995, local, state, and federal governments have allocated more than $10 billion of taxpayers' money to subsidize more than 50 new major league stadiums and arenas, and a larger number of minor league sport facilities. The practice of using public resources to support private and commercial sport enterprises is growing, and governments continue to spend more that $2 billion a year to subsidize major sport facilities. For example, construction of the Washington, D.C. ballpark that is home to the Major League Baseball (MLB) team *Nationals* cost taxpayers more that $600 million (Demause, 2007).

Critics have voiced concern about the spiraling costs that seem to be making the entire big league sports structure unworkable, and have challenged the assumption that publicly supported sports stadiums justify themselves financially. Advocates of sport facility subsidies argue that the use of public money to fund their development and operation provides the following benefits:

(a) Injection of substantial amounts of money into local economies
(b) Creation of new jobs
(c) Revitalization of urban neighborhoods.

The opposing claims have been thoroughly investigated. Economist Robert Baale conducted a study that investigated 30 U.S. cities that had built new sport facilities during the last 30 years. The findings were disappointing for proponents of subsidized sport developments. His study demonstrated that the development of new sport facility projects does not have a positive effect on local economies. In 27 of the cities examined, the effect of major sport developments on the per-capita income was not significant, and in the remaining three cases, the sport facility had a significantly *negative* impact on the local economy. Two explanations for these findings are offered: the substitution effect and revenue leakages.

The *substitution effect* measures how much money is simply transferred from other entertainment, food, and retail venues in town, as fans may decide to spend their disposable income on stadium food and merchandise instead of at the local restaurants and retail stores.

*Revenue leakage* is a measure of the degree to which stadium spending is taken out of the local economy before it can be recirculated. Leakage is taking place because team owners and players usually live, invest, and spend money outside of the local economy.

The myth of new job creation attributed to sport facilities also collapsed under the weight of evidence found in this study. Testifying to a congressional oversight committee, Demause (2007) pointed out that "where good job-development programs can cost about $10,000 for each new job created, sport facilities typically come in at as much as $250,000 in public cost for each new job, a worse ratio than some of the most infamous corporate giveaways in history." Also, the belief that sport facilities can be used to revitalize urban neighborhoods was not justified, especially for seasonal operations like baseball and football. There is no evidence that a new sport facility is going to attract further development such as restaurants, sport bars, retail space, and entertainment venues, especially when the facility is closed for most of the year.

## Television Ratings and Broadcasting Fees

The entertainment value of sporting events is evident in the large fees that television networks are paying to rightholders in order to broadcast professional or intercollegiate sporting events. The amount of money that is paid is greatly influenced by the television ratings that each professional league, game, individual athlete, and conference captures when the sporting event is aired for public consumption. Each rating point accounts for 1,102,000 households in the U.S; that is, one percent of the nation's 110.2 million houses with a television set in place. High television ratings are desirable because they mean that bigger audiences are watching the event. Advertisers and sponsoring companies are attracted to sporting events that capture high broadcast ratings, and they are willing to spend large amounts of money to secure advertising space and time when these events are broadcast.

In 2006, NBC's regular season broadcast of National Football League (NFL) games—the first after eight years of absence—captured a remarkable 12.6 household rating and a 21 percent broadcasting share (percentage of in-use televisions tuned to a given show). That same year, the Super Bowl game had attracted 90 million viewers. Similar success in securing high T.V. ratings was experienced by the other two major leagues in the U.S., the National Basketball Association (NBA) and MLB. However, Major League Baseball's World Series ratings, although high compared to other sporting events, experienced a nine percent drop from the previous year's series, and captured a 10.1 rating in 2006 (Nye, 2006). This was the lowest rating ever recorded in the history of televised World Series baseball. This ratings decline was attributed directly to the starting time of the games, the small market size of the rival clubs, and the fierce competition from other professional sports (Hart, 2006).

Television ratings are also used as a negotiation tool between network executives and leagues officials when contracts are just about to expire, or new media products, like Internet broadcasting, pay-per-view sporting events, satellite sport packages, etc., are available for bid. NFL entertainment packages have been the most successful and popular in the country. In 2006, after breaking attendance records for a third consecutive year and achieving exceptional television ratings for its broadcast games, the NFL was able to negotiate television contracts that had an overall value close to $25 billion over the succeeding six years (Covitz, 2006). For the 2007 season alone, the NFL raised more than $3.5 billion from its T.V. contracts (Molinaro, 2006). The NFL also reserved its right to broadcast selected football events through its own television channel. The scale of exchange based on television and broadcast rights and activity is indicated by the following presentation of selected contract details:

(1) NBC – Football Night in America: $3.6 billion/six-year agreement
(2) ESPN – Monday Night Football: $8.8 billion/eight-year agreement
(3) CBS – Sunday Afternoon AFC Football: $3.74 billion/six-year agreement
(4) FOX – Sunday Afternoon NFC Football: $ 4.28 billion/six-year agreement

Major League Baseball also experienced success in negotiating its own television and broadcast contracts. In 2006, MLB signed a seven-year television extension agreement with its existing broadcast partners, ESPN ($2.5 billion) and FOX Sports ($3 billion) (*Tribune Review*, 2006). The League also added TBS to its television partners after the network agreed to pay more than $3 billion in broadcasting fees (Jackson, 2006).

There are also noteworthy developments in intercollegiate sports. In 2006, the NCAA Big Ten Conference announced the creation of a new channel dedicated to showcasing sporting events and other accomplishments of its member institutions. The channel, which has its headquarters in Chicago, is a joint venture between the Big Ten Conference and the FOX Network and has signed multi-year agreements with ABC and ESPN for programming production and sharing. The goal of this venture was to dramatically increase the visibility of the Conference on television and through other electronic media (Paul, 2006).

## Franchise Values and Player Salaries

Additional evidence of the importance and magnitude of professional sports business can be found in skyrocketing values of franchises and player contracts (Naylor, 2005). Franchises in almost all major leagues have experienced significant increases in their value and, by 2007, some were worth more than $1.5 billion, with an annual appreciation rate of almost 19 percent. One NFL team, the New England Patriots, exemplifies this trend: the franchise was purchased in 1994 for $172 million. It was a record high price to pay for a team but, by 2006, its value had risen to over $1 billion (Weinbach, 2006).

*Forbes* magazine conducts an annual survey and publishes the actual market value of all professional sport franchises in the country. The survey takes into consideration a number of valuating factors, such as the franchise's annual operating income, the stadium/arena value, the size of the market in which the club operates, the aggregate value of the roster, etc. The highest valued teams in 2006 are shown in Table 3.1 (*Forbes,* 2006; Wharnsby, 2006).

Players' contracts have also been increased in value. In 2006, a star player for the New York Yankees baseball club signed a lucrative contract that guaranteed a $252 million salary over a ten-year contract, and made him the most expensive MLB contract in baseball history.

David Beckham, a star soccer player in Europe, left the famous Spanish soccer club *Real Madrid* to play for the U.S. Major League Soccer. Beckham signed a five-year contract with the Los Angeles Galaxy that guaranteed him $250 million in salaries, and additional compensation for a variety of considerations (Dell'Apa, 2007). Other star players like Lebron James and Kobe Bryant, both playing for NBA franchises, make $80 million and $136.4 million respectively over the length of their contracts. Even rookies in professional sports are signing multimillion-dollar contracts, disproportionate to their field performance and overall achievements. Mario Williams, the first

Table 3.1
**Highest valued professional sport franchises in 2006**

| Rank | Team / Value | Rank | Team / Value |
|------|-------------|------|-------------|
| | **National Football League** | | **National Basketball Association** |
| 1 | Washington Redskins $1.423 billion | 1 | New York Knicks $592 million |
| 2 | New England Patriots $1.176 billion | 2 | Los Angeles Lakers $568 million |
| 3 | Dallas Cowboys $1.173 billion | 3 | Dallas Mavericks $463 million |
| 4 | Houston Texans $1.043 billion | 4 | Chicago Bulls $461 million |
| 5 | Philadelphia Eagles $1.024 billion | 5 | Houston Rockets $439 million |
| | **Major League Baseball** | | **National Hockey League** |
| 1 | New York Yankees $1.026 billion | 1 | Toronto Maple Leafs $332 million |
| 2 | Boston Red Sox $617 million | 2 | New York Rangers $306 million |
| 3 | New York Mets $604 million | 3 | Detroit Red Wings $258 million |
| 4 | Los Angeles Dodgers $482 million | 4 | Dallas Stars $248 million |
| 5 | Chicago Cubs $448 million | 5 | Philadelphia Flyers $246 million |

overall pick in the 2006 NFL draft, signed a $54 million, six-year agreement with the Houston Texans. In Williams' contract, $26.5 million is guaranteed. The second pick, Reggie Bush, signed a six-year, $62 million contract with the New Orleans Saints, and the third overall pick, Vince Young, signed a six-year, $58 million contract with the Tennessee Titans.

## Attendance Costs of Sporting Events

Gate receipts for amateur, college, and professional sports significantly contribute to the $213 billion impact the sport industry has on the U.S. economy. In 2006, the National Football League broke its attendance record for the third consecutive year, averaging 66,453 spectators per game in its regular season, and a record-high total attendance with 17,012,000 tickets sold (Associated Press, 2006). In the same year, the National Bas-

ketball Association reported (for the second year in a row) the highest average attendance in its history (17,558 spectators per game), and the highest total attendance, with a new record of 21.6 million spectators (Business Wire, 2006). Major League Baseball experienced similar success. The league recorded the second-best record for average game attendance in the sport's history (31,381 spectators), also breaking its season attendance record (for a second consecutive year) with 75.5 million tickets sold (Blum, 2006).

With attendance in professional sports hitting an all-time high, there are some concerns about the escalating costs of attending a sporting event, especially for low-income individuals and families. The Fan Cost Index (FCI), a survey conducted annually by *Team Marketing Report*, a sport marketing company based in Chicago, provides a measure of how much a family of four will likely spend during a night out at a professional sporting event. "The FCI includes: four aver-

A day at the ballpark can be an expensive proposition.

age-price tickets; four small soft drinks; two small beers; four hot dogs; two game programs; parking; and two adult-size caps" (TMR, 2005).

According to the 2005 Fan Cost Index (FCI), the most expensive sport facility hosting an NFL game was the New England Patriots' Gillette Stadium. The average ticket price was $90.89. The Patriots' 2005 FCI was $ 477.47, which was 15 percent higher than in the previous year. The average NFL game ticket was priced at $58.95, while the league average FCI was $329.82. In 2006, the NBA average FCI was $267.37, and, in the same year, the National Hockey League (NHL) recorded an average FCI of $247.32. The 2006 FCI for Major League Baseball (MLB) was $171.19 (Barron, 2005; Perry, 2006). Sample FCIs for teams from three of the major professional leagues in the U.S. are presented in Tables 3.2—3.4. Item costs that contribute to the calculation of the FCI are also shown.

Table 3.2
Item costs ($) and Fan Cost Indexes (FCI) for selected
Major League Baseball Teams (2006)

| TEAM | Avg. Ticket | Beer | Soda | Hot Dog | Parking | Program | Cap | FCI |
|------|-------------|------|------|---------|---------|---------|-----|-----|
| Boston | 46.46 | 6.00 | 2.75 | 4.00 | 23.00 | 5.00 | 15.00 | 287.84 |
| Chicago Cubs | 34.30 | 5.00 | 2.50 | 2.75 | 17.00 | 5.00 | 12.00 | 219.21 |
| NY Yankees | 28.27 | 6.00 | 3.50 | 3.00 | 12.00 | 7.75 | 15.00 | 208.57 |
| Tampa Bay | 17.09 | 5.00 | 3.75 | 3.25 | Free | Free | 15.00 | 129.87 |
| Kansas City | 13.71 | 3.75 | 2.00 | 2.50 | 6.00 | 5.00 | 12.00 | 120.35 |
| **MLB Average** | **22.21** | **5.42** | **3.07** | **3.31** | **11.41** | **3.89** | **13.62** | **171.19** |

Table 3.3
Item costs ($) and Fan Cost Indexes (FCI) for selected
National Basketball Association Teams (2006)

| TEAM | Avg. Ticket | Beer | Soda | Hot Dog | Parking | Program | Cap | FCI |
|------|-------------|------|------|---------|---------|---------|-----|-----|
| L.A. Lakers | 79.00 | 7.50 | 3.00 | 4.00 | 13.00 | 5.00 | 10.00 | 402.84 |
| New York | 71.00 | 6.00 | 3.25 | 4.30 | 20.00 | 10.00 | 12.00 | 388.04 |
| Houston | 56.00 | 5.50 | 3.75 | 4.00 | 20.00 | Free | 18.00 | 321.34 |
| New Orleans | 29.00 | 5.00 | 4.00 | 4.00 | 10.00 | Free | 20.00 | 206.44 |
| Golden State | 24.00 | 4.50 | 2.00 | 3.00 | 12.00 | 3.00 | 16.00 | 174.27 |
| **NBA Average** | **46.00** | **5.44** | **2.95** | **3.40** | **11.67** | **3.68** | **14.00** | **267.37** |

**Table 3.4**
**Item costs ($) and Fan Cost Indexes (FCI) for selected**
**National Football League Teams (2006)**

| TEAM | Avg. Ticket | Beer | Soda | Hot Dog | Parking | Program | Cap | FCI |
|---|---|---|---|---|---|---|---|---|
| New England | 90.89 | 5.50 | 3.50 | 3.50 | 35.00 | 5.00 | 14.95 | 477.47 |
| Washington | 67.53 | 7.00 | 5.00 | 5.00 | 25.00 | 5.00 | 14.95 | 389.01 |
| NY Giants | 71.59 | 6.25 | 3.50 | 3.75 | 15.00 | 5.00 | 17.99 | 388.85 |
| Jacksonville | 40.16 | 5.00 | 3.00 | 3.00 | 10.00 | 5.00 | 9.95 | 234.55 |
| Buffalo | 39.37 | 5.50 | 3.00 | 3.00 | 15.00 | n/a | 11.00 | 229.49 |
| **NFL Average** | **58.95** | **5.52** | **3.22** | **3.53** | **16.31** | **4.53** | **15.30** | **329.82** |

*Average ticket price represents a weighted average of season ticket prices for general seating categories, determined by factoring the tickets in each price range as a percentage of the total number of seats in each ballpark. Luxury suites are also excluded from the survey. Season-ticket pricing is used for any team that offers some or all tickets at lower prices for customers who buy season tickets.*

*The Fan Cost Index™ comprises the prices of two (2) adult average-price tickets, two (2) child average-price tickets, two (2) small draft beers, four (4) small soft drinks, four (4) regular-size hot dogs, parking for one (1) car, two (2) game programs, and two (2) least expensive, adult-size adjustable caps.*

Source: Team Marketing Report (2006)

## Summary

The scale and common nature of business activity in sports is sufficiently large that it should be viewed as an industry. It is an industry that has a significant economic impact and is certainly an activity of social and cultural importance. Many large professional sport operations are subsidized, in part, by governments and public agencies. The appropriateness of public subsidization has been questioned, but such dissent has yet to play an effective role in changing current practices with respect to the private-public partnership in sport enterprises. The high cost of professional sport operations is influenced by high player salaries and other investments that increase the value of the sport franchise. Costs are recovered and profits are made through the sale of television and broadcast rights, as well as through gate receipts and other revenues from food and beverage sales, merchandise licensing and production, and parking fees.

## References

Associated Press. (5 January 2006). "NFL sets attendance record again. *The Associated Press.*

Associated Press. (1 September 2006). Five teams worth over $1 billion, according to Forbes. *Associated Press.*

Barron, D. (2005). Texans still a good value for NFL fans. *The Houston Chronicle* (17 September 2005): SPORTS

Blum, R. (1 October 2006). MLB Breaks Season Attendance Record. *Associated Press.*

Business Wire. (20 April 2006) NBA sets all-time attendance records; Regular season draws highest average attendance and highest total attendance. *Business Wire.*

Covitz, R. (2 October 2006). NFL, media battle in the trenches over access issues. *The Kansas City Star.*

Dell'Apa, F. (12 January 2007). It's a bonanza for Beckham; MLS Galaxy lure star for $250m," *The Boston Globe.*

Demause, N. (2007). Taxpayer-financed facilities. FDCH Congressional Testimony (03/29/2007). HOUSE Oversight and Government Reform.

Gangemi. J. (2006, February). A hot ticket for sports-biz rookies; B-schools are increasingly offering specialized MBAs to give sports management hopefuls a chance of making the team. *Business Week Online.*

Hart, J. (31 October 2006). Series ratings weren't a primetime success. *Morning Call*: C2.

Howard, D., & Crompton, J. (2005). *Financing sport*. Morgantown, WV: Fitness Information Technology, Inc.

Jackson, B. (12 July 2006). TBS joins MLB TV deal. *The Miami Herald.*

Li, M., Hofacre, S., & Mahony, D. (2001). *Economics of sport*. Morgantown, WV: Fitness Information Technology, Inc.

Molinaro, B. (11 August 2006). Even in the preseason, the NFL rules the waves. *The Virginian-Pilot.*

Naylor, D. (11 June 2005). Investing in a team a losing proposition; Franchise values have not gone up like they have in other sports. *The Globe & Mail (Canada):* S1.

Nye, D. (3 November, 2006). Poor TV ratings reflect MLB's popularity slide. *The State.*

Paul, J. (22 June, 2006). "Big Ten announces new TV contract with ABC/ESPN and creation of new cable channel. *Associated Press.*

Perry, D. (2006). Red Sox, Patriots in a league of their own when it comes to high price of attending a game. *Lowell Sun (Massachusetts).*

Pitts, B., & Stotlar, D. (2002). *Fundamentals of sport management* (2nd

# NOTES

# CHAPTER 4

# Financial Management in
# Tourism and Commercial Recreation Organizations

## Introduction

Managing financial resources in tourism and commercial recreation enterprises requires most of the same skills that should be applied in sport organizations or public and private not-for-profit leisure service agencies. The skills may be the same, but the purpose of the tourism and commercial recreation organization will likely differ significantly. Tourism and commercial recreation are industries. Each industry is comprised of corporations, businesses, and organizations that have a common goal of generating financial and economic benefits for the owners. Commercial recreation businesses are an important part of the community leisure service inventory, as well as to the local economy. Similarly, tourism enterprises are not public social services, but their contributions to the economic well being of a community are significant, and they are likely to have positive social impacts.

Unlike commercial recreation businesses, tourism organizations operate in the public, private not-for-profit, and commercial sectors. In some situations, local, state, and national governments fund tourism agencies and attractions, and in other situations there are private not-for-profit organizations that exist to support industry and community efforts to attract visitors and guests. Of course, commercial tourism enterprises are also plentiful. The sources of funding and financial measures of success for tourism organizations in each sector are outlined in Table 4.1.

This chapter briefly explores some of the aspects of financial management that have particular relevance to managers of tourism and commercial recreation organizations.

Table 4.1
Funding sources and measures of success for tourism
organizations in the public, private not-for-profit, and commercial sectors

| Sector | Public | Private Not-For-Profit | Commercial |
|---|---|---|---|
| Examples of tourism organizations | State or city tourism department | Destination marketing organization | Attractions, hotels, transportation, and other profit oriented businesses |
| Source of revenues | Primarily taxes (general or lodging/ meal taxes) | Grants, earned income, donations, tax transfers | Earned income (investment, sales, fees, and charges) |
| Financial measures of success | Tax revenue generated | General "health of the industry," sales statistics | Liquidity, solvency, profitability, return on investment |

## Financial Objectives

Financial decisions and operations in the tourism commercial recreation industries must address the goal of creating added value (improving the bottom line), and all appropriate accounting methods and investment activities should be applied to that end. In spite of a financial manager's passion for the destination, attraction, activity, or amenity, and regardless of any genuine interest in providing good service just because good service is the 'right' thing to do, managers in tourism and commercial recreation must remain focused on the ultimate goal of generating a measurable profit.

In these industries, decisions about facilities to build or services to offer are viewed as *investment decisions*. Whether or not a tourism or commercial recreation project is developed or a program is implemented depends on how well it will generate expected returns under expected risk conditions. For example, a waterpark feature at a resort is only worth building if it generates more short-term and long-term returns than would be realized by

simply putting the required capital development funds in the bank in a nominal interest-bearing account. As exciting as the waterpark may be, it will not be built if the financial return is greater for some other profit-generating amenity on the same site. Furthermore, investments are made not just to satisfy markets but to attract and serve those markets with the greatest spending potential. Chapter 15 discusses investment decisions and provides the tools for evaluating proposed initiatives.

## Debt and Inventory Management

In tourism and commercial recreation businesses, financial managers have two major interests: liquidity and solvency. *Liquidity* refers to the corporation's ability to meet its short-term financial obligations. In other words, it must be able to pay its bills. Assuring the availability of sufficient cash (liquid assets) for the payment of bills is an ongoing management task. *Solvency* refers to the corporation's ability to meet its long-term financial obligations. Long-term obligations include debt to creditors and the owner's claim to the corporation's assets. The entire management team of the tourism or commercial recreation organization must be concerned with maintaining an appropriate level of debt and ensuring a suitable return on the owner's investment.

Financial managers in tourism and commercial recreation enterprises must also be concerned about *inventory turnover.* An inventory turnover ratio tells the manager how effectively the costs of delivery goods to customers are being contained. For example, a low inventory ratio indicates that there may be an over-investment in inventory and, therefore, unnecessarily high storage or distribution costs.

ity to submit deposits or guarantees in local currency. Furthermore, the enterprise itself may have overseas operations that use a different currency. Not only is there the need to convert currencies, but the fluctuating exchange rate and government regulations on the cross-border flow of funds will also impact financial management in the tourism enterprise. Finally, tourism services are notoriously susceptible to differential pricing strategies. That is, many different prices may be applied to a service that differs in no substantial way between consumers or production/delivery costs. Airline ticket pricing is a well-known and somewhat mystifying example. The tourism financial manager must be able to work with highly variable revenue models based on differential pricing.

## Account Management

In the tourism industry especially, there are also some unique situations that affect the way accounts are managed. In a hotel or resort, for example, each guest has an account to which charges and payments may be made at any time of the day or night, any day of the week. Thousands of those accounts may be opened and closed each day at one property. Additionally, payments for tourism services such as cruise ship passage or air transportation may be made in advance of the service being provided, or may include some sort of deposit. Payments received and expenditure commitments made before and after a service is delivered affect cash flow and must be managed carefully. A third unique aspect of managing financial resources in tourism organizations is the use of foreign currencies. Guests come from many parts of the world and may have limited abil-

## Reporting

In many organizations, sales and expenditures are predictable and sometimes steady. This is so for tourism and commercial recreation organizations that know their markets, can control demand, and successfully attract a loyal clientele. In such cases, financial activity reports and statements of financial outcomes can be prepared relatively infrequently and for comparable periods of time. For example, monthly reports and statements may be sufficient for monitoring financial progress at a year-round reception center, even though there may be some peak periods around wedding seasons and traditional holidays.

Special events and tourism destinations, attractions, or amenities that serve many people for short periods of time usually need more frequent reports of financial activity. Reports may be required as often as hourly in some cases.

At resorts and hotels, for example, it is a common practice to prepare a daily operations report, an event report, and a night audit.

## Performance Evaluation

Profit is the goal in tourism and commercial recreation enterprises, and the ultimate evaluation criterion will always be the amount of profit generated with respect to the amount of the investment made, or in other words, the return on the investment. It would, of course, be foolish for any manager of a tourism or commercial recreation enterprise to simply wait until the end of a fiscal period and then look at the investment return for that period before deciding how well the business is doing. Along the way, there are many other ways to assess the financial health and vitality of the organization.

One important evaluation criterion that is widely used and is unique to the lodging side of the tourism industry is known by the acronym *RevPAR*. It focuses on revenue and lodging room availability, and measures how effectively the resort or hotel fills rooms during the low-rate off-season, as well as during the high-rate peak season. RevPAR, identifies the **R**evenue **P**er **A**vailable **R**oom, and differs from other measures that consider revenue per occupied room. Discussed further in Chapter 17, RevPAR is a valuable indicator of management effectiveness and is used by franchise companies, hotel owners, lenders, and management companies.

## Summary

The purpose of financial investment in tourism and commercial recreation enterprises is to generate added value for the business or industry. Financial decisions, management procedures, and reporting mechanisms must address the achievement of this purpose. Tourism and commercial recreation businesses have some unique circumstances that make managing financial resources a challenging task. Accounts may be numerous and may be opened and closed in short periods of time. Short-term and long-term financial decisions require up-to-date data, thus requiring accurate and frequent reports. Corporate success in the tourism and commercial recreation industries is measured primarily in terms of efficiency and effectiveness in generating profits and enhancing investments.

## NOTES

# SECTION B

# Organization

The next two chapters of this book examine the major functions of financial management in sport, tourism, and leisure service organizations. Organizational structures are discussed and the financial management responsibilities of a variety of positions within organizations are detailed. Organizational structures in sport, tourism, and leisure service entities are compared in the context of their public, private not-for-profit, and commercial settings.

# CHAPTER 5

# Functions

## Introduction

Effective management of financial resources in the sport, tourism, and leisure service organization requires the assumption and recognition of responsibility, as well as the deliberate assignment of authority and duties to the appropriate departments, offices, and individuals. Those who are responsible for the financial well-being of the organization are the financial decision makers. They are the ones who are the sources of authority, and they are the ones who are ultimately held accountable for the consequences of their decisions. Those to whom they delegate authority may make financial decisions within the parameters of their stewardships, but they typically function with limited responsibility as financial administrators. Financial administrators are those in the organization who are authorized to implement financial policies and follow established financial management procedures. They have specific duties and authority and are responsible not for the financial well-being of the organization, but rather for how they perform their duties and exercise their authority.

This brief chapter examines the elements of organizational structures that are designed to facilitate the integrated efforts of financial decision makers, financial administrators, and program/facility managers in sport and leisure service agencies. It also describes the roles of the different types of financial managers in a variety of settings, including public agencies operating at all three levels of government; private not-for-profit agencies with local, regional, and national programs; and commercial sport, tourism, and recreation enterprises of different sizes.

Functional distinctions between the individuals or units within an organization are most evident on the vertical dimension of the organizational chart.

Specifically, those who occupy positions at the top of the organizational chart are the financial decision makers, while those at the bottom of the chart are, in varying degrees, the financial administrators. For example, the owner of an indoor sports complex in a responsive market will, as the financial decision maker, establish policies about such things as cost recovery targets, free services, employee compensation, etc. However, the implementation of those policies is left to the financial administrators: program managers (who set prices and incur program costs), cashiers (who collect admission fees or check passes), and clerical staff (who handle the payroll).

## Financial Responsibility

In the preceding example, the owner is responsible for her decisions, regardless of the outcomes. If she sets the cost recovery target too low, authorizes too many free passes, or pays her staff too well, then she may not make a profit. On the other hand, if she has instituted sound policies on cost recovery, complementary services, and employee compensation, then she is likely to enjoy a suitable return on her investment. The owner is responsible for either outcome.

In order to realize her financial goals, the sports complex owner will delegate authority and assign duties to her staff. The likelihood of her realizing a profit is dependent on her staff exercising that authority and performing their duties in the way she expects. If they exceed the limits of their authority or fail to do their duty, the staff members are responsible for those offenses only; however, the owner is still responsible for the resulting profit or loss. In financial management, as in any other area of management, authority can be delegated, but responsibility cannot.

## Financial Functions of the Organization

Sport, tourism, and leisure service organizations facilitate two primary finan-

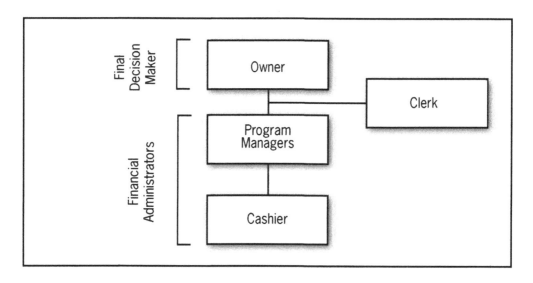

**Figure 5.1**
**Financial management functions and roles within the organizational structure**

cial functions: controlling and acquiring. *Controlling* is an internally oriented function that involves recording, monitoring, and managing the financial consequences of past and current activities. *Acquiring* is an externally oriented function that deals with securing financial resources required to meet current and future needs. The organizational chart of a sport, tourism, and leisure service agency will usually reflect these two functions by designating a *controller* and a *treasurer*. In large organizations, there may be many people working in both a controller's office and a treasurer's office; in smaller organizations, the two functions might be handled by the same person. Furthermore, that single controller/treasurer may also have other non-financial duties. Although desirable in certain situations, there is usually no requirement that a crowd of financial managers be included in the organizational structure. These two primary functions should, however, be adequately addressed in the structure.

The major financial management functions in the sport, tourism, and leisure service organization are handled by skilled individuals who have specific areas of responsibility. Several key positions and their functions are described below.

### Director of Finance

The duties of the director of finance include supervising and coordinating the activities of the Department of Finance. The director of finance serves as a financial adviser to decision-making bodies within the organization and often serves as the chief budget officer.

### Controller (also called "Comptroller")

The controller's duties include describing (by using generally accepted accounting principles [GAAP]) the fi-

nancial events that have occurred within a certain period of time. The controller develops and maintains a management information system and prepares financial forecasts for use by financial decision makers. Additional duties include pre-auditing purchase orders, handling receipts and disbursements, and issuing all payments and invoices. The controller may also be charged with maintaining inventory records.

### Treasurer

The duties of the treasurer focus on the acquisition of funds needed for the operation of the sport and leisure service organization. Private funds may come from a variety of sources, thus requiring the treasurer in the private or commercial setting to maintain and nurture relationships with lenders, stockholders, security markets, and regulatory agencies. In contrast, the treasurer in a public agency works primarily with tax collection and fund generation through special assessments. In addition to collecting all revenues, the treasurer plans cash flow, invests available funds, and recommends pricing policies/strategies that will help to achieve funding objectives.

### Assessor

Public sport and leisure service organizations receive much of their funding from tax revenues. Property taxes are collected according to assessed property values, and the establishment of those values is the duty of the assessor. Working closely with the treasurer, the assessor applies relevant state laws, studies property values, and assesses property for taxation purposes.

### Purchasing Agent

The duties of the purchasing agent go well beyond processing paperwork for ordering materials, supplies, and equipment. An effective purchasing agent establishes standards for regularly purchased items and prepares specifications for each item to be purchased. By maintaining relationships with vendors and suppliers, the purchasing agent can economize on certain bulk or special-order purchases, as well as advise program managers on new services or materials that are available. The purchasing agent purchases all materials, supplies, and equipment for the organization and then receives and inspects them to ensure that specifications have been met. Significant monetary savings can also be realized through the purchasing agent's maintaining of warehouse storage and commodity distribution systems.

### Auditor

Though not incorporated in the finance department, the auditor has a position of great importance to the financial well-being of the organization. The task of the auditor is to periodically provide an independent, objective evaluation of financial management systems and practices. The independent auditor serves as a check on executive officials by determining whether any errors (unintentional misstatements) have been made or whether there are irregularities (deliberate misstatements or unauthorized/illegal depletion of financial resources).

The auditor thoroughly reviews procedures and statements to determine and report whether:

- the financial statements present fairly the organization's financial position;
- the financial statements accurately present (in accordance with GAAP) the results of agency operations;
- the financial activities of the organization are in compliance with local,

state/provincial, and federal laws and regulations;
- the organization has established an adequate system of internal accounting and control;
- there are questionable expenditures;
- there is evidence of waste, abuse, or fraud.

Since the finance department is the primary administrative body (and subject to input by executive officials), it would be unwise for the auditor's position to be too closely associated with that department. To avoid the appearance of the finance department checking up on itself, auditors are usually directly accountable to the chief executive officer or directing authority (board of directors, city council, etc.) and may not even be an employee of the agency. Many large and small sport and leisure service organizations contract with or retain an independent accounting firm to serve as their auditor. In a few local governments, the audit function is carried out by an independently elected auditor or controller.

## Summary

The many aspects of financial management in the sport, tourism, and leisure service organization can most effectively and efficiently be addressed through an organizational structure that clearly defines the lines of authority and differentiates between financial decision-making bodies and financial administrators. Financial officers develop systems and apply standard procedures to monitor, control, and report on the financial position, activities, and future of the organization. They also implement policies that generate required financial resources, as well as relate to program-based departments. The general organization for financial management varies little between public, private not-for-profit, and commercial agencies and maintains the same basic elements in both small and large enterprises.

## NOTES

# CHAPTER 6

# Departmentalization

## Introduction

Financial management functions are the responsibility of specific financial officers (at least a controller and treasurer) and individuals within program units that receive revenues or make and approve expenditure commitments. Financial officers in large organizations might be housed (with respect to organizational structure) in a Department of Finance or similarly named unit. This chapter discusses the relationship of the Department of Finance to other organizational units, including those that also have some financial management roles. Additional discussion is devoted to developing an understanding of the extent to which financial management duties are shared by different people within typical organizations in public parks and recreation agencies, school athletic departments, private not-for-profit organizations, and tourism enterprises.

## Organization for Financial Management in the Public Sector

Figure 6.1 presents a basic organizational chart for a local government (e.g., a city, county, or town). Detailed in the chart are the relationships of the independent auditor to the elected governing body, and the Department of Finance to the institutional hierarchy and other civic departments. This model also represents the general structure of state/provincial and federal governments in the United States and Canada. Note that the responsibility and full authority to manage public finances is vested in the elected governing body. In a representative democracy, this authority comes from the people, and it is to them that the elected body is accountable.

Figure 6.1 shows an independent auditor who reports to the financial decision-making body. It is a standard practice and often a legal requirement for local, state/provincial, and federal governments to have auditors who submit public reports of their reviews to their respective legislatures. As much as possible, these auditors operate independently and without regard to personal or partisan politics.

Also shown in this basic organizational chart is the position of general manager. The general manager is the senior civil servant to whom all department heads report and through whom government policies are articulated. The director of finance reports to the general manager; thus making the latter an important figure in the financial management system. That importance is underscored by the dual role that the general manager, at times, appears to play. This top official is effectively both a financial decision maker and a financial administrator.

Technically, financial decision making or policy setting does not exist at the level of the general manager; however, it must be recognized that this person is in a position to provide selective information that leads the elected body to make certain decisions. Thus he or she has *effective* decision-making power without having formal decision-making authority. The general manager is also the top financial administrator in the government and oversees the work of the director of finance. In this oversight role, the general manager interprets the policy decisions of the elected governing body and, thereby, has further opportunity to broadly influence financial management in the organization.

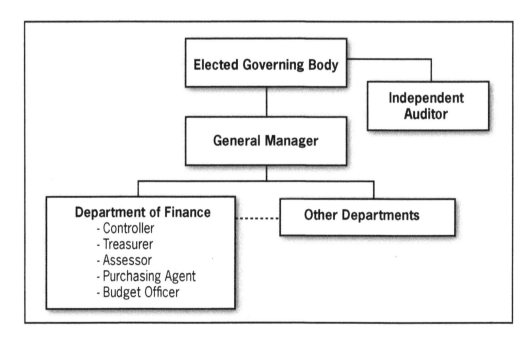

**Figure 6.1**
**Basic organizational chart emphasizing financial management unit**

Figure 6.1 uses a dotted line to represent the relationship between the Department of Finance and the other governmental departments. The dotted line indicates that one department does not take direction from the other(s), but rather, departments must communicate and work together to ensure proper management of financial resources. In reality, the Department of Finance is a support unit to the other program-based departments, yet it does maintain control over most procedures pertaining to budget implementation. In some organizations, financial administrators working within program-based departments actually report both to the program department head and to the Department of Finance. This matrix structure can be an efficient way to manage financial functions with a degree of consistency, as well as avoid duplication that occurs when other departments feel the need to keep their own financial records and develop their own financial management information systems.

## Organization for Financial Management in the Private Not-for-Profit and Commercial Sectors

Whether large, small, private not-for-profit, or commercial, most nonpublic organizations will have a similar basic structure to the government organization typified in Figure 6.1. Instead of from an elected governing body, the private not-for-profit agency will receive policies and directives from an appointed board of directors. In the commercial sector, the decision-making body will be the owner(s) or board that represents the shareholders.

The value of an independent auditor is just as great for not-for-profit organizations as it is for public entities. The independent auditor position is frequently mandated by the organization's charter or by-laws. Some small private not-for-profit sport, tourism, and leisure service agencies rely on local volunteers to conduct their financial audits, while major commercial enterprises may have large in-house auditing departments.

As in the public agency, the day-to-day management of the private not-for-profit or commercial organization is entrusted to the general manager. The title used for this top management position varies, but the most common alternatives are "chief executive officer" or "president."

Finally, the finance division is also an important part of private not-for-profit and commercial sport, tourism, and leisure service organizations. In these nonpublic settings, the finance division continues to fulfill the basic functions of acquiring funds and controlling internal financial activities while relating in a supportive way to the organization's program-based departments.

### *Program Unit Involvement in Financial Management*

Though not designated as financial managers, some individuals in the sport, tourism, and leisure service organization do manage financial resources. They are most likely program personnel who recommend and implement pricing strategies, collect fees, make expenditure commitments, and ensure that program activities are consistent with established fiscal parameters. In a public leisure service organization, for example, the Parks and Recreation Director is responsible for developing and implementing an operating budget. The Recreation Manager makes purchases and wages commitments, as does the Parks Manager. The Administrator and positions within the administrative support unit manage financial resources by controlling petty cash, purchasing, accounting, and reporting.

In a school or college setting, an athletic department has a director who oversees all operations, including the use and acquisition of financial resources. The Athletic Director develops and implements a budget for athletic operations and oversees other areas that also manage finances. One important area for school athletic departments is fundraising and development. The Associate Athletic Director for External Affairs spends a great deal of time and effort identifying and recruiting donors and sponsors, thus assuring an important source of income for the school. Managers of the Athletic Fund record and account for revenues into and expenditures from that account, but are also involved in helping the fund grow (through additional donations and investment). The Associate Athletic Director for Administration and Finance makes certain that all bills are paid and that earned income is properly managed. This individual and others in subordinate units handle a wide variety of expenditure accounts, such as travel, lodging, licensing, staff compensation, marketing, administrative operations, accreditation/affiliation, etc. Income accounts that they manage include ticket sales, sponsorships, concessions, licensing, merchandising, etc.

In a private not-for-profit sport, tourism, or leisure service organization, the Executive Director prepares and implements the budget. This individual also has a somewhat unique responsibility for encouraging fund-raising success and philanthropic support. In representing the not-for-profit organization, the Executive Director works closely with the Development Manager to nurture giving

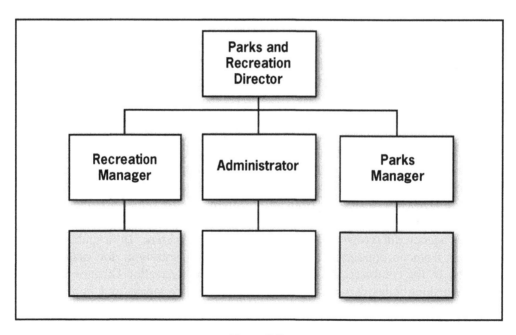

**Figure 6.2**
**Units within a public leisure service agency that are involved in managing financial resources (shown as unshaded blocks)**

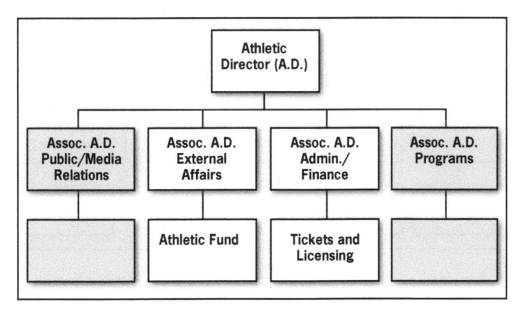

**Figure 6.3**
**Units within a school athletic department that are involved in managing financial resources**
**(shown as unshaded blocks)**

relationships with individuals, foundations, and corporations. The Facility Manager manages financial resources as an expenditure officer and is expected to keep costs down and enhance the revenue potential of the facilities. The Office Manager records financial transactions, makes payments, issues invoices, receives revenue, handles payroll issues, and generates financial status reports and projections. The Program Coordinator provides programs while making expenditure commitments within the limits of the approved budget. The Program Coordinator is also involved in financial management when setting prices and determining the number and nature of revenue-generating programs and services.

It is reasonable to expect that, in a commercial setting, financial resource management is shared by a wider range of positions within the organization than would be the case in public or private-

not-for-profit sport, tourism, and leisure service organizations. The General Manager (GM) of a resort hotel, for example, *must* make the property earn a profit. The GM's job depends on it. Financial management becomes the primary concern of the GM, and he or she ensures that all subordinate managers and staff share that interest. The use of profit centers in resort hotels and other commercial enterprises pushes the concern for and involvement with financial procedures and results to all levels of management. The role of the Human Resources department is limited to salary and benefit issues, and meeting the costs of training requirements. The Accounting Office is involved in financial management in an obvious way, and the Marketing and Sales Department spends money for marketing and generates revenues through group and individual sales. Marketing and sales goals are expressed almost entirely in monetary terms. The Food and Beverage Division plans and

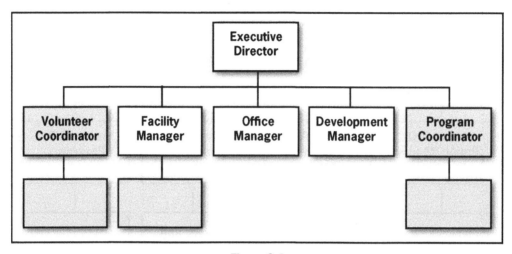

**Figure 6.4**
**Units within a private not-for-profit organization that are involved in managing financial resources (shown as unshaded blocks)**

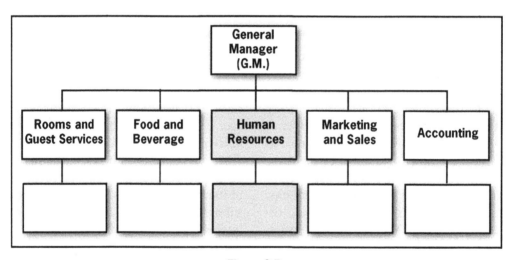

**Figure 6.5**
**Units within a hotel/resort organization that are involved in managing financial resources (shown as unshaded blocks)**

follows a budget for every catered event and for the operation of the restaurant, lounge, snack bar, café, food vending machines, and room service. Food and beverage managers must be smart purchasers and experts in limiting expenses by accurately estimating demand and consumption. The Rooms and Guest Services unit generates revenue through the services they provide. This area includes resort recreation services, to which appropriate pricing structures should be applied and for which expenses should be kept to an appropriate minimum. The staff in each of these areas is usually keenly aware of the impact of their activities on the management of financial resources. Many of their operational decisions are, in fact, financial decisions.

Figures 6.2—6.5 illustrated the slight differences in organizational structures in sport, tourism, and leisure. There are very few organizations, if any, that do not decentralize the management of financial resources, at least to some degree. Likewise, there are very few, if any, sport, tourism, and leisure service organizations that leave all financial management activities up to just one office or person.

## Politics and the Financial Management Organization

Managers of public sport, tourism, and leisure service organizations are generally quick to point out that there is no work environment where politics so much influences day-to-day management as it does in government agencies. Private not-for-profit managers would likely disagree and describe the many frustrations that they experience in their own politically sensitive positions. Further claims to the title of "Most Political Organization" could also be made by managers of commercial sport, tourism, and leisure service organizations who feel that too much of their time and energy is spent on keeping the owners happy rather than doing the job properly.

A reality of management life is the constant exposure to and influence of corporate politics: It is a part of public service management. It is a part of management in the private not-for-profit sector. It is a part of how the commercial sport, tourism, and leisure service organization operates. It is natural, and it is not necessarily bad.

Financial decision makers are usually in such a position because their political viewpoint is consistent with that of the power base (i.e., the voters or the shareholders). It is believed that the management philosophy of the financial decision maker will lead to desired results, and the decision maker is, therefore, empowered to establish fiscal policies for the organization. Financial administrators are expected to reflect that management philosophy in their implementation of the fiscal policies. In reality, it is just as important for the financial administrator to be responsive to the political context as it is to be efficient and effective in performing the technical finance functions of the organization. To underscore the importance of this responsiveness, most financial administrators serve "at the pleasure of the board," and their job security depends on how well they reflect political ideologies and achieve desired results.

In some public organizations, however, there is a stated need for and an interest in achieving nonpartisan, technical competence in financial management. In other words, the voters want to be sure that their tax dollars are managed by the most competent financial administrator, regardless of political party affiliation. In such cases, the organizational structure may include a variety of autonomous or semiautonomous elected fiscal agencies (ranging from boards of tax appeal to boards of assessors) and elected officers such as controllers, treasurers, and assessors. However, the more integrated financial system and organizational structure (with the general manager as the chief steward and distributor of authority) is most common in the public sector and almost universal in the private not-for-profit and commercial sectors.

It should be noted that, while financial managers might not serve a political (policy-making) function in the organization, they are working in an environment that is influenced by political philosophies, structures, and behaviors. Financial management requires a set of skills that goes beyond accounting and forecasting, and includes interpersonal skills that allow the financial manager in sport, tourism, and leisure service organizations to respond to directives that don't always make the most financial sense. An important function of the financial manager is to advise about the 'right' course, and about potential problems with politically motivated decisions. This responsibility is one that cannot be shirked, but it must be understood that the final decision is often made by somebody else in the organization.

## Summary

Financial management specialists may be assigned to a distinct organizational unit and be directed to assist and support program units in such matters as payroll, invoicing, payments, and purchasing. Program specialists in other organizational units usually do have financial management responsibilities, but financial management is not the major skill that they possess, nor is it considered to be a defining element of their assignment.

A variety of organizational structures can support financial management relationships in sport, tourism, and leisure services. Typical structures vary and reflect the public, private not-for-profit, or commercial nature of the enterprise. They also reflect the political realities of the corporate environment and emphasize the importance of hierarchy in financial resource management.

# NOTES

# SECTION C

# Economics

The first six chapters of this book lay the foundation for detailed discussions of the most important aspects of managing financial resources in sport and leisure service organizations. Although we could have provided the reader with a thorough introduction to and exploration of the principles of economics as a preface to an examination of the structural or technical aspects of financial management, we have waited and chosen to highlight and discuss in Chapter 7 those basic economic principles of most immediate concern to managers in the field.

# Economic Principles

## Introduction

An effective sports, tourism, and leisure service manager is not only capable of establishing, directing, and implementing procedures of sound financial management, but is also aware of the basic economic and accounting principles that relate to those procedures. This chapter introduces some elementary economic concepts that are particularly relevant to financial management in sports, tourism, and leisure service organizations. It should be noted that this is a very basic discussion of a few key principles and in no way is meant to supplant the valuable learning that can be gained from a full course of studies in economics. While financial management and accounting require development of technical proficiency, we gain from their parent discipline an understanding of the human element of resource allocation. Economics is a social science that contains specific assumptions about the way people behave as they al-

locate available resources for the purpose of realizing their wants and needs. Economics involves the measurement and quantification of observed or expected relationships and transactions between economic agents. Individuals, families, teams, government departments, and not-for-profit and business organizations are all examples of economic agents.

When, for example, an event manager predicts the attendance at a championship baseball game for which the admission price is $8.00, he applies his understanding of the economic principles of supply and demand. If a public recreation administrator is trying to decide whether investing today in a particular recreation facility or piece of equipment will provide the future returns that she feels are appropriate, she will need to apply her understanding of the economic concepts of inflation, interest, and future values. Furthermore, accounting for the changing value of facilities or equipment over time requires a manager to understand the notion of depreciation, and articulating the benefits of a sports, tourism, or leisure program or enterprise will require an understanding of multipliers, leakage, and inter-industry purchasing as they relate to economic impact assessment.

These key economic principles are important to the effective management of programs, events, attractions, destinations, and facilities. Among other benefits to be gained from studying economics and understanding these few principles is an increased ability to recognize and measure the probable financial outcomes of decisions that might be made with respect to product development, pricing, and promotion. Exploring and understanding these principles can help managers of sport, tourism, and leisure services to see the full effect and impact of specific financial decisions, thereby enhancing their ability to successfully meet their respective financial objectives.

## Supply and Demand

The terms supply and demand have more precise meanings than are suggested by their everyday use. In casual conversation, for example, reference is made to the supply of gasoline, and an opinion might be expressed that, after learning about the huge oil reserves in the Persian Gulf, there is a large supply of gasoline—certainly enough to meet the public demand. More correctly, the assertion is that there is a large stock of gasoline—enough to meet current needs. The difference between stock and supply is subtle, but important. *Stock* refers to the quantity of a product or resource that exists. *Supply* refers to the quantity of a product or resource that the owner is willing to offer or make available at a given price. Oil-producing nations with large

petroleum reserves have extensive stock, but may have a very small supply when the price being offered is only $10 per barrel. Without any change in the stock of oil, the supply would increase significantly if the price rose to $50 per barrel. Similarly, there is a very small supply of excellent basketball players who will play for a professional team when offered a salary of $5,000 per year. The supply will, however, increase considerably when the annual salary offer goes to $50 million. In this illustration, the number of excellent basketball players did not increase, but the supply for the professional league did. The relationship between quantity made available and the price offered is graphically represented in Figure 7.1 and is referred to as the supply curve.

From the data presented in Figure 7.1, it appears that there are only about 25 excellent basketball players who are willing to play for a professional team for $20,000 per year. There are, of course, many more equally talented players, but they probably will choose to pursue more lucrative careers for which their college education has prepared them. When the invitation to join the team comes with a $40,000 salary offer, there are many more players (about 40) willing to consider the opportunity. Teams that offer $90,000 per year find an even greater number of excellent players (approximately 70) from whom to recruit. The supply curve illustrates the human behavior expected in situations of exchange. The supply curve shows how the quantities that are available increase and decrease in relation to the prices offered for the product or resource.

In discussing demand, it is common to refer to the amount wanted or needed. The more traveling a team wants to do, the more it wants gasoline for its bus. However, the precise meaning of

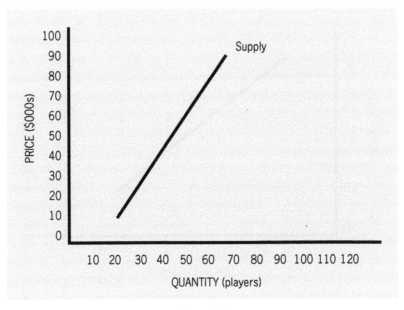

**Figure 7.1**
**The supply curve for athletes in a professional sport**

demand is the amount of a product or re-source wanted at a given price. When the consumer price of gasoline is $1.90 per gallon, the team is more inclined to travel, and the quantity of gasoline wanted is greater than when the price is $3.40 per gallon. Similarly, if would-be professional athletes are demanding annual salaries of $20 million to play, the number of teams and the number of player positions will be less than if players could be contracted for $50,000 per year. The relationship between quantity wanted and the price of the resource is graphically represented in Figure 7.2 and is referred to as the demand curve.

Using the demand curve represented in Figure 7.2, it is observed that when players demand $80,000 salaries, the league is only interested in or able to acquire approximately 25 players. If the salaries are only $20,000, perhaps smaller markets can afford to have teams, team rosters can be expanded, and more players (approximately 100) will be needed.

As the price goes down, the demand goes up. The supply and demand curves shown in Figures 7.1 and 7.2, respectively, appear to be straight lines rather than arc-like curves. The extent of curvature will vary according to the nature of the resource and the behavior of the market. A straight line may, in fact, be the best representation of the price/quantity relationship and is, for convenience and simplicity, used in our discussion of supply and demand. All curves shown in Figure 7.3 can be accurate reflections of either supply or demand.

It might also be observed, when comparing the above supply and demand curves, that the supply and demand curves slope in opposing directions. Supply curves have a positive slope; that is, they show that the quantity made available increases when the price offered increases. Conversely, demand curves have a negative slope. This means that increases in price are associated with decreases in the quantity wanted. If the

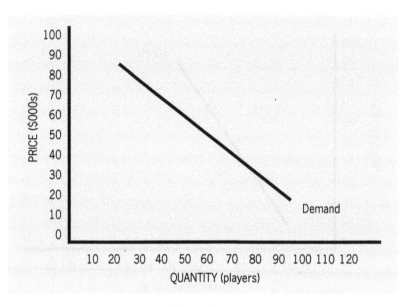

**Figure 7.2**
**The demand curve for athletes in a professional sport**

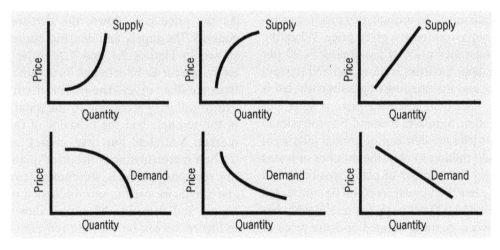

**Figure 7.3**
**Examples of supply and demand curves**

supply curve and the demand curve for a particular product or service are both drawn on the same field, they will intersect at some point. This point is called the equilibrium point. At the equilibrium point, the corresponding price motivates the supplier to make available the same quantity of a resource that is wanted by the consumers at that price. At any price above the equilibrium point, there is insufficient demand (i.e., too much supply). At any price below the equilibrium point, there is inadequate supply (i.e., too much demand).

Supply and demand curves are constructed using data that describe the availability of and the want for resources at different prices. They are the result of experimentation, simulation, and observation of behaviors in similar exchange situations. In the following example, some very simple data will be used to illustrate three different approaches to the estimation of supply and/or demand.

## Estimating Supply and Demand

Data:

A marina developer calculated that appropriate revenues could be generated if he offered 20 boat slips for $10 each. If, somehow, his customers could be convinced to pay $90 for a slip, the developer could build a larger facility and realize appropriate revenues by offering 73 boat slips. After studying marina operations at another waterfront in the area, he found that one that charged only $20 was able to attract 100 customers, and another that charged $80 attracted only 25 boat owners. These data are summarized in Table 7.1.

Problems:
• How many boat slips should he build if he decides to charge $40 per slip?
• How many customers would want his $40 boat slips?
• At what price will the supply of boat slips equal the demand?
• How many boat slips should he build in order to take full advantage of the demand without creating more capacity than is necessary? (Alabama State Parks, Department of Conservation and Natural Resources, 2000.)

There are two approaches to solving these problems: (1) approximation through graphing, and (2) algebraic calculation. These approaches are explained in the following examples.

1. Approximation through Graphing

Using graph paper, plot the known data points and draw the supply and

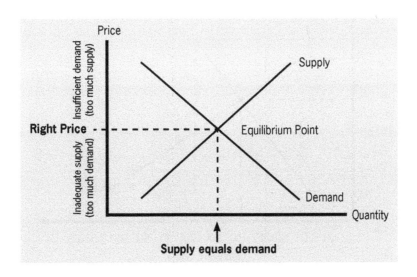

**Figure 7.4**
**The supply/demand equilibrium point**

**Table 7.1**
**Summary of supply and demand data for proposed marina**

| Price | Supply | Demand |
|-------|--------|--------|
| $90 | 73 | |
| $80 | | 25 |
| $40 | ? | ? |
| $20 | | 100 |
| $10 | 20 | |

demand curves (Figure 7.5). For a given price, find its intercept on the supply or demand curve and identify the corresponding points on the horizontal axis representing units of supply/demand. For example, at $40, it appears that the supply will be about 40 units and the demand will be for about 75 units.

It also appears that the equilibrium point (where the supply and demand curves intersect) is somewhere around the $60 mark, with supply and demand at that price being approximately 50 units.

Obviously, this method has the advantage of simplicity, but it results in approximate values. In most cases, the approximation is sufficient, especially in consideration of the fact that the supply and demand curves themselves are somewhat imprecise.

### 2. Algebraic Calculation

The second method provides more precise results, but these too are based on somewhat imprecise values for points along the supply and demand curves. This method involves the use of basic algebra as follows:

Use the formula for calculating any point on a straight line. In this case, the straight lines are slopes.

$$y=ax+b$$
- where: y is a given price
- x is the quantity supplied or demanded at that price
- a is the slope of the supply or demand curve
- b is a constant

First calculate the slopes of the sup-

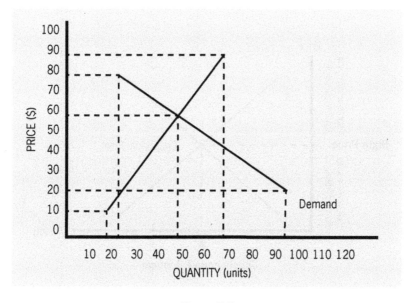

**Figure 7.5**
**Supply/demand curve graph**

ply and demand curves:

Slope (supply) = Change in price /Change in quantity

=(90-10) / (73-20)
=1.5

Slope (demand) = Change in price / Change in quantity

=(80-20) / (25-100)
= -0.8

Next, calculate the constants for both the supply and demand curves.

For the supply curve, use the known coordinates of any point on the line. For example, use $10 and 20 units and a slope of 1.5. Thus:

10 = 1.5 (20) + b
b = -20

Likewise, for the demand curve, use the known coordinates of any point on the line. For example, use $20 and 100 units and a slope of -0.9. Thus:

20 = -0.8 (100) + b
b = 100

To estimate the supply and demand when the price is $40, simply use 40 as the value for y, use the same values for the slope and the constant, and solve for x.

(ignore the minus sign)

Supply Demand
y = 1.5x - 20 y = -0.8x + 100
40 = 1.5x - 20 (40) = -0.8x + 100
x = 40 units x = -75 units

Therefore, if the price is set at $40, the supply will be 40 units, but the demand will be for 75 units. It would be useful to find a price where the supply meets the demand and to know what that supply/demand quantity will be.

With slopes and constants already established, x (the quantity at equilibrium) can be calculated by equating y (price), even though its value is not yet known.

If y(supply) = y(demand), then

1.5x - 20 = -0.8x + 100
- x = 52 (the quantity supplied/demanded at the equilibrium point)

To calculate the price at equilibrium, substitute the calculated value for x in either of the equations for supply or demand.

Supply: y = 1.5 (52) - 20 Demand: y = -0.8 (52) + 100

y = $58

It has now been determined that, at a price of $58, the supply and demand will both be 52 units.

(Note that this result is very close to the result from approximation through graphing [$60 and 50 units] and, in most circumstances, is close enough.)

It is important to note that supply and demand curves are not fixed for eternity. Rather, they reflect the behavior of a certain market or industry at a particular time. Either curve or both curves may change in response to common circumstances or conditions. For example, the pattern of demand for spectator seating at a high school football game may move to the right (i.e., more will be demanded at a given price) if it bcomes to be apparent that the team has a good chance of qualifying for the state championship for the first time in 25 years. Likewise, the curve can move to the left (i.e., less will be demanded at a given price) if the football team consistently loses by 30 or more points to competitors who play their second string for three quarters of the game. Such movements in patterns of demand do not necessarily change the supply curve, but they will likely affect stock. Refer to the new equilibrium point shown in Figure 7.6 and notice how the number of seats that can be sold and the price at which they can be sold increase solely as a result of change in demand.

Not only can shifts in demand occur, but also attitudes about and opportunities for supply can change. For example, a Boy Scout camp may, because of surplus capacity and a generous operating grant, be able to substantially reduce individual participation fees for the usual number of campers. This price reduction also means that the camp administrators will be under pressure to serve more campers because of the increased demand at those lower prices. Figure 7.7 illustrates the impacts of changes in supply conditions.

There are many conditions that can influence shifts in supply and demand curves. Generally, they relate to capacity and production opportunity, or to consumer need and sentiment. Some of the most common influences of supply and demand for leisure and sport services are identified in Table 7.2.

Managers of tourism, leisure, and sport organizations who understand the economic principles of supply and demand are well equipped to deal with the relative uncertainties of forecasting revenues and anticipating expenses. They are better able to apply the art of anticipating human behavior in exchange situations to the technical process of budgeting and other aspects of financial management.

## Inflation

In discussing the principles of supply and demand, it is evident that decisions with regard to the offering of or desire for stock reflect the natural desire of both producers and consumers to maximize their

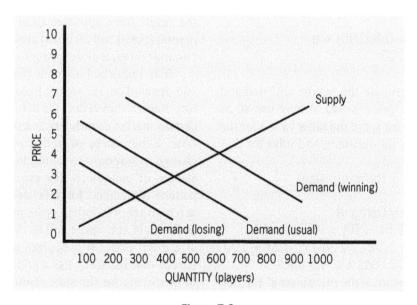

**Figure 7.6**
**Illustration of shifts in the demand curve**

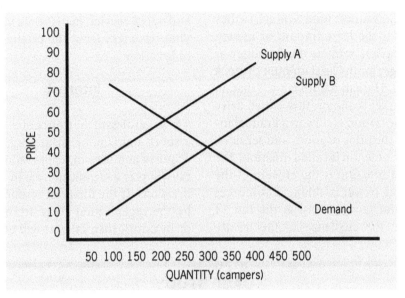

**Figure 7.7**
**Illustration of shifts in the supply curve**

**Table 7.2**
**Common influences on supply and demand for leisure and sport services**

| Condition | Influence |
|---|---|
| Increased ability to offer services due to:<br>—new or expanded facilities<br>—new or expanded staff<br>—new equipment<br>—staff with new skills/certification | Move supply curve to the right. |
| Reduced capacity of physical plant | Move supply curve to the left. |
| Realization of greater efficiency due to economies of scale | Move supply curve to the right. |
| Revised operational mandate or mission. | Move supply curve in either direction. |
| Change in market need/problem resolution | Move demand curve to left if problem resolved or need reduced. New problems or needs move demand curve to the right. |
| Change in market resources | Move demand curve to the right if time, money, transportation, etc., more available. Move demand curve to left if constraints increased. |
| Panic/Perception of scarcity | Move demand curve to right. |
| Competition | Move demand curve to the left. |

returns. Consumers want as much as they can get for the least amount of money, while suppliers want as much money as they can get for the least amount of stock depletion. Human nature is such that, in a free market economy, this valued drive for maximization results in a gradual increase in the price of goods and services. This phenomenon is called inflation. The impact of inflation is the erosion of the purchasing power of financial resources that do not grow at least at the rate of inflation. The challenge to the leisure and sport service manager is to protect vital resources from the eroding effects of inflation.

## Interest

Regardless of the source of money that a sport, tourism, or leisure organization acquires and uses in its operation, interest will play a significant role in financial decisions. If the financial resources used by the organization come from lenders or investors, then interest will be paid to

---

### CASE STUDY
#### The Alabama Experience

In the mid-1980s, the Alabama State Park system stopped receiving tax revenues from the state general fund. This included money for their operational budget and capital improvement budget. By 2000, the state park system was in desperate trouble. The parks were in poor shape, almost no money had been spent on improvements, personnel were poorly paid, morale was low, and their lodge system was in such poor shape that few people stayed in their facilities.

By 1990, the state park system received $4 million in cigarette tax funds and generated $24.3 million in revenues from entrance fees, lodge room rentals, campground reservations, restaurants, and similar outdoor recreation services. By 1999, the total operating budget had risen to $28.8 million (or about $500,000 over a 10-year period). It seemed a rea-

State parks are dependent upon multiple sources of income for successful operations.

sonable amount of money to operate the state budget until inflation's impact is measured. During the same 10-year period the rate of inflation averaged 2.8 percent per year. Inflation's impact on purchasing power can be measured through the use of an inflation calculator. The impact of inflation on the operating budget was measured by converting each year's budget (from 1991 to 1999) to 1990 dollars. The calculator applied the impact of inflation on each year's operating budget and converted the value of each year's budget to 1990 dollars. When this was applied, it was discovered that the $28.8 million 1999 operating budget only had a purchasing power of $23.8 million, or $5 million less purchasing power in 1999 then in 1990. Alabama's operating budget, while appearing to hold steady, had actually decreased in purchasing power a total of 8% over the 10-year period. The actual loss in purchasing power over the 10-year period exceeded $25 million.

them in addition to the original amount borrowed or invested. If the funds used come from internal reserves, then their use will reduce the interest that could have been earned by those reserves. The impact of interest should not be ignored. In fact, this point is emphasized in the unofficial definition: *"Interest—those who understand it, get it; those who don't, pay it."*

Interest is the time value of money. It represents what it costs an economic agent to consume immediately by using funds that it does not have. It represents what an economic agent receives for postponing consumption by lending or investing funds that it does have. Interest is typically expressed as a percentage of an original amount (called principal) that is paid by a borrower or earned by a lender on a per-annum basis. For example, 7% interest on a principal of $2,000 would oblige a borrower to pay the lender the original $2,000 plus $140 interest after one year. The lender may extend the loan period for one more year, after which the borrower would repay the $2,000, plus another $140 (if interest was also paid after the first year). In this case, the time value of the money was $280. If the borrower did not make the $140 interest payment after the first year, that amount would be considered as an additional loan and be added to the principal to be repaid after the second year. After the second year, the borrower would, in addition to the $2,140 principal, pay an interest charge of $149.80 (7% of $2,140). The total time value of the money when the interest is compounded (i.e., carried over and included in the principal) was $140.00 + $149.80 = $289.80.

## Future Value

Unless the owner of money hides it in a sock or under the mattress, that money will be invested and thereby has the potential to grow or increase in value over time. Such is the effect of interest. However, the effect of inflation is the erosion of the purchasing power of money over time. Obviously, it is hoped that the rate of growth will be greater than the rate of inflation. The financial manager works to protect the purchasing power of the sport, tourism, or leisure organization's money. In other words, the financial manager's first goal is to ensure that the future value of a sum is sufficient to overcome the impact of inflation. Earlier in this chapter, it was shown how a sum of money increases in value over time, thanks to interest. The *future value* of an investment can be calculated as follows:

If interest is paid each year for a given number of years, the future value (F) of an original sum is P+n (Pi), where P = the principal (the original amount invested), n = the term (number of years until repayment of the principal), and i = the interest rate. After two years, the value of $2,000 earning 7% paid annually is:

$$F = P+n \ (Pi)$$

$$\$2,000 \ + \ 2(\$2,000 \ \times \ .07) \ = \ \$2,280$$

If the interest is compounded, the future value of the original sum is calculated using a more complicated formula:

$$F = P(1+ i)^n$$

Fortunately, table values can be used to avoid calculation of $(1+i)^n$. Interest Table A (which can be found at the end of the book and is excerpted here in Table 7.3) provides interest factors ($T_A$) to be substituted in a restated formula for the future value of a sum with interest compounded. The restated formula is:

$$F = PT_A.$$

Note that the product of P (the original $2,000 investment) and $T_A$ (the table value for $n = 2$ years and $i = 7\%$) is $2,000 x 1.145 = $2,290. This outcome is essentially the same as was earlier determined to be the future value of the sum after two years earning 7% interest.

The foregoing discussion of future values helps the sport, tourism, and leisure organization determine the future value of resources that it currently has and is willing to invest. For example, an agency that plans to fund a future building project by setting aside (investing) $10,000 at the beginning of each year for the next five years is able to calculate the expected balance of that earmarked account at the end of the five-year period.

Assuming a stable interest rate of 8% for five years, the future value of the first amount invested (F1) will be:

$$F1 = P(T_A) = \$10,000 (1.469) = \$14,690$$

To this amount, add the future value of the next $10,000 installment (F2) invested at 8% for four years:

$$F2 = P(T_A) = \$10,000 (1.360) = \$13,600$$

Continue calculating the future values for the remaining installments (while paying attention to the fact that the $T_A$ value should reflect the declining $n$ [years of investment]). Sum the future values to determine the money that will be available for the project after five years.

$$F1 = P(T_A) = \$10,000 (1.469) = \$14,690$$
$$F2 = P(T_A) = \$10,000 (1.360) = \$13,600$$
$$F3 = P(T_A) = \$10,000 (1.260) = \$12,600$$
$$F4 = P(T_A) = \$10,000 (1.166) = \$11,660$$
$$F5 = P(T_A) = \$10,000 (1.080) = \$10,080$$

### Table 7.3
### Excerpt from Interest Table A $(1+ i)^n$

| n\i | 6% | 7% | 8% | 9% | 10% | 12% | 15% |
|---|---|---|---|---|---|---|---|
| 1 | 1.060 | 1.070 | 1.080 | 1.090 | 1.100 | 1.120 | 1.150 |
| 2 | 1.124 | 1.145 | 1.166 | 1.188 | 1.210 | 1.254 | 1.323 |
| 3 | 1.191 | 1.225 | 1.260 | 1.295 | 1.331 | 1.405 | 1.521 |
| 4 | 1.262 | 1.311 | 1.360 | 1.412 | 1.464 | 1.574 | 1.749 |
| 5 | 1.338 | 1.403 | 1.469 | 1.539 | 1.611 | 1.762 | 2.011 |
| 6 | 1.419 | 1.501 | 1.587 | 1.677 | 1.772 | 1.974 | 2.313 |
| 7 | 1.504 | 1.606 | 1.714 | 1.828 | 1.949 | 2.211 | 2.660 |
| 8 | 1.594 | 1.718 | 1.851 | 1.993 | 2.144 | 2.476 | 3.059 |
| 9 | 1.689 | 1.838 | 1.999 | 2.172 | 2.358 | 2.773 | 3.518 |
| 10 | 1.791 | 1.967 | 2.159 | 2.367 | 2.594 | 3.106 | 4.046 |
| 15 | 2.397 | 2.759 | 3.172 | 3.642 | 4.177 | 5.474 | 8.137 |
| 20 | 3.207 | 3.870 | 4.661 | 5.604 | 6.727 | 9.646 | 16.367 |
| 25 | 4.292 | 5.427 | 6.848 | 8.623 | 10.835 | 17.000 | 32.919 |

Total $62,630

By setting aside $10,000 per year for the next five years, the organization will have $62,630 for its building project.

## Present Value

The calculation of future values requires knowledge of a beginning amount (principal), a term of investment, and the applicable interest rate. There are, however, situations wherein the financial manager has a target future value but needs to know how much to invest at a given rate for a specified term to achieve that target. In a sense, the manager needs to reverse the procedure for determining future value in order to calculate a present value. For illustrative purposes, assume that an athletic team has been invited to travel to and participate in a prestigious tournament in just a little more than two years from now. The team's manager has worked with a transportation agency, hotels, and others to secure a firm price for services needed at the time of the event. The estimated team expenses to be paid at the time of the trip total $40,000. Team members are required to have 50 percent of the trip funds deposited in the team's interest-bearing account two years before the event. The remainder is payable at the end of the two years, just prior to departure. How much money has to be deposited now? The amount of $20,000 comes to mind quickly, but, after considering what was just discussed about future values, it becomes evident that all that is needed is an amount that in two years will have become $20,000. The question is actually, "What is the present value of the future sum of $20,000?" Using, for example, 6% as the interest rate, the present value can be calculated in the following manner:

$$P = F[1/(1+i)^n ] = \$20,000$$
$$[1/(1+.06)2] = \$20,000 (0.890) =$$
$$\$17,800$$

The team needs to deposit only $17,800 now and $20,000 later to have the full $40,000 at the time of the trip.

Once again, a formula has been introduced that may look a bit intimidating. Fortunately, there is another table that eliminates the need for cumbersome calculations. Interest Table B (which can be found at the end of the book and is excerpted here in Table 7.4) provides values from the solution of $[1/(1+i)^n]$ when calculating present values.

In the previous illustration, solution of the formula $[1/(1+i)^n]$ generated an interest factor of 0.890. The Table B value corresponding to $i =.06$ and $n = 2$ also generates the interest factor of 0.890. The formula for calculating present value can, therefore, also be expressed as:

$$P = F(T_B)$$

## Depreciation

Physical assets used by sport, tourism, and leisure organizations do have a finite life span. With the exception of land, assets such as buildings and equipment eventually wear out or become obsolete because of market or technological developments. The loss of or reduced productivity of these resources is recognized and quantified as *depreciation*. In accounting, depreciation is considered as an expense, but not in the same way as is the cash outlay for the purchase of production supplies or services. The precise accounting procedure for dealing with depreciation is discussed in Chapter 17.

**Table 7.4**
**Excerpt from Interest Table B $1/(1+i)^n$**

| n\i | 6% | 7% | 8% | 9% | 10% | 12% | 15% |
|---|---|---|---|---|---|---|---|
| 1 | 0.943 | 0.935 | 0.926 | 0.917 | 0.909 | 0.893 | 0.870 |
| 2 | 0.890 | 0.873 | 0.857 | 0.842 | 0.826 | 0.797 | 0.756 |
| 3 | 0.840 | 0.816 | 0.794 | 0.772 | 0.751 | 0.712 | 0.658 |
| 4 | 0.792 | 0.763 | 0.735 | 0.708 | 0.683 | 0.636 | 0.572 |
| 5 | 0.747 | 0.713 | 0.681 | 0.650 | 0.621 | 0.567 | 0.497 |
| 6 | 0.705 | 0.666 | 0.630 | 0.596 | 0.564 | 0.507 | 0.432 |
| 7 | 0.665 | 0.623 | 0.583 | 0.547 | 0.513 | 0.452 | 0.376 |
| 8 | 0.627 | 0.582 | 0.540 | 0.502 | 0.467 | 0.404 | 0.327 |
| 9 | 0.592 | 0.544 | 0.500 | 0.460 | 0.424 | 0.361 | 0.284 |
| 10 | 0.558 | 0.508 | 0.463 | 0.422 | 0.386 | 0.322 | 0.247 |
| 15 | 0.417 | 0.362 | 0.315 | 0.275 | 0.239 | 0.183 | 0.123 |
| 20 | 0.312 | 0.258 | 0.215 | 0.178 | 0.149 | 0.104 | 0.061 |
| 25 | 0.233 | 0.184 | 0.146 | 0.116 | 0.092 | 0.059 | 0.030 |

At this point, the techniques for calculating depreciation will be presented.

One way of calculating depreciation is to divide the original value (sometimes referred to as the starting book value) of an asset by its expected life span. For example, a $6,000 electronic notice board at a community center may have a five-year life span, after which any repairs needed would be too expensive or may be impossible because of changing technology.

Table 7.5 illustrates the steady reduction in value of the bulletin board during the five years. This is called *straight line depreciation.* Note that the bulletin board has no book value or salvage value at the end of its life span.

Not all assets depreciate to zero value at the end of their projected life spans. Furthermore, only some will depreciate at a constant rate, as was expressed in the preceding example of straight-line depreciation. In reality, many assets will decrease in value more at the beginning of their use than later on, and many will outlast projected life spans, as well as maintain some salvage value, even when obsolete or nonfunctional. *Declining bal-*

**Table 7.5**
**Annual starting values, depreciation, and remaining book values after straight line depreciation**

| Period | Starting Book Value | Depreciation Amount | Remaining Book Value |
|---|---|---|---|
| Year 1 | $6,000 | $1,200 | $4,800 |
| Year 2 | $4,800 | $1,200 | $3,600 |
| Year 3 | $3,600 | $1,200 | $2,400 |
| Year 4 | $2,400 | $1,200 | $1,200 |
| Year 5 | $1,200 | $1,200 | $0 |

*ance depreciation* reflects these realities. With declining balance depreciation, a depreciation rate is set for an asset based on industry standards. This rate affects both the amount of annual depreciation and the salvage value.

To calculate first-year depreciation and remaining book value (salvage value), divide the starting book value of the asset by its life span, and then multiply that number by the appropriate depreciation rate. Expressed as a formula:

(Starting Book Value/Life Span) x Depreciation Rate = Depreciation

For example, a $6,000 pitching machine with a five-year life span and 150% depreciation rate would depreciate ($6,000/5) x 1.5 = $1,800 in the first year and have a remaining book value of $6,000 – $1,800 = $4,200. After the second year, it will have depreciated ($4,200/5) x 1.5 = $1,260 and have a remaining book value of $4,200 – $1,260 = $2,940. As shown in Table 7.6, the final year's depreciation will be much lower (only $432), and there will be a salvage value of $1,009.

An important advantage of declining balance depreciation is the tax shelter it offers to profits generated early in an enterprise. Since depreciation is considered an expense, the taxable profits are reduced, but not the cash that is generated from operations. These cash reserves are more critical in the early stages of an enterprise than later, when the depreciation amount is reduced.

Table 7.7 provides a comparison of the depreciation amounts and remaining book values of a $6,000 asset that is straight-line depreciated, and declining-balance depreciated at 150 percent and 200 percent. The choice of depreciation method and seemingly small differences in depreciation rates clearly have significant impacts on how the sports, tourism, or leisure service organization accounts for the mortality of its physical resources.

## Sensitivity to Changes in Price

Consumers of sport, tourism, and leisure services respond to changes in prices in several different ways. In some cases, an increase in price will result in an increase in consumption because the price increase is thought to be an indication of improved service quality. Most often, however, increases in price have the opposite effect on consumption. When the price goes up, consumption goes down.

The degree to which consumption decreases with a given increase in price

**Table 7.6**
**Annual starting values, depreciation, and remaining book values after declining balance depreciation (150%)**

| Period | Starting Book Value | Depreciation Amount | Remaining Book Value |
|---|---|---|---|
| Year 1 | $6,000 | $1,800 | $4,200 |
| Year 2 | $4,200 | $1,260 | $2,940 |
| Year 3 | $2,940 | $882 | $2,058 |
| Year 4 | $2,058 | $617 | $1,441 |
| Year 5 | $1,441 | $432 | $1,009 |

**Table 7.7**
**Comparison of depreciation amounts and remaining book values for straight line declining balance (150%) and declining balance (200%) depreciation of a $6,000 asset**

| Period | Straight Line | 150% | 200% |
|---|---|---|---|
| Year 1 | $1,200 | $1,800 | $2,400 |
| Year 2 | $1,200 | $1,260 | $1,440 |
| Year 3 | $1,200 | $882 | $864 |
| Year 4 | $1,200 | $617 | $518 |
| Year 5 | $1,200 | $432 | $311 |
| Total Depreciation | $6,000 | $4,991 | $5,533 |
| Remaining Book Value | $0 | $1,009 | $467 |

will differ between consumer markets. Some groups of consumers are more sensitive to price changes than others, and it is important for the financial manager in sport, tourism, and leisure service organizations to understand and be able to make sound decisions based on an understanding of price-induced fluctuations in demand.

The measure of demand fluctuations is referred to as *elasticity of demand*. The measure of price-induced demand fluctuations is called *price elasticity of demand*. More specifically, price elasticity of demand is defined as the percentage change in a quantity consumed that is caused by a percentage change in price. For example, suppose that a 1.0 percent increase in the admission price results in an 0.5 percent decrease in sales to a particular market segment. The price elasticity of demand for this market segment and this product would be –0.5.

Allowing that an increase in price practically always results in a decrease in demand, the calculated value of price demand elasticity would always be negative. An important academic/practical contradiction deserves attention at this point. Because elasticities are always negative

values (and to avoid confusion when comparing those values) economists usually ignore the negative sign. Thus, an elasticity of –2.5 would be considered greater than –2.4 (in spite of what is learned in elementary school mathematics).

Consider the following illustration, which uses admission price and attendance data from A.J.'s Aussieland Theme Park.

To calculate the price elasticity of demand for any of the four market segments, use the appropriate data from Table 7.8 and apply the following formula:

Price Elasticity=

$$\frac{\text{Change in attendance/(Sum of attendance/2)}}{\text{Change price/(Sum of prices/2)}}$$

Example: For the child market segment in 2004-2005, the price elasticity of demand would be:

Price Elasticity =

$$\frac{(120,000 - 150,000) / ((120,000 + 150,000)/2)}{(3.50 - 3.00) / ((3.00 + 3.50)/2)}$$

$$= -1.44$$

**Table 7.8**
**Sample price and attendance data for four market segments**

| Market Segment | Season | Price | Attendance |
|---|---|---|---|
| Child | 2004 | $3.00 | 150,000 |
| Child | 2005 | $3.50 | 120,000 |
| Child | 2006 | $4.00 | 100,000 |
| Youth | 2004 | $4.00 | 105,00 |
| Youth | 2005 | $5.00 | 99,500 |
| Youth | 2006 | $6.00 | 92,000 |
| Adult | 2004 | $7.00 | 60,000 |
| Adult | 2005 | $8.00 | 52,500 |
| Adult | 2006 | $10.00 | 42,000 |
| Senior | 2004 | $6.00 | 35,000 |
| Senior | 2005 | $6.50 | 28,000 |
| Senior | 2006 | $7.00 | 23,000 |

Other elasticities were calculated in an identical manner and are presented in the Table 7.9.

Note that the calculated elasticities for the child and senior markets are both "greater" than 1.0 (remember to ignore the minus sign). This means that a greater percentage of change was observed in attendance than was affected by price. As demonstrated by their change in demand, the children and the seniors appear to be relatively sensitive to price changes. In fact, they are so sensitive that the additional revenue received from increased admission fees paid by the 120,000 remaining customers in 2003 was $30,000 less than the amount received in 2001 from the 150,000 customers who paid the lower fee. Market segments with an elasticity of greater than 1.0 are said to be *relatively elastic*. They are markets for which a change in price results in an opposite change in revenue (i.e., increasing prices produces decreasing revenue; decreasing prices produces increasing revenue).

The calculated elasticities for the youth market segment are "less" than 1.0, which indicates that the youth market is relatively insensitive to price changes at A.J.'s Aussieland. Market segments with an elasticity of less than 1.0 are said to be *relatively inelastic.* They are markets for which a change in price results in a parallel change in revenue (i.e., increasing prices produces increasing revenue; decreasing prices produces decreasing revenue).

The adult market is called a *unitary elastic* market segment because price changes, although they cause a decrease in attendance, do not result in either an increase or a decrease in revenues. Unitary elastic markets have a price demand elasticity of approximately 1.0. For the purpose of comparison, the linear demand curves for three markets that share a common point on their demand curves are presented in Figure 7.8.

**Table 7.9**
**Sample data and computed elasticities for four market segments**

| Market Segment | Season | Price | Attendance | Elasticity |
|---|---|---|---|---|
| Child | 2004 | $3.00 | 150,000 | |
| Child | 2005 | $3.50 | 120,000 | -1.44 |
| Child | 2006 | $4.00 | 100,000 | -1.36 |
| | | | | |
| Youth | 2004 | $4.00 | 105,000 | |
| Youth | 2005 | $5.00 | 99,500 | -0.24 |
| Youth | 2006 | $6.00 | 92,000 | -0.43 |
| | | | | |
| Adult | 2004 | $7.00 | 60,000 | |
| Adult | 2005 | $8.00 | 52,500 | -1.00 |
| Adult | 2006 | $10.00 | 42,000 | -1.00 |
| | | | | |
| Senior | 2004 | $6.00 | 35,000 | |
| Senior | 2005 | $6.50 | 28,000 | -2.78 |
| Senior | 2006 | $7.00 | 23,000 | -2.78 |

From Figure 7.8, it is evident that markets that are less sensitive to price changes (inelastic) are represented by steep demand curves. Conversely, the demand curves for more price sensitive (elastic) markets will be less sloped.

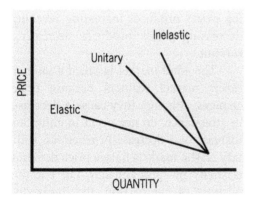

**Figure 7.8**
**Comparison of demand curves for elastic, inelastic, and unitary elastic markets**

## Economic Impacts

A common strategy for winning support for a major tourism, recreation, or sports development project is the declaration of economic benefits that will be realized in the community by virtue of that particular project. A city council considering the construction of a major sports stadium might be influenced by the promise of hundreds of new jobs in the community and millions of dollars of additional sales, household income, and tax revenues. Because of the influence that such promises may have, it is important for the sport, tourism, and leisure service manager to understand the basics of economic impact analysis and be able to critically evaluate such considerations.

A simple illustration will lay the foundation for this discussion. Assume that Maurice visits the small town of Striderville and spends $100 on crafts made and sold locally by Jean. Jean needs a new display case, so she hires Stefan to build one for her. She pays Stefan $80 and spends the remaining $20 at Vicki's produce stand at the Farmer's Market. Stefan pays $35 for materials bought in New York City, spends $30 on computer software from a mail order company in St. Louis, and buys $15 worth of produce from Vicki. Vicki pays $35 to her lawyer, Susan, who hires Rufus to tend her garden while she attends a professional meeting in Orlando. Rufus is paid $20, while the remaining $15 of Susan's income goes toward her trip. Rufus spends his $20 on garden tools manufactured in Seattle by Ethel & Pen Tool Co. Figure 7.9 diagrams this series of transactions.

Note that, in the above scenario, money was introduced into the Strider-

ville economy by Maurice and was respent by several people. Some of the money was spent on locally produced goods and services and some was spent outside the community. Eventually, all the money introduced by Maurice was sent to New York City ($35), St. Louis ($30), Orlando ($15), and Seattle ($20). The exogenous funds had circulated within the economy and then leaked out through outside spending. However, Maurice's $100 did result in $270 of spending (economic activity) in the community. Its direct impact was multiplied 2.7 times, and it contributed to the employment income of five people in Striderville.

Economic impact assessment measures the amount of local respending of money that comes into the economy

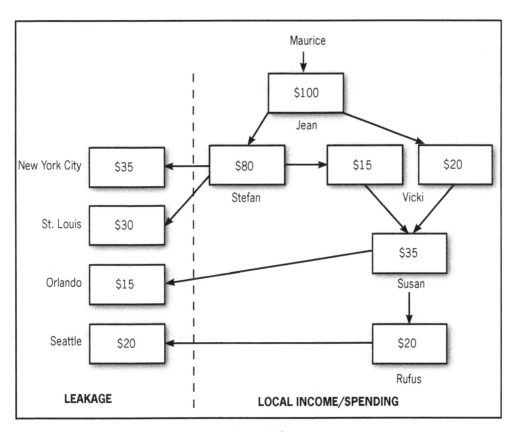

**Figure 7.9**
**Transaction series showing local re-spending and leakage**

because of a particular event or project. It results in a description of the local income, local sales, and local tax revenues generated by exogenous funds. It results in quantification of the employment created by new income, sales, and tax revenues. Figure 7.10 details the flow of dollars from non-local sources as they move through the local economy and affect government, industry, and household spending activity.

The direct effect of money spent on a major tourism, sports, or leisure project is the local purchasing and employment required for that project. The indirect effect is the local purchasing and employment that results from direct sales and employment income. Induced effects result from third and subsequent rounds of economic activity having their genesis in the project. Economic impact studies are occasionally conducted to provide justification for

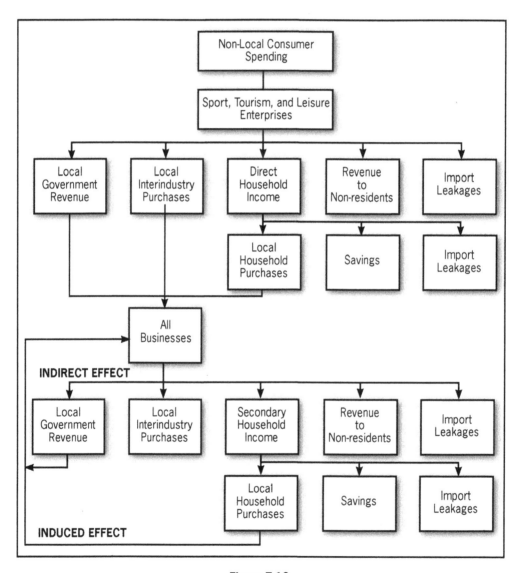

**Figure 7.10**
**Flow of exogenous funds through the local economy (adapted from Liu and Var, 1983)**

a "dream" project. Such studies must be viewed with a critical eye, as the results may reflect more of a political will than an economic reality. When evaluating the results of an economic impact study, the sports, tourism, and leisure service manager should consider the following:

- Does the study focus on the impact of money coming from outside the community? This is an important distinction, because the impact of spending local funds is, in most respects, independent of the project. In fact, a project that only stimulates spending of local money may create more import leakage than it does new sales, income, and employment.

- Are the multipliers that are used truly reflective of economic conditions within the community? Extreme caution should be exercised when applying a sales, income, or employment multiplier that was computed for another community that may have a more diverse economic base or may be less subject to seasonal constraints and market fluctuations. While it may be convenient or less expensive, a "borrowed" multiplier just may not fit.

- Are projections of direct spending based on solid market research or on unsubstantiated optimism? Invest-

ment decisions that would require an economic impact analysis are much too important to make on the basis of unreliable or biased information.

## Summary

As an introduction to the economic principles that underlie the successful management of financial resources in the sport, tourism, and leisure service organization, this chapter has emphasized the need to develop an understanding and working knowledge of the concepts of supply and demand. Additionally, attention has been devoted to the impact of interest on decisions about present or future use of money. The concepts of depreciation and economic impact assessment were also introduced. The economic principles presented help the financial manager to understand how individuals and society work; that is, they provide insights into basic human behavior. Furthermore, the technical aspects of the discussion also serve as a review of the basic mathematical skills that are needed for procedures discussed later in this book. An understanding of basic economics is important to the development of skills and the strengthening of the decision-making ability of financial managers in sport, tourism, and leisure service organizations.

# NOTES

# SECTION D

# Revenue Management

The next five chapters of this book examine the need and opportunities for revenues to be used in support of the sport, tourism, and leisure service enterprise. Revenue management is a crucial skill to develop because without the acquisition and management of revenues, there can be no expenditures and therefore no activity. Chapter 8 identifies major sources of income for organizations in the public, private not-for-profit, and commercial sectors. It provides a detailed discussion of compulsory income and introduces other sources, including earned income. Pricing is an important consideration in the generation of earned income and is the topic of Chapter 9. Pricing principles and strategies are presented, and the impacts of price and price adjustment on consumer behavior are described. Gratuitous income is discussed in Chapters 10 and 11, and the process of grantseeking is carefully detailed. Because grants are usually awarded by foundations or other philanthropic organizations, this section includes an exploration of philanthropy and fundraising. In the sport industry, sponsorship is a particularly important source of revenue and it is discussed in Chapter 12. Thanks to a firm foundation in the principles and practices of revenue management, the financial manager will then be prepared to focus on expenditure management through budget development and administration, and through accounting and reporting.

# CHAPTER 8

# Revenue Sources

## Introduction

Income is essential to all sport, tourism, and leisure service organizations. Without income, they would not be able to function. Regardless of whether it is a private fitness center, a not-for-profit sport stadium, or a state park system, each uses similar, and yet different, sources of income. The different types of sport, tourism, and leisure service organizations rely on different types of income in different ways, and in some cases, their sources of income will be unique. Initially, this chapter will discuss the types of income common to the three sectors: commercial, private not-for-profit, and public. Governments have different ways to secure income, and the methods of achieving it may vary on a state-by-state level. This uniqueness of government sources will receive particular attention.

## Types of Income Sources

There are multiple sources of income available to any organization. In this section, five of the most common types of income will be discussed. They are compulsory income, gratuitous income, earned income, investment income, and contractual receipts. While these are the most commonly accepted terms, not all organizations use the same terminology. For example, the National Association of State Park Directors (a not-for-profit organization) uses revenues appropriated, revenues unappropriated, general funds, dedicated funds, and federal funds to describe sources of income for the various state park systems. The meanings are similar, but this example of a different classification system emphasizes the point that while there is a general acceptance among terms, they are not universal. Table 8.1 illustrates the five most common sources of income for sport, tourism, and leisure service organizations and identifies the level of importance each source has to the sectors. It also emphasizes the uniqueness of compulsory income to the public sector and the relative importance of earned income to all three sectors.

Compulsory income consists of funds secured by government organizations that are generated through taxes, licensing, or some other sort of government-instituted income source that requires all or specific individuals or organizations within a legislative jurisdiction to contribute.

Gratuitous income is received without expectation of a return. Sources for gratuitous income include grants, bequests, gifts, and blind and open sponsorships. In each case, the giver typically does not receive a direct benefit or compensation for the gift. Much of what is discussed in Chapters 10 (Grantwriting) and 11 (Philanthropy and Fundraising) is

considered to be gratuitous income.

Earned income consists of cash resources generated from fees and charges instituted by the sport, tourism, or leisure service organization. These can include program fees, charges for use of areas and facilities, income from sales of supplies, equipment, gift shops, entrance fees, admission fees, rental fees, and user fees. Fiscal investments that earn interest are also considered earned income.

Investment income includes new money generated from investment in the form of interest, dividends, and capital appreciation. Investment income is the result of investing a fixed amount of dollars (principal) in such a way as to generate new money. The increase in wealth is the investment income available to sport, tourism, and leisure service organizations.

Contractual receipts are revenues generated from legal agreements with other organizations. Agreements can include the management of resources, rent-

### Table 8.1
### Income sources and their level of importance to the three sectors

| Sector | Compulsory Income | Gratuitous Income | Earned Income | Investment Income | Contractual Receipts |
|---|---|---|---|---|---|
| *Commercial Sector* | None | Minimal | Major source of income for operations | Key source of income for some business enterprises | Can be a major source of income, dependent upon scope of enterprise |
| *Nonprofit Sector* | May have some impact when tied to public funding, but limited | Essential and major source | Becoming a major source of income for some types of nonprofits | Limited, based on organization's capability to secure gratuitous income and invest the income | Growing importance through partnerships |
| *Public Sector* | Essential source of income | Growing importance as an income source | Essential source of income | Limited source of income, but frequently used | Growing source of income among some agencies |

al of facilities, rental of equipment, management of special operations such as golf courses or marinas, concession operations, tennis centers, zoos, stadiums, gift shops, or other types of enterprises. They can also include arrangements generally referred to as privatization, a practice of contracting out for the delivery of a specific service.

## Compulsory Income Sources

Compulsory income includes cash and non-cash sources collected through the taxing and regulatory powers at different government levels as prescribed by state and federal law. Government sources of income have changed dramatically for sport, tourism, and leisure service organizations since 1978, when California voters passed Proposition 13 (a landmark initiative that cut property taxes by almost 50 percent). Prior to that, public agencies gained the vast majority of their income from the general fund, which was primarily supported through property tax revenues. Since 1978, governments across the United States have responded to voter demands for lower taxes with sometimes massive tax cuts. In some cases these have been prompted by voter-initiated propositions, as in California, Oregon, and Massachusetts. In other states, the legislatures responded to what they saw as a growing trend. Even the federal government has not been immune to the trend, as the President and Congress have sometimes competed with each other over who could appear to cut taxes more. The declining availability of general fund dollars has required public sport, tourism, and leisure service organizations at all levels to rethink how they secure and use income.

Taxes continue to represent the largest single source of income to government. There are several different types of taxes, including real property tax, personal property tax, excise tax, use tax, income tax, local option tax, special assessment tax, and impact tax. Each has a specific purpose and is discussed in the next two sections.

### Types of State and Municipal Taxes
Real Property Taxes

Real property taxes are assessed in all 50 states and their subordinate jurisdictions (counties, cities, municipalities, etc.). Jurisdictions can set the tax at the local level in compliance with state law. Real property is defined as land and whatever is developed or erected or growing on the land. This includes subsurface features such as oil or mineral deposits. Tax assessors (see Chapter 5) are appointed at the local level and have primary responsibility for determining the value of the property.

In 1957, real property taxes represented 69 percent of the total local government tax base. By 1995, property taxes had shrunk to 22 percent of the tax base and has remained constant. Other types of taxes increased over the same period and became a larger part of the mix of revenues available to sport, tourism, and park and recreation organizations. In spite of the recent changes in compulsory income sources, property taxes remain the single largest source of revenue for local governments. Table 8.3 depicts the various sources of revenue utilized by state and local governments in 1990, 1995, and 2003.

It can be seen that, while property taxes as a source of revenue declined minimally over the period, total taxes paid has almost doubled. Because this table represents both state and local governments, not all results can be universally applied.

## CASE STUDY
### Alabama State Parks Focus on Increasing Revenue

In 1999 Alabama State Parks determined they needed to enhance their revenue. In 1987 the state parks converted from an agency that received 60 percent of its operating budget from the general fund (compulsory income) to 14 percent from an excise tax on cigarettes. By 1999 the $28 million operating budget received only 14% of the budget from the excise tax on cigarettes, a declining source of revenue in most states. The director of the Department of Natural Resources, the administrative location of state parks, determined the future of tax support was, at best, tenuous.

Consultants were brought in to assess the current revenue in the state park system and how it might be enhanced. It was determined the state park system generated most of its revenue from earned income. Two key sources of income were entrance fees ($1.3 million annually) and camping ($3.9 million annually), and were identified, along with concession operations ($117,000 annually), as targets for increased revenue.

Alabama's actual income for the targeted income areas was compared with national averages and suggestions were made for increasing income. The table below depicts the findings of the study. Alabama had assumed the income from entrance and camping fees provided considerable income to the state park system while concession operations provided minimal income. When compared to national averages the Alabama revenues were poor performers. From just the three sources studied it was suggested that over $9 million in potential revenues were not captured.

Such a study of mean collections of all states versus a single state presents some problems, but for state park and department of natural resource executives it was immediately apparent that changes needed to be made. The data, when compared to state park political realities, suggested entrance fees could not be changed. They had been raised two times in recent years. Closing of the entrance fee gap, however, could be affected by implementing more fee stations at state parks. Many state parks were not collecting entrance fees for a variety of reasons.

Camping was immediately embraced as a source of improved income. An initial $5 million in capital improvement funds was targeted and applied to key state parks where the potential for increased revenue could be achieved. Concession operations were a bigger challenge. There was no consistent state-wide policy for establishing concession contracts and operations. A multiyear strategy was adopted.

The Alabama State Park case study reflects changes in public park and recreation

### Table 8.2
**Comparison of Alabama state parks' sources of revenue compared to national trends**

| Category | Operating Revenue | | | | | |
| | Entrance Fees | Camping | Facilities | Concessions | Beaches & Pools | Total |
|---|---|---|---|---|---|---|
| Alabama | $1,334,525 | $3,897,545 | $5,526 | $117,107 | $72,627 | $26,159,506 |
| % of income | 5.10% | 14.90% | 0.10% | 0.45% | 0.28% | 100.00% |
| National Average | 21.46% | 27.00% | 0.35% | 8.13% | 0.83% | 100.00% |
| Difference | -16.36% | -12.10% | -0.25% | -7.68% | -0.55% | |
| Revenue | $4,279,527 | $3,166,221 | $65,333 | $2,009,074 | $143,975 | $9,664,130 |

---

## CASE STUDY
### Alabama State Parks Focus on Increasing Revenue (continued)

income sources over the last 30 years. These agencies have moved from a compulsory income model to a mixed model including compulsory income, gratuitous income, earned income, contractual receipts, and state and federal entitlement funding (another source of compulsory income). The model continues to change as compulsory income sources lessen and expectations for earned income increase.

---

Municipal governments are allowed, by law, to establish different tax rates for different classifications of property. Decisions about the levels at which different properties are taxed are made by the local legislative body. Personal homes, undeveloped land, businesses, and farm property are typically taxed at different levels. Permanent tax-exempt status may be granted to certain types of land uses, such as governments, school districts, and religious and charitable organizations. A tax abatement, which is an exemption from paying taxes, can be granted to an organization for a specified period of time.

Tax abatements are generally granted as an incentive to firms considering moving to a particular region.

Determining the value of real property is based on an estimation of its taxable worth or assessed value. Assessed value is different from market value. In many states, assessed value is much lower than fair market value. Fair market value is that at which a home may be valued for sale, whereas its assessed value for taxation purposes may be as much as 30 percent to 50 percent lower. For example, a home with a fair market value of $240,000, which is assessed at 50 percent

### Table 8.3
**Amount and percentage of state and local government revenue from selected sources, comparative years (in millions of dollars; 712,700 represents 712,700,000,000)**
(Source: 2007 Statistical Abstract of the United States, U.S. Census Bureau)

| Revenue Source | 1990 | | 1995 | | 2003 | |
|---|---|---|---|---|---|---|
| | Amount ($) | Percent Distribution | Amount ($) | Percent Distribution | Amount ($) | Percent Distribution |
| General Revenue Total | 712,700 | 100.0% | 940,733 | 100.0% | 1,374,948 | 100.0% |
| Taxes | 502,619 | 70.5% | 660,557 | 70.2% | 938,372 | 68.2% |
|   Property | 115,613 | 21.8% | 203,451 | 21.6% | 296,683 | 21.6% |
|   Sales & Gross Receipts | 177,885 | 25.0% | 237,268 | 25.2% | 337,787 | 24.6% |
|   Individual Income | 105,640 | 14.8% | 137,931 | 14.7% | 199,407 | 14.5% |
|   Corporate Income | 23,566 | 3.3% | 31,406 | 3.3% | 31,369 | 2.3% |
|   Other | 38,915 | 5.5% | 50,521 | 5.4% | 74,726 | 5.4% |
| Charges & Miscellaneous | 211,061 | 29.6% | 280,156 | 29.8% | 434,976 | 31.6% |

of the fair market value, would have an assessed value of $120,000.

Each potential jurisdiction with real property taxing powers has a tax base. The tax base is the total assessed value of all taxable property in a community. Assessed values of communities will differ considerably and are difficult to compare within a state and almost impossible for comparison between states.

Tax rates are based on revenue needs of the government and the value of the tax base. To understand how tax rates are determined, consider the following illustration. A government decides that it needs $4 million from taxes to pay for its operations in the upcoming fiscal year. This decision is made after the public agency has completed its budgeting process and identified what portion of its operating budget needs to come from real property taxes. For example:

Total amount needed to operate:
    $4,650,000
Subtract revenue (from user fees, grants, permits, etc.):
    - $650,000
Equals revenue (to be collected from taxes):
    $4,000,000

The tax rate is then determined by dividing the property tax requirements ($4 million) by the assessed valuation. Note that assessed valuation does not include all real property within the jurisdiction because some organizations or groups have a tax abatement. When the tax abatement property is removed from the total assessed value, what remains is a net assessed value. For example:

Total assessed valuation of the community:
    $450,000,000

Subtract tax-exempt property:
    $10,500,000
Equals net assessed valuation:
    $439,500,000

The tax rate is based on net assessed valuation. If this community requires $4 million from taxes to operate, the following formula is used, and the example tax rate is calculated:

Required Taxes / Net Assessed Valuation = Tax Rate
$4,000,000 / $439,500,000 = .0091

There are three ways in which tax rates can be expressed: (1) as a percent of the value of property; (2) as a mill rate; or (3) as mills. The tax rate from preceding illustration would be expressed in the three alternatives as:

Tax Rate Expression
Percent Tax Rate        0.91%
Mill rate               0.0091
Mills                   9.1

The relationship between "Percent Tax Rate" and the "Mill Rate" is obvious. The 0.91 percent means 0.91 per hundred, which is 0.91/100, which equals .0091. A "mill," on the other hand, is equal to 1/1000 of the assessed property value. The net assessed property value is $439,100,000, which means that the value of 1 mill is $439,100,000/1,000, which equals $439,100. How many mills (valued at $439,100) does it take to make the $4,000,000 to be collected from taxes? It takes 9.1. Figure 8.1 shows the conversion factors for the three tax rate expressions.

Knowing the tax rate, the owner of a property can calculate the property tax that is owed. If the owner of a home with an assessed value of $240,000 is subject to the tax rate used in the above example, the tax bill will be $2,184. This amount is calculated as follows:

A. Applying the 0.91% Tax Rate

(% Tax Rate/100) x Assessed Value = Property Tax
   (0.91/100) x $240,000 = $2,184

B. Applying the 0.0091 Mill Rate

Mill Rate x Assessed Value = Property Tax
   0.0091 x $240,000 = $2,184

C. Charging 9.1 Mills
Mills x (Assessed Value/1000) = Property Tax
   9.1 x ($240,000/1,000) = $2,184

The property tax system is based on the idea that the more a person owns, the more that person should pay. The methods of tax calculation previously illustrated follow the principle that a property owner's contribution to the tax revenue total should be proportionate to his or her share of the value of the taxable property in the community.

Other Types of Taxes

Personal property taxes are allowed in 41 states. Taxing of personal property occurs in three common forms: (1) household tangible property (e.g., automobiles, recreational vehicles, and sport transportation devices); (2) business tangible property (e.g., inventory, business fixtures, furniture, equipment, and machinery); and (3) intangibles (e.g., stocks and bonds). In most states, individuals declare the value of their personal property to tax assessors.

Sales tax is administered at the state level, but there may be provisions for additional local sales taxes. State sales tax rates vary from three percent to eight percent. In some states, a portion of the tax may be reserved for state and local sport, tourism, or leisure service func-

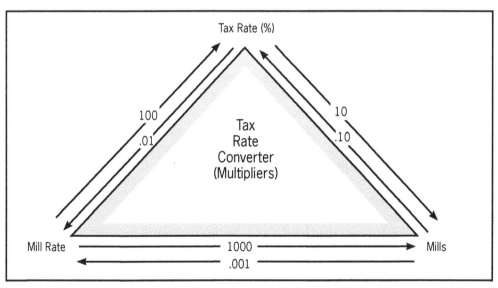

**Figure 8.1**
**Conversion factors for three expressions of the tax rate**

tions. For example, Missouri voters supported the allocation of one-tenth of each cent collected through the state sales tax for operation of their state park system. Eighty-five percent of Missouri's state park system's operating expenses are now covered by the dedicated sales tax. Sales tax is applied to a broad range of goods and is determined by state legislatures. Only four states (Delaware, Montana, New Hampshire, and Oregon) do not have a state sales tax.

A use tax is imposed in some states on individuals who purchase items outside of their state of residence and who do not pay any state sales tax on those otherwise taxable items. The use tax is designed to replace uncollected sales taxes for items purchased outside of the taxing jurisdiction. Use tax is gaining popularity in some jurisdictions.

Excise tax is imposed on the sale of specific goods, such as gasoline, cigarettes, and alcoholic beverages, and specific services, such as those provided by hotels and motels (sometimes called a lodging tax), restaurants, and auto rental agencies. These taxes may be levied at the state or local level. Excise taxes, which are authorized at the state level and collected at either the state or local level, are never popular with those who have to pay.

Income taxes are administered at the municipal, state, and federal levels. There are two types of income taxes—personal and corporate. Personal income taxes are present in 43 states. Personal income taxes are typically levied on individuals residing in the state and/or earned income in the state. Corporate income taxes are prescribed by state law and administered at the state and/or the municipal level.

Local option taxes are applied at the local level, but legislatively enabled at the state level. One of the most popular local option taxes is a local sales tax that is added to the state sales tax. In 2005, local option sales taxes accounted for about 12 percent of all local government revenue. There is enabling legislation for some type of local option taxes in every state. Supporters of local option sales taxes argue the taxes allow local governments (city and county) to diversify their revenue bases. They also argue that this form of taxation allows geographically large areas to provide programs and services from local funds rather than tapping state resources. Local hotel/motel taxes are also a common form of the local option tax. These taxes were initially focused on convention and travel destination localities, but have become much more widespread. Local option taxes are used for a broad variety of purposes. In most cases, the enabling legislation is very specific about the use of these taxes, while in other instances, the legislation can provide for almost unrestricted use of the funds collected.

## Other Sources of Compulsory Income

Special assessment taxes are enabled at the state level and administered at multiple levels. Most often, however, they are administered at the local level. These types of taxes focus on a specific geographical area, such as the downtown or a particular residential neighborhood. Consequently, the taxes collected may be spent only in the source neighborhood. They may be used for improvements in a particular area, for land purchases, or for salaries to maintain an area. The introduction and elimination of special assessment taxes are generally agreed upon by those who will be taxed.

Dedication ordinances and regulations are available to local governments and are typically instituted by county and city councils within guidelines established

## CASE STUDY
### *Who Should Pay for Sport Stadium Construction?*

A major debate prevalent in many large American cities revolves around who should finance the construction of new sport stadiums, primarily for professional sport teams. Recent research suggests new stadiums do not enhance tourism or produce new economic growth in urban areas, but rather affect local patterns of economic activity. The sport team rather than the community appears to benefit most from the increased economic activity is as a whole. For example, in New York City it was projected thar enhancements to Shea Stadium and Yankee Stadium would add an additional $111 million in economic output for the city, of which $76 million would be new revenues for the teams (mostly in earned income) and $5 million in new tax revenues (compulsory income).

Regardless of the debate about who should pay for new stadiums, cities regularly move ahead with the construction for new stadiums and place the bulk of the burden upon residents. The Indianapolis Colts are moving in 2008 from the current RCA Dome, built 20 years ago at a cost of $94 million, to the new Lucas Oil Stadium projected to cost $625 million. Negotiations for financing the stadium took several years to accomplish and were finally concluded after the state stepped in to assist in the financing. The projected funding sources for the stadium include $100 million from the Indianapolis Colts (gratuitous income). Marion county, where Indianapolis is located, raised taxes (compulsory income) for food and beverage sales, auto excise taxes, innkeeper's taxes and admission taxes. Additionally, a small increase in food and beverage taxes (compulsory income) in the eight surrounding counties and the sale of Colts license plates (earned income) completes the total revenue required to construct the stadium.

Not all stadiums are built with public funds or in partnership with private developers. Most recently, the San Francisco Giants baseball team financed their new stadium after efforts to secure public funding failed. It was the first major league baseball stadium built with private money since the Los Angeles Dodgers in 1962. The Giants do lease the land from the Port of San Francisco, a public agency, but pay fair market value for the use of the land. The Giants, in cooperation with the city of San Francisco and private developers, built their new ballpark on a former landfill that was eligible for reduced taxes under a law titled Federal Brownfields Tax Incentive. Taxes on the site were reduced equivalent to the cost of the cleanup, making the financing plan more attractive to investors. In addition to the 13-acre stadium site an additional 102 acres are planned for development as residential and commercial sites. The city put $15 million into the larger project and has realized $10 million annually in new tax revenues. The Giants

*Construction of a new stadium is most often wholly or partially financed by compulsory income sources.*

---

**CASE STUDY**
*Who Should Pay for Sport Stadium Construction? (continued)*

were able to leverage the project into $1 billion in investments for the entire 115 acre site. Actual construction costs exceeded $300 million for the stadium. The Giants and their partners have seen increased revitalization of a formerly blighted waterfront area, validating their belief that private financing, when creatively applied, can be an effective income source.

---

by state legislatures. When dedication ordinances and regulations were initiated, they required developers of neighborhoods to set aside a portion of the land for park and recreation use. While this was commendable, all too often the land set aside was not acceptable for park and recreation use, but was land the developer could not use. Local governments quickly began to look at alternatives to land dedication. In some instances, they tightened up local ordinances and became more specific in the type of land they deemed acceptable. In other instances, they began to accept money in lieu of land dedication. The money generally had to be used to improve or add to existing property or to purchase new property for parks and recreation. One common use was to purchase greenbelts linking the community and its parks together.

The imposition of impact taxes is another method of recovering development costs, and has been in use for over 30 years. Impact taxes are intended to require developers and new home owners to help pay for public improvements that may be needed as a result of new construction. It is argued that existing city residents should not have to pay for the development of new home and commercial sites, but that the cost should be borne, at least in part, by those who will benefit most directly from the development. Impact taxes are most frequently used for infrastructure costs such as streets, utilities, schools, and other essential services. Sport, tourism, and leisure service organizations have successfully argued in a number of communities that they are an essential service and, therefore, eligible recipients of funds collected as impact taxes.

### Licenses and Permits

Licenses and permits are a relatively small source of income for sport, tourism, and leisure service organizations. A license is an authorization to act or to engage in an activity. Probably the most common example is a driver's license. Licenses in sport, tourism, and park and recreation organizations are frequently granted for the distribution or sale of a particular product. For example, the National Football League entered into an exclusive agreement with Pepsi, guaranteeing exclusive rights to the sale of its products in NFL stadiums.

A permit is an authorization for a person to engage in a particular activity—not necessarily recreational—or to use a facility or equipment. A common permit is a building permit issued by a local jurisdiction. In sport, tourism, and leisure service organizations, a permit might be issued for the serving and consumption of alcoholic beverages at a public facility, for the rental of a facility, or for the use of a significant natural resource. Usually, permits are good for a shorter period of time than licenses.

## Federal Government Sources

The federal government has long been a source of revenue for state and local governments. Funds collected by the federal government and redistributed to state governments are called transfer payments. In 1980, the federal government made transfer payments worth $83 billion. By 1995, that amount had risen to $229 billion, and in 2003, it was $389 billion. The greatest share of transfer payment money is used for public welfare, but other programs, such as highways, education, health and hospitals, and housing and community development have also received significant amounts. Historically, sport, tourism, and leisure service organizations are well served by transfer payments and federal government programs. However, federal government fiscal support for state and local sport, tourism, and leisure service organizations has been on the decline in recent years. For example, state parks received $31 million in 2006 from federal sources, but that is a major reduction from the $630 million they received just two decades earlier.

Some of the legislation and programs that the federal government transfer funds to states and local jurisdictions include the Land and Water Conservation Fund, the National Recreational Trails Act, the National Highway System, Intermodal Surface Transportation Efficiency Act of 1992 (ISTEA), highway safety programs, scenic highway programs, and metropolitan planning. Each program has provided varying levels of funding to sport, tourism, and leisure service organizations. The Land and Water Conservation Act (LWCF) has been in place for more than 40 years. During its early years, it provided significant levels of revenue to state and local governments. Beginning in the mid-1980s, levels of funding declined to the point where it now provides minimal funding at the state and local levels. The National Recreation Trails Act has received limited funding since 1993. It is set up so that 30 percent of the funds go to motorized trails, 30 percent to non-motorized trails, and 40 percent to multipurpose trails. The money can be spent on maintenance, as well as on construction

Impact fees and other taxes and fees can be one-time sources of income to offset new construction.

of trails. The National Highway System provides a potential source of money for trail development next to any National Highway System highway (excluding the interstate system). The ISTEA has been the steadiest federal government source of income for public sport, tourism, and leisure service organizations in recent years. As with other transportation sources, ISTEA focuses wholly on trail development and maintenance.

## Gratuitous Income

Gratuitous income receives significant attention in Chapters 10 and 11. Grants are an important source of potential income for sport, tourism, and leisure service organizations. In 2005, $30.3 billion in grants were awarded from public and private grant sources, and it is estimated that sport, tourism, and leisure service organizations received almost $950 million (3.1%) of that total.

Fundraising is an organized process of seeking out gifts to support leisure service organization and capital improvements. The growth of fundraising and support organizations for sport, tourism, and leisure service organizations has been dramatic over the last 15 years. Many community park and recreation agencies have created their own foundations or a sport promotion corporations thatt are financially supported by a companion foundation or a corporation through its own philanthropic mechanism. In 2005, individuals, bequests, and foundations gave over $260 billion, and of that total, individuals were responsible for $180 billion (69%) of all giving. Grant-seeking and fundraising are intertwined, and entrepreneurial sport, tourism, and leisure service organizations look to both of them as important elements of their income structure.

## Earned Income

Earned income consists of cash resources generated from fees, as well as charges assessed by the sport, tourism, and leisure service organization. Types of fees can include program fees; charges for use of equipment, areas, and facilities; income from sales of supplies; gift shop and pro-shop revenues; entrance fees; admission fees; rental fees; and user fees. Fiscal investments that earn interest are also considered earned income. In recent years, the greatest growth in revenues for sport, tourism, and leisure service organizations has been from earned income. For most tourism and sport organizations, earned income is the primary source of operational funds, and the emerging emphasis on earned income has helped to reshape public leisure service organization management over the last 20 years. As a result of this emphasis, management has become more entrepreneurial and business focused. Even charitable not-for-profit organizations report that as much as 73 percent of their operating budgets come from program service revenues.

Earned income comes primarily from fees and charges. The Government Finance Officers' Association, suggesting a technical difference between fees and charges, agrees that in most cases, the terms "fees" and "charges" are used interchangeably. A fee may be imposed as a result of a public need to regulate activities, safety, or other protective measures. Fees constitute the purchase of a privilege or an authorization and are applied to services rendered, such as an inspection or the issuance of a building permit. In sport, tourism, and leisure service organizations, the term "fees" has come to be associated with the delivery of programs and services. Examples of major classifications of earned income include entrance and admission fees, rental fees, user or program fees, sales revenue, and special fees. Entrance and admission fees are charged for entrance to any public or private sport or leisure facility, movie theater, art museum, children's museum, monument, historical building, etc. Income from fees may be used to cover the cost of operations, but in some cases, it may also be intended to provide additional revenue for such needs as debt retirement and capital improvement funding.

Rental fees are charged for the exclusive use of a tangible property, such as a Santa suit, park pavilion, sport equipment, sport complex, picnic equipment, game equipment, public address system, stroller, lawn chairs, paddle boats, coin telescopes, cabin, lodge, resort room, horse, camping equipment, bicycles, and golf clubs. The list of potential rental revenue sources can be very long indeed. Revenue from rental fees may be used to recover the cost of the purchase and replacement of the rental item(s), storage and handling, or maintenance and cleaning. Sport, tourism, and leisure service organizations may also use rental fees to offset operational costs in other areas, provide renters with additional recreation opportunities, and/or contribute to profits.

User and program fees are defined as charges made for the use of a facility or for participation in an activity, program, or service. The fee may be used for capital development, debt retirement, maintenance operations, and operation of the facility or program. User and program fees could be charged for almost any type of program offering, such as figure skating classes, pottery classes, modern dance classes, tie-dyeing classes, child care, etc. The 75-page brochure for one service organization that serves a community of 150,000 included (for a three-month period) over 900 programs with fees attached to them. In this instance, fees were different for residents and non-residents, with the latter paying a higher rate. User fees can also be charged for the use of facilities and might, on the surface, appear to be just like rental fees. However, user fees grant access to facilities whereas rental fees usually grant exclusive use thereof.

Sales revenue comes from the sale of goods and services through gift shops, stores, concessions, restaurants, and similar types of operations. Many professional teams own apparel and souvenir shops located at the sport arena, local malls, and airports. Concession operations are becoming a major source of income for sport, tourism, and leisure service organizations. Sales activities are almost always implemented in conjunction with some other service operated by the sport, tourism, and leisure service organization. In a fitness center, for example, there may be a pro shop, a snack bar, and a full-service restaurant. In Tacoma, Washington, the city parks and recreation department contracts with an outside organization to operate a full-service restaurant on the recreational waterfront. Many golf courses have pro shops and restaurants as part of their operations. Museums have gift shops, restaurants, snack bars, and other revenue-generating amenities. State and national parks may accommodate grocery stores, gas stations, motels, and lodges. The purpose of sales activity is to provide a service to the user and to generate revenue for the organization.

Special fees are generally charged for providing some extraordinary service to consumers. In many cases, special fees might also be included in one of the previously identified fee types. Examples include lights for tennis courts, park security for special events, and use of por-

*State resort parks provide opportunities for users to experience state parks who choose not to camp and provide the agency with earned income.*

table stages, sound equipment, etc. In some communities, a fee is charged for after-dark use of facilities, such as night softball, where teams are charged a fee to recover the cost of lighting and additional maintenance. Other examples include fees charged for special camps (basketball, baseball, cheerleading, computer, etc.), equipment storage, and facility reservation privileges (group picnic shelters, for example).

## Investment Income

Investment income represents those funds generated from the investment of currently available resources. Most public, not-for-profit, and commercial enterprises are allowed to invest either all or portions of their available funds according to sound investment strategies. Some of the most common investment strategies and opportunities are municipal and corporate bonds, money market certificates, stock transactions, and mutual funds. The investment of any money is almost

always made in consultation with an investment professional who has expertise in the public, not-for-profit, or commercial sector. In some instances, especially with public agencies, the investment is for short periods of time (less than six months). Even investments over a short period of time allow the organization to realize additional income for its operations. Investment income reduces the need for other types of income, such as compulsory income. Such investments are usually made in opportunities that are "safe," in the sense that they are less strongly affected by major downturns or upturns in the stock market. Not-for-profit organizations may use investment income as a major source of revenue for their operations. Many state park and recreation associations and universities have made investments in mutual funds, bonds, or other sources and then used the annual interest income to fund scholarships.

## Contractual Receipts

Contractual receipts are revenues that are generated from legal agreements with other organizations. Income-generating agreements are entered into for the management of resources, rental of facilities, rental of equipment, and the management of special operations, such as golf courses, marinas, food concessions, tennis centers, zoos, stadiums, or gift shops. They can also include those varied operations collectively referred to as subjects of privatization—a concept that has become popular in the management of public organizations.

A contract is a term that describes a unit of trading for a financial or commodity future. Contract management requires proficiency in a set of business and fiscal management skills from both the contractor and the owner. In the early years of contract management, it was not uncommon for a public agency to unwisely "give away" potential for revenue from the contract and then provide inadequate oversight to contract compliance. In response, one city eventually canceled the private contract for its golf course operations after the facility regularly posted annual losses of over $500,000. The city managers determined that they could no longer justify using tax dollars to support golf operations with such major losses. In the first year after canceling the contract, the city discovered that the driving ranges actually had revenues of over $250,000 and expenses of only $40,000. Under the previous contract, all of the driving range profits had been going to the golf pro. In this case, the golf pro had done nothing wrong (according to the terms of the contract), but the city had failed to manage the contract closely enough to see how it was limiting the revenue potential and forcing the city to assume too much financial liability. Good contract management requires time and expertise.

## Partnerships and Collaborations

Partnerships and collaborations are becoming more common approaches to generating income. The terms *partnership* and *collaboration* are frequently used interchangeably; however, they have very different meanings. Partnerships are formed through agreements between two or more parties with a mutual interest and common need. A partnership may be for a fixed or indeterminate length of time. The key to success in a partnership is for all parties to clearly understand and easily identify their needs. By contrast, in collaborative arrangements, different organizations may work together to achieve a common goal, but they do not entirely share the same vision, resources, or risks. The foundation of collaborations is the hope that, by working together, several organizations will have a better opportunity to resolve an issue than would a single organization. Sport, tourism, and leisure service organizations use both partnerships and collaborations, but partnerships are more likely to produce income.

A partnership results from a formal or informal agreement between two or more organizations to work together to provide a service or to fund a project. Partnerships can include any combination of public, not-for-profit, and commercial organizations. For example, a partnership may result from co-sponsorship of a 5K run by the public parks and recreation department, the YMCA, a women's shelter, a local bank, a sporting goods dealer, the convention and visitor bureau, and the local hospital. The parks and recreation department plans and jointly conducts the event with the YMCA; the hospital's marketing department develops brochures, logos, T-shirt designs; the convention and visitors bureau distributes advertising and sets up lodging and sightseeing opportunities for out-of-town participants; the bank and sporting goods store provide the awards to the runners and help pay for advertising costs; and the women's shelter receives the bulk of the revenues earmarked for its operations.

Each of the partners receives some benefit from the partnership. In the preceding example, the parks and recreation department, the YMCA, the hospital, the sporting goods store, the convention and visitor bureau, and the bank all received recognition for their efforts. The parks and recreation department, the convention and visitor bureau, and the YMCA were perceived as fulfilling their mission to serve the community. The bank, the hospital, and the sporting goods store succeeded in enhancing their image as socially responsible entities. The women's shelter received financial support, additional legitimization as a social service agency, and a positive image boost. Each participant received support, recognition, and a feeling of contribution that it might not have been able to secure independently.

Partnering is about working toward common goals and outcomes. It brings to the table unique resources from each organization that may be unavailable to the other organizations. It strengthens the assertion that "the whole is greater than the parts" and reinforces the concept of working together so that all partners can receive a positive return on their respective and collective investments. The return does not always need to be a financial benefit and could be an intangible benefit, such as image, good-

will, or legitimization.

Further examples of partnerships and the benefits of partnership can be found in numerous communities, such as Indianapolis, Indiana, and Naperville, Illinois. The Indianapolis Parks and Recreation Department worked with neighborhood community groups to formalize their involvement and leadership in local parks. Community groups and local churches accepted a shared responsibility for maintenance and the general upkeep of the parks (mowing, trash removal, graffiti reporting, etc.). As partners, they received a stipend of either cash, special services, or availability of department resources to the church or neighborhood association. The work was done at a lower cost than department maintenance crews, and local involvement has resulted in a higher level of maintenance and lower levels of vandalism. In Naperville, Illinois, the city and park district (the park district is a separate taxing district) have partnered with the Riverwalk Foundation to develop and maintain a downtown riverwalk. In celebration of the city's 1981 sesquicentennial anniversary, volunteers developed the riverwalk, and since then, it has become a focal point of the community. Its covered bridges, fountains, landscaping, and distinctive shepherd's-crook light poles have become symbolic of Naperville's ties to its historic past as the oldest settlement in DuPage County. The city, the park district, and a community foundation worked together to ensure the continued success. Fittingly, city hall and the park district headquarters are adjacent to the riverwalk, and the high school is within walking distance. Numerous major park and recreation facilities are linked to the riverwalk, and it continues to figure prominently in community festivals and special events, as well as provide one more feature to attract visitors to the area.

## Revenue Structure Plan

The amount of revenue that an organization needs, and the source of that revenue, is detailed in the revenue structure plan. The purpose of the revenue structure plan is to help the financial manager understand the organization's expenditure needs and potential sources of revenue. A revenue structure plan is typically prepared for each fiscal year. Commercial and not-for-profit sport, tourism, and leisure service organizations might identify a small number of income sources, but the expenditures may be distributed across multiple divisions or profit centers. Conversely, public agencies might identify many different sources of income to cover expenses in

a single leisure service enterprise. Figure 8.2 illustrates an example of the different types of revenue sources reported by state park agencies.

The revenue structure plan focuses attention on the need to strive for an acceptable balance of income sources. Table 8.4 shows how one municipality's income is derived. As might be expected, property taxes constitute the largest source of income for the municipality, and sales tax is the second largest source of revenue. In today's changing fiscal environment, some public sport, tourism, and leisure service organizations are generating more than 50 percent of their income from non-tax sources. In this illustration, there are 11 sources of income for the municipality.

A private not-for-profit or commercial sport, tourism, or leisure service organization's revenue structure would be different and would likely show a higher

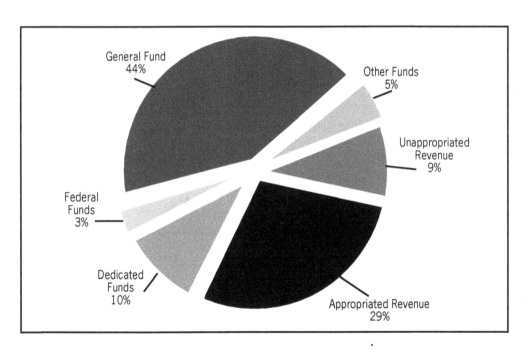

**Figure 8.2**
**Example revenue structure for state parks**

percentage that is derived from charges for services or other types of earned income.

It is important that any revenue structure plan be based on an established fiscal policy. That policy should articulate the revenue goals and describe, in general terms, how revenue should or may be generated. For example, Indy Parks developed its revenue structure model and identified two major funding categories: enterprise funding and underwriting (Table 8.5). The establishment of these two categories helped to further identify and classify revenue sources and place them on a service continuum with fair market pricing (where user fees cover full costs) at one extreme and city budgeting (where all costs are covered by tax revenues) at the other. Each program or service can be matched to a point on the continuum, depending on a variety of factors, such as need, ability to pay, community willingness to support, consistency with the mission of the city and the department, vision of the city and the department, consistency with the core principles of the organization, appropriate revenue sources for those programs, and services emphasized.

Developing the revenue structure plan as guided by fiscal policy maintains consistency and promotes efficient exploitation of revenue sources. Furthermore, following the fiscal policy ensures revenue generation activities will be supported by policy makers.

## Summary

Income generation is an important aspect of financial management in sport, tourism, and park and recreation organizations. The various revenue sources discussed in this chapter can provide the funds necessary to conduct programs, offer services, and maintain equipment and facilities. There are five types of income: compulsory income, gratuitous income, earned income, investment income, and contractual receipts. All of them provide different levels and types of funding for sport, tourism, and leisure service organizations. Not all sport, tourism, and leisure service organizations will secure income from the same sources. Understanding and awareness of income sources, along with the relating of that knowledge to policy directions, allow sport, tourism, and leisure service managers to more effectively meet the revenue demands of their organizations.

### Table 8.4
### Example of a revenue structure for a municipality

| Property Tax | Utility Tax | Sales Tax | Shared State Tax | Other Taxes | Licences & Permits |
|---|---|---|---|---|---|
| 16.7% | 7.4% | 15.2% | 34.0% | 5.0% | 1.4% |
| $17,854,577 | $7,906,570 | $16,317,115 | $36,420,521 | $5,316,027 | $1,448,228 |

| Fines & Forfeittures | Investment Income | Inter-governmental Services | Charges for Services | Other | Total |
|---|---|---|---|---|---|
| 1.4% | 3.0% | 3.7% | 3.3% | 9.0% | 100.0% |
| $1,551,597 | $3,221,994 | $3,976,524 | $3,574,485 | $9,602,968 | $107,190,606 |

**Table 8.5**
**Revenue structure for enterprise funding for Indy Parks.**

| | |
|---|---|
| *Enterprise Funding* | Fair Market Price (fee covers total cost) |
| | Fee Schedule (fee covers partial cost) |
| | Sponsorships (sponsor receives exposure as benefit) |
| *Underwriting* | Self Funding (funds shift from another internal budget) |
| | Donor Base (corporate, individual giving, and grants) |
| | City Budget (compulsory income) |

## References

Crompton, J. L. (1987). *Doing more with less in parks and recreation services.* State College, PA: Venture Publishing, Inc.

McLean, D. D. (Ed.). (1993). *Models of change in parks and recreation: Proceedings of a national conference.* Bloomington, IN: Department of Recreation and Park Administration, Indiana University.

McLean, D. D. (Ed.). (1993). *Models of change in parks and recreation: A 2-part training video.* Bloomington, IN: Department of Recreation and Park Administration, Indiana University.

# NOTES

# CHAPTER 9

# Pricing

## Introduction

One of the most challenging tasks associated with financial management in sport, tourism, and leisure service organizations is that of setting prices. In setting prices, the financial manager must be able to collect and appropriately analyze relevant data, make reasoned predictions about consumer behavior, and be creative in developing pricing strategies to help achieve the financial objectives of the organization. This chapter discusses the purposes of pricing in sport, tourism, and leisure service enterprises and explores the ways in which prices are established and adjusted. In addition, this chapter examines the effects of pricing on consumer behavior. Price quantifies the financial and other resources that a consumer of sport, tourism, and leisure services exchanges with the provider of those services. The nature, amount, and source of the resource that is exchanged vary tremendously, but there will always be an exchange in the consumption process. Every service has a price, and every pricing strategy is designed to achieve particular purposes.

## Purposes of Pricing

In most situations, pricing is used to recover the costs of production, but it can also be used to create new resources, establish value, influence behavior, and promote efficiency and equity.

### Pricing to Recover Costs

Cost-recovery pricing is best illustrated by its application in public, private not-for-profit, and commercial organizations. Though not exclusively, commercial organizations produce and deliver services on a for-profit basis, which means that the agency uses pricing to recover more resources from the consumer than were used in production and delivery. Organizations in the public and private not-for-profit sectors typically price their services on a break-even basis (i.e., approximately the same amount of resources are recovered through pricing as are expended in production and delivery), and public sport, tourism, and leisure organizations frequently offer subsidized services which are priced in order to recover only a certain portion of their production and delivery costs.

Cost-recovery pricing assumes that the production costs are known and can be apportioned and assessed to a known number of consumers who are to pay the price. Production and delivery costs include fixed and variable costs, and the consumers (i.e., those who pay the price) may include non-users as well as direct users of the service. The method for calculating prices based on cost recovery will be described in detail later in this chapter.

### Pricing to Create New Resources (Added Value Pricing)

Where pricing is used to recover more resources than constitute the cost of production and delivery, value is thereby added to the service, and new resources (profits) for the organization are created. The sport, tourism, and leisure service organization can retain those new resources to develop additional services, support other existing services, or maintain the support of investors by paying dividends or increasing the value of stock.

### Pricing to Establish Value

While most people like to believe that "the best things in life are free," they also accept that, usually, "you get what you pay for." The latter assertion reinforces the suggestion that price is used as an in-

dicator of the relative quality or value of a product. For example, a sporting event for which the admission price is $40 is expected to be much better than one that charges $2 at the gate; a $19 resort room is not likely to be as nice as a $200 room; a golf putter that sells for $15 is inferior to one that sells for $150; and so on. When the price for a particular sport, tourism, or leisure service is determined, the value of that service is established in the mind of the consumer. It is not unusual, therefore, to find sport, tourism, and leisure services that are priced well above the full cost-recovery level simply to establish and maintain a perceived level of value or quality.

### Pricing to Influence Behavior

When consumers pay a price for a sport, tourism, and leisure service, they recognize that the service has value to them. The price is considered fair; otherwise, they would not have paid it. If, however, that fair price is increased because of failed performance or irresponsible behavior on the part of the consumer, the price may no longer be consistent with the value of the service. For example, $50 for 10 canoeing lessons may sound like a good price, but only if the student attends all 10 lessons. If he attends only one lesson, it is a very expensive lesson. In this case, the student is encouraged to attend all 10 lessons because of the price. He would not likely be so motivated if the price of all 10 lessons were only 49 cents. Similarly, the price of admission to a session of roller skating may seem reasonable, unless the skater violates safety or other rules of conduct and is ejected from the facility without a refund of the admission price. The fear of having the experience reduced, but not the price, of having to pay the full admission price for re-admission to the same session strongly influences the value-conscious skater to conduct himself according to the established standards. Many sport, tourism, and leisure service organizations use pricing to promote desired behaviors. Consider the following examples:

- Lower early-registration fees are charged as an incentive to participants to sign up for programs early enough to give the agency adequate preparation time.
- Late fines or replacement fees are charged by libraries or movie rental stores to encourage users to return books and videos promptly and in good condition.
- Performance bonds are required of teams to make it seem too costly to withdraw from a tournament at the last moment.
- Care of facilities and equipment is promoted through the assessment of damage/cleaning deposits from groups renting recreational facilities and areas.
- Discounts are given for season tickets to promote regular attendance.
- Special prices are available for travelers who book their transportation or lodging on-line, thus avoiding the costly commissions that providers would normally pay to travel agents or other intermediaries.

### Pricing to Promote Efficiency

The sport, tourism, and leisure service industry is subject to seasonal and other fluctuations in demand. There are times when the demand for certain services or products exceeds the supply, and there are times when the supply far exceeds the demand. Pricing is often used to shift the demand from peak periods to low periods and, thereby, promote ef-

ficiency. For example, the summertime demand for a commercial campground with 100 sites will normally exceed its capacity, but many sites will be empty during the spring and fall (especially on weekdays). If the campground operator added 50 new sites to accommodate the summer campers, he would be offering an inefficient solution, because the off-season surplus would then be even greater. A more efficient response might be to raise prices during the summer and lower them during other times. Some campers have flexibility in their vacation and travel plans and can be enticed, by the price differential, to camp during the off-season rather than during the busy summer months.

*Bulk pricing*, in the form of season passes or ticket blocks, can also promote efficiency by reducing the cost of selling individual tickets and reducing the uncertainty in estimating demand. Many amusement theme parks, for example, have abandoned the inefficient practice of selling individual tickets or coupons for attractions in favor of the all-inclusive admission price.

Efficiency can also be promoted through the use of *two-tiered pricing* structures. While some amusement parks, for example, have an all-inclusive admission price, others have the standard admission price that grants park guests access to most of the rides and services. However, an extra ticket or pass must be purchased to go on some of the more popular or thrilling rides, or to have guaranteed access to the ride regardless of how busy the park is.

### Pricing to Promote Equity

Equity refers to fairness in the allocation of resources. Equity decisions are based on response to need and merit and, therefore, may result in unequal allocation of services. Pricing can be used to promote equity by redistributing the wealth of those who pay a higher price for a service to more needy or deserving people who would pay a lower price for the same service. For example, an adult may pay $5 to use a public swimming pool, while a child may pay only $2 for the same opportunity. This price structure is considered fair because children have fewer financial resources than adults, and because they need to develop aquatic safety skills and have available healthy recreation activities in their growing years. Pricing promotes equity by making the swimming pool more accessible to a needy or deserving market (the children) through fees that are made more affordable by the higher financial contribution of a more resourceful and less needy market (the adults).

## The Appropriateness and Feasibility of Pricing

As stated earlier, every sport, tourism, or leisure service has a price. That price, however, may be or may include a non-monetary resource that the consumer is required to give up in exchange for the service. Only certain types of services can appropriately or feasibly be priced in direct monetary terms. In other words, charging a fee for a service is not always desirable or practical.

An example of a type of service for which it may not be desirable or practical to charge a user fee is a public service. Public services, such as neighborhood parks and playgrounds, trails, parades, and ecological reserves, are of value and benefit to a broadly defined community and, for that reason, have traditionally been supported by public funds (i.e., taxes) rather than user fees. The customary

practice of having no direct user charges, coupled with the difficulty or inefficiency of limiting access for the purpose of charging admission, makes public services unlikely candidates for pricing.

A type of service for which pricing may be more appropriate and feasible is a merit service. Merit services are those that indirectly benefit the community, but are most beneficial to those who receive the service. Many of the facilities and programs provided by public recreation agencies qualify as merit services. For example, a minor soccer league is good for the community because it provides positive, wholesome outlets for the energy of young girls and boys. It also promotes many of the qualities of leadership and responsible citizenship.

Aside from benefiting the community indirectly, participation in the soccer league promotes the physical health of those who participate and also provides a great deal of personal enjoyment. Because of the benefit received by the community, it is appropriate for some community resources (e.g., playing fields built and maintained with tax dollars) to be used in support of the league. On the other hand, the individual participant benefits the most, so it is also considered appropriate and desirable for each boy or girl to pay a fee in order to play on a league team. Because player registration and game scheduling are required for the successful operation of the soccer league, it is feasible to charge a fee for individual participation.

Public, private not-for-profit, and commercial sport, tourism, and leisure service organizations might also provide what are classified as private services. Though more common in commercial agencies, private services are those that are exclusive and that benefit only the individuals who use the service. It is, therefore, considered to be both desirable and feasible for the agency to charge a fee. Tennis lessons, dog grooming classes, weight training, movies, amusement parks, lake or ocean cruises, sky diving, river rafting, and professional sporting events are just a few of the thousands of private sport, tourism, and leisure services available to consumers. Participation in them is at the discretion of the consumer, and while they may be highly enjoyable and beneficial to the participant, their value to the general community is not readily apparent, so there is little reason for financial support of the services by anyone but the direct consumers.

It is important to recognize that a service is not inherently public, merit, or private. A weight-training facility at a particular university, for example, may be open to all students by virtue of the mandatory activity fee. Viewed as a benefit to all, it would be considered a public service in that campus community. Another university may provide access to its weight-training facilities only to those who pay the voluntary student activity fee. In recognition of the extended value of personal physical health to the university community, the university may subsidize the activity fee. In this case, the weight-training facility is a merit service. A third university, meanwhile, may determine that weight training benefits only the user of the facilities and that all costs of maintaining and operating a weight-training center need to be recovered from single usage or semester pass fees charged to individual users. The sometimes challenging task of classifying sport, tourism, and leisure facilities, programs, and activities as either public, merit, or private services is central to the debate about whether user fees should be charged.

## The Nature of Price

Price, as a quantification of the resources exchanged by a consumer for a desired service, is usually expressed in monetary terms. The price of a hot summer afternoon at the swimming pool, for example, is said to be $3—the amount charged by the pool owner for admission to the facility. Likewise, the cost of taking a cruise might be $750—the cost of the cruise ship ticket. There are, however, other non-monetary elements of price that may play an equal or more important role in the decision about whether or not to purchase the service than the dollar amount displayed on the price tag. In addition to the monetary cost, the consumer of a sport, tourism, and leisure service will incur opportunity costs, psychological costs, and effort costs.

### Monetary Price

The monetary price of a sport, tourism, or leisure program or event includes direct and indirect expenditures attributable to participation in that activity. Obviously, the registration or admission fee will be one part of the monetary price. Another part will be money that had to be paid for services that facilitate the individual's participation in the program. These facilitation costs include the following:

- Transportation: all the costs of getting to and from the activity, including fares, gasoline, maintenance, depreciation, and insurance.
- Clothing and Equipment: the costs of specialized clothing and/or equipment required for participation in the activity.
- Proxy: the costs of someone else fulfilling other obligations of the par-

ticipant while he or she is engaged in the activity (e.g., expenses for child care, pet boarding, house sitting, employment substitution).

- Refreshment/Sustenance: the additional cost of purchasing meals or refreshments during the time of the activity.
- Qualification: the costs directly associated with making the individual eligible to participate in the activity (includes preparatory training and/or certification, medical clearance, membership fees, etc.).
- Reference: the costs of acquiring artifacts, such as souvenirs and photographs, that help the participant to later recall and describe the experience.

## Opportunity Price

By participating in a sport, tourism, or leisure activity, an individual dedicates to that activity time and other resources that could have been utilized in alternate ways. The participant always pays the price for lost opportunity. Fathers who go out in the evening to play basketball with their co-workers give up the opportunity to spend that time with their families. College students who spend the weekend skiing lose the opportunity that those two days presented for rest, study, and preparation for an upcoming exam. Children who take piano lessons forfeit the opportunity to watch after-school cartoons on television. A recreational seamstress may spend carefully saved money to take a quilting class but, in so doing, lose the opportunity to buy a new sewing machine. The opportunity cost of time can be measured in hours and minutes; the opportunity cost of lost wages or spent savings can be measured in dollars and cents; and the opportunity cost of not studying can be measured in grade points. There

are, however, opportunity costs that defy quantification, such as family cohesiveness, spiritual health, a clear conscience, a sense of accomplishment, and so on. Though not always measurable, the opportunity price is perceivable by the consumer and is considered in the purchase/participation decision.

## Psychological Price

Participants in sport, tourism, and leisure activities experience a certain amount of psychological stress. The stress may result from the uncertainty of a contest's outcome or the anxiety associated with performing at a level near the limits of the participant's capabilities. Other forms of stress manifest themselves as boredom, fear, or even embarrassment. All these conditions are a part of the psychological price of the activity. Participation may require the individual to step out of his or her personal comfort zone and place his or her self-esteem or social position at risk. By participating, the individual exchanges the psychological position of comfort for the expected stresses and anticipated outcomes, thereby paying the psychological price.

## Effort Price

Sport, tourism, and leisure activities usually require substantial physical or mental exercise, and by so doing, exact a price of personal energy. Some programs may be too expensive for certain individuals—not because the monetary, opportunity, or psychological price is excessive, but because the prospective participant is "just not up to it."

Figure 9.1 presents a summary of the many costs that constitute the price for a man to spend his hot summer afternoon at the community swimming pool. It provides examples of the monetary, opportunity, psychological, and effort prices that

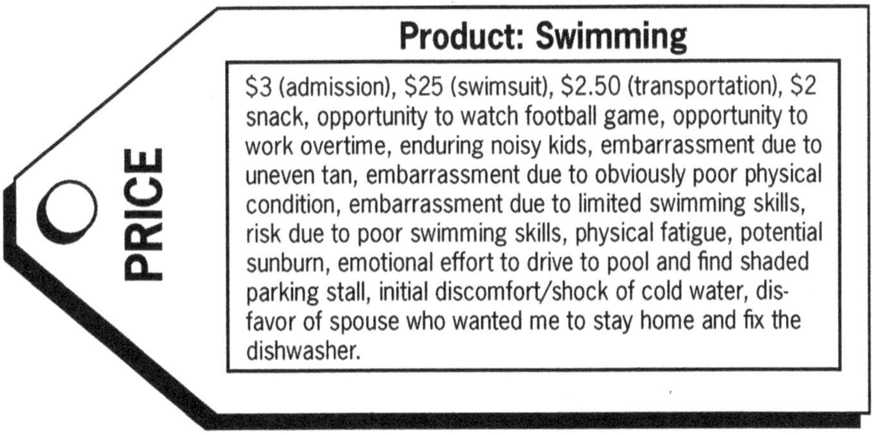

## Product: Swimming

$3 (admission), $25 (swimsuit), $2.50 (transportation), $2 snack, opportunity to watch football game, opportunity to work overtime, enduring noisy kids, embarrassment due to uneven tan, embarrassment due to obviously poor physical condition, embarrassment due to limited swimming skills, risk due to poor swimming skills, physical fatigue, potential sunburn, emotional effort to drive to pool and find shaded parking stall, initial discomfort/shock of cold water, disfavor of spouse who wanted me to stay home and fix the dishwasher.

**PRICE**

**Figure 9.1**
**The varied elements of the price tag for going swimming**

the man must be willing to pay in order to go swimming.

## Approaches to Establishing Price

One of the easiest ways to establish a price is to just pick a number and decide that it will be the dollar price for the service. This *arbitrary approach* ignores market conditions and requirements for cost recovery, and settles on a price with which the financial decision maker is most comfortable. For example, the director of a summer sport camp may decide to charge $20 just because $20 is a nice round number. Unfortunately, the positive simplicity of this approach is usually overshadowed by the negative ineffectiveness of such a strategy in meeting the financial goals of the organization.

Another relatively simple approach is to establish a price that is consistent with the price charged for the same or a similar service by a competing service provider. *Competitive pricing* can be an efficient and effective strategy if the competing provider has similar goals, production

resources, costs, and market conditions. For example, the price for a recreational swimming session at a new YMCA Family Fitness Center may reasonably be set at the same amount as is charged for admission to the local public swimming pool because the costs of operation are comparable, the range of aquatic services is similar, the market is identical, and both agencies are pricing their services at the break-even level. If, however, the YMCA has a wave machine in the new pool and requires more lifeguards than the public recreation agency, then charging the same as the public agency would likely result in reduced profits or increased operating deficits.

A third approach to pricing sport and leisure services is to charge whatever the market is *willing to pay*. This *market pricing strategy* assumes that consumers are willing to pay at least the amount required by the organization for cost recovery and then seeks a higher amount that will optimize financial returns. Using the market pricing approach, a college athletic department with a nationally ranked basketball team may decide to charge non-student spectators $20 per game because that is the amount that these basketball fans have demonstrated a willingness to pay. These same fans, however, may only be willing to pay $5 per game if the basketball team goes for three seasons losing every game by as many as 50 points.

Finally, a *cost-recovery pricing strategy* is based on the principle of seeking a return from the consumers that represents a predetermined portion of the resources that are required to provide the sport, tourism, or leisure service to them. That portion may be less than, equal to, or greater than 100%, depending on the organization's financial objectives and how the service being priced is supposed to help achieve those objectives. Clearly, two pieces of information are essential before determining price based on cost recovery. The first is accurate information about the costs of providing the service, and the second is information about the extent to which the pricing strategy is expected to generate revenues equal to those costs. The latter item of information is referred to as either the *subsidization rate* or the *mark-up*.

## Calculating Costs for Unit Pricing

In order to calculate the costs incurred in the provision of service to each consumer, the financial manager needs to know what the *fixed* and *variable* costs are, how much *contingency* is required, and how many consumers are likely to participate in the program or purchase the service at a given price. Estimating demand (i.e., the quantity desired at a given price) requires an understanding of the needs, interests, capabilities, constraints, and opportunities of the target market. Although demand has been discussed in

detail in Chapter 7, it is appropriate here to emphasize that estimation of demand is an art founded in science and measurement. In other words, "knowing" how many people will participate in a sport, tourism, or leisure program requires an educated guess.

Contingency refers to being prepared for the unexpected. There is obvious wisdom in adding to the itemized costs of a product an amount that can be used if additional costs arise. How many contingencies should be built into the costs? Some managers are comfortable with only five percent of the costs being contingent, while other more cautious financial managers may want to have an amount as much as 15 percent of the itemized costs be available to deal with contingencies. For long-standing, established programs, or for programs requiring limited financial investment, the reduced risk would justify a relatively small contingency, but new, untried, or short-term programs, as well as those for which the consequences of financial failure are severe, should have a relatively high contingency built into their cost estimates.

Fixed and variable costs are the financial resources that are used in production and delivery of the sport, tourism, or leisure service. They can be itemized and are the basis of cost-recovery pricing. Fixed costs are those financial costs that the sport, tourism, or leisure service organization incurs, regardless of the status of the program. They are unavoidable, even if nobody registers for the program or attends the event.

Figure 9.2 identifies the fixed costs associated with the maintenance of a skating rink. If the facility is maintained as a rink, but nobody comes to skate, there will still be mortgage installments due and bills to be paid. There will still be a portion of the agency administrators' salaries that are actually rink-related costs, because maintaining the rink partly justifies the administrator's position. There will be the direct costs of installing and removing the ice surface at either end of the skating season. And even this unused and empty facility would require repairs and upkeep, as well as basic utility services.

Variable costs are those costs that result from the actual operation of the sport, tourism, or leisure service. The more the service operates, the greater the variable costs will be. Operating at full capacity, the skating rink lights would be on, the dressing rooms and spectator areas would be heated, showers would deliver thousands of gallons of hot water, floors would need cleaning, supervisory staff would be retained, and so on. The cost of operating the rink will vary depending on its use; hence, the term variable costs.

Figure 9.2 identifies sample variable costs for the rink to operate for a seven-month skating season.

The actual cost of one unit of a product is calculated by applying the formula: $P=(F+V)/N$ where $P$=the cost of a unit, $F$=the total fixed costs, $V$=the total variable costs, and $N$=the number of units expected to be sold.

Using the data from Figure 9.2, the recoverable hourly cost of operating the ice rink is calculated by applying the formula:

$$P=(F+V)/N$$

$$P=(\$56,425 + \$45,000)/2,250 \text{ hours}$$

$$P=\$45.09/\text{hour}$$

To calculate the price that should be

---

## Kotkawagan Ice Rink
### COST SUMMARY
(October - April)

**Fixed Costs**

| | | |
|---|---|---|
| Capital cost | $4,300/month x 7 months | $30,100 |
| Administration (overhead) | $375/month x 7 months | $2,625 |
| Ice installation/removal | | $2,000 |
| Basic maintenance | $2,000/month x 7 months | $14,000 |
| Basic utilities and services | $1,100/month x 7 months | $7,700 |
| TOTAL FIXED COSTS | | $56,425 |
| HOURLY FIXED COSTS* | | $25.08 |

**Variable Costs**

| | | |
|---|---|---|
| Utilities and maintenance | $11/hour x 2,250 hours | $24,750 |
| Staff | $9/hour x 2,250 hours | $20,250 |
| TOTAL VARIABLE COSTS | | $45,000 |
| HOURLY VARIABLE COST* | | $20 |
| TOTAL COSTS | | **$101,450** |
| HOURLY COST* | | **$45.09** |

*based on expected 2,250 hours of ice time sold

**Figure 9.2**
**Sample cost summary for ice rink**

charged in order to recover all costs, a revised formula that considers contingency may also be used. *Contingency costs* are the unforeseen costs or revenue shortfalls for which the host or sponsoring organization needs to be prepared. For example, if the price is based on an estimation that ten people will participate and only nine actually do, then a contingency cost that was added to the price will at least partially cover the revenue shortage. Similarly, if a piece of equipment breaks down or additional materials need to be obtained after the program or event begins, then a contingency cost that was included in the price will help to pay for the unexpected expense. The formula for calculating the price, with a built-in contingency, is:

$P = C(F+V)/N$

where P=the average price per unit, and C=the contingency rate.

If the operator of the ice rink chooses to build a 5% contingency into the pricing model, then the average price for one hour of ice time will be:

$P = ((F+V) + C(F+V))/N$

$P = (($56,425 + $45,000) + .05($56,425 + $45,000))/2,250$ hours

$P = ($101,425 + $5,071.25)/2,250$ hours

$P = $47.33/hour$

Note that the $47.33 per hour cost calculated in the preceding example includes all of the costs associated with providing the specific activity. This approach to cost quantification is referred to as *activity-based costing* (ABC) and is different from traditional approaches to accounting, which often ignore major fixed costs

(e.g., capital, administrative overhead) and often do not relate costs to specific activities or program components.

The advantages of ABC over traditional cost measurement strategies include the following:

- ABC helps to identify manageable contributing factors to cost (thereby facilitating improvements to operational efficiency).
- ABC allows cost comparisons for the same activity provided by different units within the organization or for different market segments.
- ABC generates data for benchmarking and comparing the cost of an activity provided in-house or by contracting out.
- ABC tells the true story of cost and facilitates appropriate pricing based on cost recovery objectives.

### Subsidization and Unit Pricing

Once the cost-based price has been determined, the next step in establishing the unit price for a particular consumer or target market is the application of a rate of subsidization. The rate of subsidization refers to how much of the unit cost is going to be recovered from sources other than the consumer. In the public sport, tourism, and leisure service organization, subsidization means using tax revenues to reduce or eliminate user fees for services. Private not-for-profit and commercial sport, tourism, and leisure service organizations may subsidize some programs or services by using the profits generated by another of their enterprises to reduce or eliminate the consumer's contribution to meeting the costs of the programs or services.

Using the profits of one program to reduce the price of another is often called *cross-subsidization*. A common pricing strategy involves subsidizing different market segments at different levels. For example, the pricing strategy for the public skating rink could reflect a political decision to keep skating activities very affordable for special populations in the community while, at the same time, expecting commercial ventures to pay the full share (or more) of the costs of any public facilities or services that they use. The sample subsidization rates displayed in Table 9.1 demonstrate a commitment to youth recreation. Subsidization rates are used to convert the average per unit cost of a sport or leisure service to the final consumer price(s) for the product. The appropriate formula for calculating price is:

$$Pm=(1-Sm)(((F+V)+C(F+V))/N)$$
where Pm=the price to be charged to a specific market (m) for one unit, and Sm=the subsidization rate applied to market m.

Note that the subsidization rate can be as high as 100% (a free service) or as low as a minus percentage (a profit-generating service). A service that is "marked up" 30% is subsidized at -30% and priced at 130% of its cost.

The prices charged to various skating groups for one hour of ice time are shown in Table 9.1. The price for youth programs such as minor hockey, figure skating, and ringette are subsidized 35% and calculated as follows:

$$Pm=(1-Sm)(((F+V)+C(F+V))/N)$$

$$Pm=(1-.35)(\$47.33/hour)$$

$$Pm =\$30.77/hour$$

The subsidization rate for the Junior A hockey club (a commercial enterprise) is -25%, which means that the hourly cost will be marked up to establish a price for this user group. The formula given above can be used to calculate the price to be charged (\$59.16/hour, which is 25% greater than the cost to be recovered).

$$Pm=(1-Sm)(((F+V)+C(F+V))/N)$$

$$Pm=(1-(-25))(\$47.33/hour)$$

$$Pm =\$59.16/hour$$

## Other Considerations in Establishing Price

While cost recovery is usually the most important consideration in establishing prices, there are other factors to

Table 9.1
Sample subsidy rates and hourly prices for ice rink rental

| User Group | Subsidy Rate | Price |
|---|---|---|
| Minor Hockey | 35% | \$30.77/hour |
| Figure Skating | 35% | \$30.77/hour |
| Ringette | 35% | \$30.77/hour |
| Public Skating | 0% | \$47.33/hour |
| Open Skate | 100% | free |
| Gentlemen's Hockey | 10% | \$42.60 |
| Junior A Hockey (practice) | -25% | \$59.16/hour |

keep in mind when determining how much to charge for a sport, tourism, or leisure service. The potential customers' willingness to pay the established price is certainly an important consideration, as is their sensitivity to price changes.

## Willingness to Pay/The Going Rate

When cost-recovery goals are easily met because the calculated unit price is below an amount that all or most consumers are accustomed to paying or willing to pay, it may be appropriate (and, perhaps, necessary) to price the sport, tourism, or leisure service at a higher "going rate." Conversely, a service that costs more to produce than the consumers are willing to pay may also need to be priced at a going rate that results in a financial loss. In either case, the reasons for pricing at the going rate may be varied and may also include protection of perceived value, protection of consumer self-esteem, and promotion of competition.

A sport, tourism, or leisure service that is highly valued by consumers may not necessarily be costly to produce. However, if that low-cost service is priced too low, the potential appeal of and commitment to it may actually be diminished because of the commonly held belief that "you get what you pay for, and if it doesn't cost much, then it's probably not very good." Even if a private not-for-profit organization's excellent fitness program incurs a cost of $10 per participant, it might be wise to charge around $30 per participant if that is what he or she is used to paying for services of similar value (i.e., perceived personal benefit) or for similar services offered by another provider. In this example, the consumers have indicated a willingness to pay $30 and thereby have implicitly suggested that a significantly lower price would probably generate doubts about the quality of the product. The $30 price tag helps to protect the perceived value of the service. The "problem" of what to do with the $20 profit that would be realized by this not-for-profit organization may be quickly resolved if the organization also has a worthwhile program for which the production costs exceed the price that consumers are willing to pay. All the organization needs to do is to shift the profits of the former program to cover the losses of the latter. Clearly, consideration of the willingness of patrons to pay the going rate is important in pricing decisions, especially when the sport or leisure service organization uses cross-subsidization to achieve its financial objectives.

Consideration of the going rate in pricing decisions is also important for protecting the self-esteem of consumers. Generally, people like to feel that they have earned what they receive. When they receive benefits from a sport or leisure service, they feel better about themselves if they worked, sacrificed, or somehow paid a fair price for those benefits. Pricing decisions should allow for consumers to maintain or enhance their self-esteem in the knowledge that they will have "paid their dues." At the same time, pricing decisions should protect consumers' self-esteem by demonstrating sensitivity to the desire to believe that all basic needs and, perhaps, a few leisure wants are available and affordable to everyone. In other words, prices should not make a consumer feel that it is impossible to satisfy perceived needs, but instead should make him or her feel that paying the price is an appropriate way to demonstrate deservedness of the benefits derived from consuming the sport, tourism, or leisure product.

Sometimes the going rate is used as a means to promote competition. For example, a state park agency may be able to provide serviced campsites at an average cost of $8 per night, but will choose to charge the going rate of $15 per night in order to help the neighboring commercial campground stay in business. The commercial campground also charges $15 per night, but its average campsite costs are $12. The state park is able to produce campsites at a lower cost because it does not pay off a mortgage on the land, does not pay local property taxes or sales and income taxes, and does not pay directly for marketing. In some respects, the state park has an unfair advantage and could exploit that through its pricing. The state park, however, cannot always satisfy the demand for camping, but is required to facilitate extensive use of the park. It needs the commercial campground to stay in business in order for the state park to continue to attract visitors and to avoid expanding the public campground to the detriment of protected natural areas. By establishing prices that are consistent with the going rate, regardless of production costs, the state park promotes competition and ensures adequate camping opportunities for overnight visitors.

It should be noted that the going rate for a particular service might vary according to product and market conditions. Products that are seasonal in their appeal will have a lower going rate in the off-season than during periods of high demand. Products oriented toward children or economically disadvantaged population segments also tend to have a lower going rate than those offered to adults and wealthier persons. There are several appropriate justifications for differential pricing that are based on willingness to pay and the going rate:

- Customer Characteristics. Both the willingness to pay and the going rate may vary because of age limitations/opportunities, income, ability, intensity of consumption, etc.
- Product Levels. Consumers are willing to pay more for advanced levels or elitist tourism, leisure, and sport opportunities and less for basic services.
- Distribution. Differential pricing may reflect the advantages of one service location or time over another. For example, concert tickets are priced according to the location of reserved seats, and rental fees for sports facilities are higher during prime-time hours.
- Merit. Prices and expectations of price differentials may reflect the historical contribution of the consumer to the product. For example, lower program registration fees for club or association members serve as recognition and expectation resulting from the earlier payment of membership. Bulk pricing (such as season passes and ticket packs) is also a practice based on recognition of the contribution and merit of the high-quantity/frequency customer.

## Sensitivity to Changes in Price

The measure of price-induced demand fluctuations is called price elasticity of demand, and was discussed in Chapter 7. It is clear from that discussion that any change in price is going to have an impact of consumption and, most likely, on revenue. As a general rule, price increases should be avoided when dealing with an elastic market, but may be applied more liberally when dealing with a market or market segment that is relatively inelastic.

## Adjusting Prices

It is natural to expect that a drop in sales or attendance will result from an increase in price. When a price increases, there will inevitably be a portion of the market that feels that the new price is too high, and therefore cannot or will not pay the higher amount. Some of those customers will need time to adjust to the new price and may eventually find the resources or the will to return and continue participating. Others will not be able to convince themselves that the higher price is worth paying, but could be convinced by the service provider. In doing so, the sport and leisure service provider is challenged with finding a way to adjust or redefine the consumer's reference price. Reference price is the amount that the consumer feels that the service might or should cost and is derived from the consumer's experience with similar services and/or from introductory information provided by the sport, tourism, and leisure service organization. The *reference price* for a youth soccer camp, for example, might be $40. Last year the consumer paid $45 for a basketball camp with a similar format, and her neighbor reported paying $38 to register his daughter in the children's soccer camp offered by the YMCA. Hence, $40 seems to be a reasonable expectation (reference price).

The sport, tourism, and leisure service organization only needs to adjust the soccer moms' reference price if it is significantly different from the objective price. The *objective price* is defined as the actual price charged for the service. For example, the registration fee for youth soccer may be $55. Expecting to pay $40 and then being presented with a bill for $55, the consumer would be inclined to consider the program to be a bit expensive. She may even consider it to be much too expensive. The words or expressions that a consumer uses to describe the difference between the reference price and the objective price are referred to as the *subjective price*. Essentially, the subjective price is how the consumer feels about the objective price, based on his or her reference price. The subjective price is a word or expression, not a number. Examples include the following: "expensive," "reasonable," "cheap," "bargain," "rip-off," "prohibitive," "a good deal."

There are several effective approaches to adjusting the consumer's reference price. One approach is to *inform the consumer of the actual costs* that the price is supposed to recover. For example, the soccer camp may cost the agency $65 per participant. Knowing this, the consumer would be inclined to adjust her reference price upward and recognize that the objective price ($55) is really a pretty good deal. A second approach to changing the consumer's reference price is to *emphasize the value or the benefits of the product* to the consumer. In the youth soccer camp example, the sponsoring agency could point out that participation in the program provides the boy or girl with a wholesome, health-promoting way to spend time, a positive social environment, opportunities to experience success and failure (and help in learning how to deal with them), skill development, leadership experience, etc. Surely these benefits are worth at least $55! The third approach involves *comparing the cost of the service* with a similar service or activity offered elsewhere. The consumer could be informed that the price for the local soccer camp is $55, but that a similar program in a nearby community would cost $80. Furthermore, the soccer camp is $15 cheaper than both the basketball and volleyball camps offered by the same agency. The fourth approach to adjusting the reference price is to *enhance the image of the product* in the eyes of the consumer. In order to raise the reference price for the youth soccer camp, promotional emphasis could be placed on the success achieved by camp alumni or on the international reputation of the camp director.

Figure 9.3 shows the relationship of past experience and direct communications to the establishment of reference prices. It also identifies four approaches to adjusting reference price. The opportunity to influence the reference price is important to the sport, tourism, and leisure service manager, because the reference price is the price with which the objective price is compared in order to establish a subjective price. Purchase decisions are based on subjective price.

## Summary

The price of a sport, tourism, or leisure service is the quantification of the level of exchange between the service provider and the customer. It is what the customer gives up in order to receive the service. In addition to financial resources, the price includes opportunity, effort, and psychological stress. Monetary pricing helps the organization to recover costs of production, manage consumer behavior, and establish value for the service. Pricing of certain services is desirable and necessary, but others may not be suitable for direct pricing. There are several ways to establish a price, but the most common approach is to determine

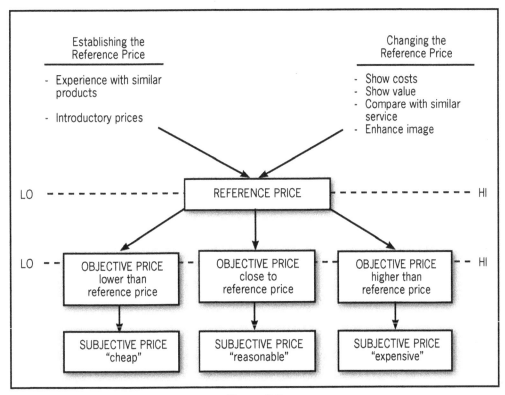

**Figure 9.3**
**Relationship of reference price to subjective price**

production costs and then price according to particular cost-recovery objectives. It is important for financial managers to understand and consider the sensitivity of sport, tourism, and leisure service consumers to price changes. Price changes will affect demand and consumption, which will ultimately affect revenue and profits.

## NOTES

# CHAPTER 10

# Grantseeking

## Introduction

Grantseeking is an area of financial management in which many sport, tourism, and leisure service professionals must develop proficiency. Grantseeking is a systematic, logical process of articulating and matching needs with the goals and expectations of a granting agency. Unfortunately, many sport, tourism, and leisure service managers are deterred from grantseeking by a process that they believe is complicated. While some granting organizations do require detailed proposals that are strongly supported by additional sources of information or money, there are many simpler grant proposals that can lead to equally successful results. There is no guaranteed formula for success, but there are procedures that, when followed, increase an applicant's potential for success. In today's competitive budget environment, it has become more common to use grantseeking as part of the sport, tourism, and leisure service organization's revenue plan. Successful grantseeking provides opportunities to extend programs and services in ways that might not otherwise be possible. This chapter describes the grantseeking process and suggests approaches that have proven to be successful in a variety of situations.

The terms *grantseeking* and *grantwriting* are frequently used interchangeably, but have different meanings. Grantseeking refers to the broader process of finding and securing a grant, while grantwriting is a particular reference to the process of writing a proposal.

## Why Pursue Grants?

Indiana University's Bradford Woods Outdoor Center is a 2,600-acre outdoor campus located about 20 minutes south of Indianapolis. During its 55-year history, it has evolved from a youth camp facility to a multifaceted outdoor education resource and demonstration center that includes camping, professional development, environmental education, a retreat center, and a training center. For its first 35 years, Bradford Woods operated with little change. Its primary function was to provide summer camping opportunities and dedicated areas for outdoor youth-serving agencies. By 1978, Bradford Woods was operating with a significant financial deficit. The university determined that changes needed to be made and Bradford Woods was expected to become more financially self-sufficient. Divestiture of the property, which had been bequeathed to the university in 1941, was not an available option. A new director was hired and given a charge to diversify operations and create new opportunities. One of the early strategies for increasing financial strength was the use of grants to support operations, programs, and capital improvements. This approach has made Bradford Woods increasingly more effective in securing short-term and multiyear grants. For example, the 1998–99 revenue budget for Bradford Woods was more than $2.25 million, of which about 20 percent came from the parent institution. Another 15 percent came as gratuitous income through an ongoing aggressive program of grantseeking. The 1998–99 capital improvement budget for the outdoor education center was $150,000, of which 80 percent came from grants. Bradford Woods is more successful in receiving grants in some years than it is in others. The management team's approach to grantseeking has yielded very positive results. Bradford Woods' need for and approach to grantseeking is typical of that experienced by many public and not-for-profit organizations.

## The Granting Environment

According to the Foundation Center's 2006 edition of *Foundation Growth and Giving Estimates*, the United States had nearly 68,000 granting foundations in 2005. That year, granting organizations awarded $33.6 billion in grants. Of that amount, the largest portion of grants (26 percent) went to human service organizations, and the largest share of money (24 percent) was given to education. Granting organizations can be viewed as potentially important sources of income for sport, tourism, and leisure service organizations.

Foundation granting organizations are divided into three categories: independent foundations, corporate foundations, and community foundations. *Independent* or *private foundations* are self-defining. They are not specifically connected with an organization, corporation, or community. Private foundations are usually created by a single individual or family through a bequest of funds. These bequests frequently have restrictions placed on the granting. These independent foundations make grants to other tax-exempt organizations to accomplish their charitable purposes. They do not program directly, but provide money to organizations that do program.

A foundation invests its assets to generate revenue that is used primarily to provide money for grants. Independent foundations must make charitable expenditures of approximately five percent of the market value of their assets annually. If an independent foundation has assets totaling $100 million, it will need to award at least $5 million in grants. Of course, it may award more than that.

A foundation is generally organized as a not-for-profit organization under appropriate state codes and registered as a (501 (c) (3)) charitable organization with the Internal Revenue Service. It typically has a board of directors and may hire an executive director. The board of directors makes decisions for grant awards. As shown in Table 10.1, independent foundations are the largest single source of grants. In 2005, independent foundations accounted for 89 percent of all granting organizations and awarded 73.3 percent of all grant dollars.

A *corporate foundation*, as the name suggests, is linked to a corporation and frequently focuses its giving in those communities where the corporation has operations such as offices, factories, or other interests. Funds for these foundations come primarily from the corporation, but granting decisions are, in most cases, separate from corporate decision-making processes and officers.

*Community foundations* represent a relatively new phenomenon. The focus of these locally instituted foundations is on their communities and on investing into the community. Some large corporate foundations, such as the Lilly Foundation, have made major commitments to community foundations as a way of enhancing their efforts to achieve their purposes. The purposes of community foundations vary somewhat, and may appear as those articulated in the following example mission statement:

"The Community Foundation is committed to improving and strengthening the community of the metropolitan region. Our mission is to:

- Develop the widest range of endowed funds and services to donors on behalf of the region and its counties and communities;
- Administer a growing granting program focused on helping where the needs are greatest and the benefits to the region are most extensive;
- Support the development of the services and institutions of the charitable sector of the region; and,
- Serve as a catalyst for community-based convening consensus building and problem solving in the region."

In today's rapidly changing and competitive society, securing grants is essential to fulfilling the missions of public and not-for-profit sport, tourism, and leisure service organizations. The availability of traditional funding sources has forced organizations such as Bradford Woods to seek alternative funding opportunities. Simultaneously, the diminishing role played by government in social service areas has increased the demand upon granting organizations. It is, therefore, essential that grantseekers

### Table 10.1
### Foundation statistics for 2005 (Foundation Center, 2005 giving)

| Foundation Type | Number | Grants* | Assets* |
|---|---|---|---|
| Independent | 60,520 | $24,528 | $454,574 |
| Corporate | 6800 | $5,712 | $16,644 |
| Community | 6880 | $3,360 | $38,782 |

* thousands of dollars

learn the art of matching their seemingly infinite needs with the finite offerings of grantmakers. The following step-by-step discussion of the grantseeking process is designed to help sport, tourism, and leisure service managers achieve proficiency as grantseekers.

## The Grantseeking Process

Successful grantseeking preparation involves far more than just asking and writing. A well-planned grantseeking process involves six steps (Figure 10.1) that take the applicant from idea generation to grant administration. Each step requires the development and assessment of time-tested approaches to grantseeking. Grantseeking is an opportunity to increase resources and thereby allow the organization to accomplish its mission in ways not normally possible.

### Step 1: Identifying a Potential Idea

Beginning with the end in mind is a key element of grantseeking. Step 1 involves identifying an idea that lends itself to the grantseeking process. The identification of an idea is not as difficult as it may at first appear. There are many good ideas that are worthy of a grantseeking, but the key is to work the idea into a problem statement and then match it to a willing grantmaker.

The development of a good idea is a problem-solving process. It does not initially seek to match ideas with potential grantmakers, but instead seeks to identify ideas that cannot be met with existing resources. The following questions can assist an organization in determining whether the idea might have merit with a potential granting organization:

- Is the idea new or innovative, and does it meet an identified need among potential or existing constituents? Can it solve an existing problem or enhance the potential for the solution of a problem?
- Is there a general recognition of the need within the community or among organizational members?
- Is funding available within the organization to support the idea? If

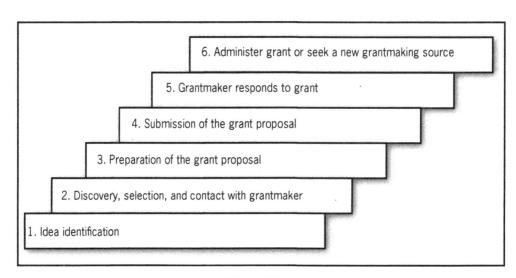

**Figure 10.1**
**Steps of the granting process (adapted from Smith & McLean, 1988)**

no, then what external sources and amounts can be considered?

- Are local or organizational funds available as a matching support for a potential grant (e.g., other government or not-for-profit organizations, individuals, in-kind contributions, etc.)?
- Are the community and the organizational members willing to support a grantseeking process?
- Does the idea support the organization's mission and strategic plan?

Once an idea is generated, it needs to be refined. The most important part of this phase of the process is to clearly identify and describe the problem. This phase will require sound research to show that a problem exists. Just because someone may "think" this is a problem does not make it a problem in the eyes of the granting organization. It is becoming more common for grantmakers to require documentation of the needs and to justify the problem. If other, similar types of projects already exist in other organizations, the grantseeker may be asked to show how his proposal is different. At this stage of the process, the development of the idea should be the primary focus. Collection of data to justify the need should be started, but only sufficient to begin phase 2 of the process.

### Step 2: Discovery, Selection, and Contact with a Granting Agency

Of the thousands of grantmakers serving U.S. communities, grantseekers must identify those that are most closely linked in their purposes for applying for the grant. Grantmakers can be classified as (1) government organizations, (2) corporations, (3) national or international philanthropic organizations, (4) regional or local or community philanthropic or-

ganizations, and (5) individual foundations. Identification of the philanthropic organization that best fits your problem can be daunting, but fortunately, assistance is available.

There are several organizations that assist grantseekers in their search for the perfect match. For example, the Foundation Center has branch libraries with staff in Atlanta, Cleveland, New York, San Francisco, and Washington, D.C. In addition, there are cooperating collections in over 200 public and university libraries, where support materials and publications are available. The Foundation Center publishes several directories, including the two-volume *The Foundation Directory*, the single-volume *National Guide to Funding in Arts and Culture*, and *The Foundation Grants Index*. The Foundation Center suggests that, through its resources, searches can be accomplished by using one of three criteria: geographic location, subject, or type of support.

*The Chronicle of Philanthropy* is another source of information about grants. The *Chronicle* is especially useful if the intent is to make grantseeking a part of the organization's funding and growth strategy. The *Chronicle* is a bi-weekly newspaper that tracks what is going on in the philanthropy arena and provides detailed information about grantmakers, types of grants that are being awarded, trends in grants, and so forth.

The same resources are available on the Internet. Users can access the Foundation Center (foundationcenter.com), *The Chronicle of Philanthropy* (philanthropy.com), and The Grantsmanship Center (tgci.com). Each site provides information for the grantseeker to assist in this search for granting organizations. Most grantmakers also maintain a web presence. These are accessed by conducting an Internet search for a specific

---

**CASE STUDY (part 1):**
*Identifying and securing a grant*

The case study presented in this section carries throughout the chapter. It appears at the conclusion of each step and provides an example. The case study applies to securing a grant for a public park and recreation agency and focuses on providing programming for people with disabilities.

**Identifying the Need**

The director and assistant director were discussing upcoming issues facing the recreation division when there was a knock at the door. The aquatics director walked in, obviously concerned about something. Her first words were, "The local job agency,for people with disabilities is no longer going to provide support for its employees to participate in Special Olympics. This is terrible."

The job agency had a long history of providing support for Special Olympics and had become a mainstay in the community's support of individuals with disabilities. The loss of their support would leave a big gap in services. The aquatics supervisor was appropriately concerned and saw the loss as a community failure. The director and assistant director saw an opportunity. The department had done little in providing services for people with disabilities. It was an issue of funding and staff.

The aquatics supervisor had additional responsibilities for people with disabilities during the aquatics off-season, but this gave her little time to provide programming. The director had indicated the department would not initiate any programs for people with disabilities if the department could not provide adequate and sustained support. As long as the aquatic supervisor could not provide year-round support to the programs, it was not feasible to initiate new programs. Instead, the strategy developed involved creating strategic partnerships, facilitating programming with other agencies, and taking the lead for special projects, but not for sustained programming.

The loss of sponsorship for Special Olympic funding provided an appropriate and viable problem for a grant. The issues of funding and staff could be resolved with an appropriately constructed grant. As the director and assistant director laid out their ideas, the aquatics supervisor saw distinct advantages to securing a grant.

After some discussion a problem statement was arrived at: *"Adult members of the community with physical and mental disabilities need recreation opportunities to make their lives more fulfilling. The act of preparing for and participating in Special Olympics provides unique opportunities for this population to experience leisure. The loss of the opportunity to the community significantly erodes their quality of life."*

---

foundation, for a specific type of grant, or for a type of foundation. Searches can be conducted through a foundation support site, such as the Foundation Center, or using a traditional Internet search engine such as Yahoo!, Google, or others.

Searching for Grantmakers

There is no single best way to search for a foundation that supports an iden-

tified problem. Finding the right grant-maker can be a time-consuming and sometimes frustrating process. This discovery phase is a necessary second step. The search can be conducted by looking through the various resources available from one of the previously mentioned sources, by making direct contact with foundations, or by securing support and ideas from other individuals. No single source will be sufficient. It requires a combination of sources to identify and select the one or more grantmakers that match a particular problem statement.

The search will likely turn up several potential grantmakers, from whom some basic information should be secured. First, the name, contact person, and address of the foundation should be noted. Second, financial information related to the organization should be collected. This information should include the total assets of the grantmaker, the total grants awarded in the most recent reporting year (many foundations issue annual reports), the dollar value range of grants awarded (high to low), and the average period of time for which the grantmaker is willing to fund a project. Total assets consist of the economic resources available to the grantmaker. They make up the principle that the grantmaker has available for investment purposes and from which they draw interest income. Third, the grantmaker's areas of focus (in order of importance). Fourth, the grantseeker needs to know if funding is restricted on the basis of geographic locations. Private grants are frequently restricted to the area where the benefactor either lived or had some special ties. Fifth, there may be restrictions or specific types of support that are identified by the grantmaker. The population that is served, such as children, the disabled, or the elderly, is another important piece of information. Finally, identify the types of recipients that the grantmaker has made awards to in recent years. Figure 10.2 depicts the results of this information search as applied to The National Parks Foundation.

## Selecting a Grantmaker

Selection of the appropriate grantmaker is based on the research completed in the early part of this step. If the research

has been thorough, then the grantseeker can make an informed judgment. Most likely, several grantmakers will emerge as potential sources of funding. If this occurs, the grantseeker must determine how to select the grantmakers with the highest potential to fund the project. Using the collected information, the grantseeker compares the various grantmakers with the specific criteria for the grant and the grant's goals and outcomes.

Table 10.2 provides an example of how to evaluate the gathered information. The decision to select a single grantmaker is based on finding the one most closely matching the funding problem. If there are no foundations matching the funding problem, then maybe it is appropriate to rethink the problem or to rethink the type of grantmaker being sought. While some grantmakers may seem better suited to a particular problem or idea, there may be other grantmakers who have not yet been considered.

1.  Name of the Foundation:
     The National Parks Foundation
2.  Assets: $81,588,053 (June 30, 2005)
     Expenses:
       Program Grants – $20,099,877
       Program Support – $8,200,892
     Grant Ranges: $400,000 to $1.5 million
     Funding Periods: up to 5 years
3.  Broad Focus:
     Education
     Community Engagement
     Volunteerism
     Visitor Experiences
     Priority Projects
4.  Local Focus:
     African American Experience
     Crater lake
     Flight 93 Memorial
     Greater Washington
     Glacier National Park
     Mississippi River Fund
     Shenandoah National Park Trust
     South Florida
     Washington's National Park Fund

**Figure 10.2**
**Example of a search result**

Figure 10.3 is a prospect worksheet that grantseekers can use to assist in the decision-making process. Grantseekers could carefully deselect potential grantmakers at this stage in the process. Keeping options open and being creative in the approach to seeking a grantmaker allows an organization a higher degree of potential success. Many grantseekers are not successful in their first try, so an attitude of perseverance becomes an essential quality for all good grantseekers.

### Contacting the Grantmaker

Depending on the type of grantmaker that is contacted, the nature of the relationship between the would-be grantseeker and the potential grantmaker will vary. Large grantmakers may send a packet with a form letter telling about themselves and their expectations. Smaller, specialized, or regional grantmakers may take a more personal interest. In one community, the grantseeker made personal contacts with the grantmaker over a period of several years and had established a credible relationship. Many have done the same thing with local foundations in their areas.

When contact is made, some questions need to be addressed by the grantseeker. The questions include the following: (1) How do they want the proposal written? (2) Do they provide technical assistance, including a review of proposal drafts? (3) How are proposals reviewed and decisions made? and (4) Are there budgetary requirements and preferences (examples include matching funds, in-kind services, payment preferences, and so forth)? The contact is an important source of information and future reference for the grantseeker.

### Securing Grant Guidelines

It is important to secure a copy of the grantmaker's published grant guidelines from the potential grantmakers. Many grantmakers have their guidelines printed and available for distribution. Figure 10.4 provides an example of the grant guidelines from a philanthropic organization that supports not-for-profit agencies.

Table 10.2
Grantseeking selection criteria

| Grantseeker | Grantmaker | Criteria |
|---|---|---|
| Problem Statement | Focus | The problem statement and grantmaker primary focus should match. |
| Appropriateness | Examples of Recipients | Examples provide additional information to the grantseeker depicting how previous resources were awarded. This is a guide to the grantseeker who recognizes funding priorities do change. |
| Location of needed | Geographic limits | Many grantmakers geographically restrict their awards. Use this as a quick eliminator of potential grantmakers. |
| Required support | Types of support | Provides detailed discussion of types of support the grantmaker might provide. Grantseekers need to match needs with willingness. |
| Population | Population served | Requires addressing at who the grantmaker is targeting their funding. Does the grantseeker population in need match the grantmaker population willing to serve? |

| Date: | Funder: | Your Organization |
|---|---|---|
| 1. Name Address, Contact Person | | |
| 2. Financial Data:<br>    Total Assets<br>    Total Grants Paid<br>    Grants Ranges/Amount Needed<br>    Period of Project Funding | | |
| 3. Subject Foucs | | |
| 4. Geographic Limits | | |
| 5. Type(s) of Support | | |
| 6. Population(s) Served | | |
| 7. Type(s) of Recipients | | |
| 8. People (Officers, Trustees, Staff) | | |
| Application Information<br>    Does the funder have printed guidelines/applications forms?<br>    What type of initial approach is required?<br>    What are the deadlines?<br>    Board meeting dates? | | |
| What are the sources of information? | | |
| Notes: | | |
| Followup: | | |

**Figure 10.3**
**Funding prospect worksheet (after Foundation Center worksheet)**

## Step 3: Preparation of the Grant Proposal

A grant proposal has several elements. Collectively, they provide a comprehensive justification and plan for what the grantseeking organization sees as a problem and for which it hopes to secure funding. Unfortunately, there is no standardized format for preparing grant proposals. One grantmaker may require an extensive funding proposal, while another may require a single-page summary of the proposal. Paying careful attention to the grantmaker's guidelines increases the chances that the proposal will be given serious consideration. Figure 10.5 illustrates elements of a grant proposal as suggested by four different grantmakers and grantwriting support organizations.

The elements of a grant proposal will vary according to the grantmaker's requirements, but there are some commonly agreed upon elements of a proposal. The eight common elements are a cover letter, an executive summary, a statement of need, a project description, organizational information (including key personnel and/or credentials), a budget, an

## CASE STUDY (part 2):
### Identifying Funding Sources

The task of identifying a potential funding source was not as difficult as it might have first seemed. When the current recreation director was new to the position, a former recreation director introduced him to his friend of 50 years who was also the executive director of a foundation located in the community. The foundation had a history of providing support to good causes in the community. When a proposal for a new public library could not get past a bond referendum, the foundation had paid for it and provided $500,000 each year for five years in support of library acquisitions.

With this history of community support the recreation director felt that the search for a funding source for a disability services was over. To engender interest in the project, the director met with the foundation executive director and discussed the project's purposes and needs. The foundation's executive director felt that it was a worthy project and believed that the foundation board would be positively inclined to support it. However, he could not speak officially for the board, since it made the ultimate decision.

The recreation director felt encouraged by the response and gathered the assistant director and aquatics supervisor together to build a strategy for the grant proposal.

evaluation process, and the grantseeker's commitment and ability to complete the project.

### Cover Letter

The cover letter is the formal introduction of the grantseeker to the grantmaker. It should be a clear and concise statement about the organization's pur-pose and why a grant is being sought. The grantseeker's needs are written in a manner that matches the grantmaker's purposes. This match clarifies the grantseeker's intentions and provides a gateway to the grantmaker's goals and objectives. The cover letter should be addressed to a specific person, rather than to the grantmaking organization, and it should in-

We strongly recommend that prospective applicants submit the following in the form of a letter of inquiry before a full proposal is sent:

- Information about the organization's purposes and specific activities.
- A brief description of the program for which funds are being sought, including the time period to be covered.
- The principal outcome(s) expected.
- Budgets for the program for which funds are sought, as well as for the organization.
- The amount being requested of the Foundation.
- Funding received to date for the program, as well as sources from which funding is being sought.
- The names and qualifications of the key personnel who will be responsible for the program.
- The most recent audited financial statements of the organization and its operating subsidiaries, if any.
- IRS certification of 501(c)(3) status of the organization.
- E-mail address for contact person at the organization.

**Figure 10.4**
**Grant guidelines from a typical foundation**

| The Foundation Center | Corporation for Public Broadcasting | LRR.net | The Grantsmanship Center |
|---|---|---|---|
| | | Cover letter | Cover letter |
| Executive summary | | Summary of cover sheet | Abstract/Summary |
| | | | Introduction |
| Statement of need | Statement of need | Problem statement | Need |
| Project description | Approach | Methodology | Plan of operations |
| | Methods of evaluation | Evaluation | Evaluation |
| | Project timelines | Program goals and objectives | Budget and cost effectiveness |
| Budget | Budget | Budget | |
| Organizational information | Credentials | Qualifications | Key personnel |
| Conclusion | | | Commitment and capability |
| | Supporting materials | Appendices | |

**Figure 10.5**
**Comparative analysis of elements of a grant proposal**

clude a brief description of the content of the proposal. The letter should not be overly long. One page normally suffices.

### Executive Summary

The executive summary is a one-or two-page descriptive summary of the project. It contains all of the essential information present in the full proposal. This snapshot of the proposal allows the grantseeker to set the stage for the proposal in a clear and concise way. It provides a narrative explaining the problem, its importance, the proposed solution (the projects and anticipated results), budget needs (including what has already been committed), and information about the organization and its competence. The executive summary should be written last and requires considerable thought and framing. It is often easier to write the proposal than an executive summary. It takes practice and several rounds of editing to write a good executive summary.

### Statement of Need

The statement of need is the most critical part of the grant proposal. It provides a description and justification of the need and/or description of the problem the project will resolve. The statement should enhance the reader's understanding of the issues. It presents facts in support of the project's need and validates the grantseeker as the best organization to meet the need. It provides information about five areas: (a) involvement of beneficiaries of the grant; (b) statement of need in terms of the participants or beneficiaries; (c) explanation of how needs were identified; (d) supporting statements and statistical data and authoritative documentation or statements; and (e) linking the needs and proposed solutions to the goals and strategic plan of the organization. The Foundation Center's Proposal Writing Short Course suggests six points to follow in preparing the arguments:

1. Determine which facts or statistics are going to best support the project. Emphasis in this section is on accuracy and detail to ensure that a valid case is built for the issue or problem. Eliminate information that is not germane to the proposal.
2. Determine whether it is reasonable to portray the problem as acute. If this is an acute problem, then explain why the organization should receive the grant.
3. If the problem is an issue that may seem unsolvable, then give the reader hope about the organization's involvement and potential to solve the problem.
4. Could the project be presented as a model solution? Determine if that is the best approach for this grant. If the grantseeker has a model solution and it fits the grant proposal, then include it. If not, then don't make it part of the proposal. Using a model solution can increase the base of potential grantmakers.
5. Demonstrate that the project addresses the need differently or better than other projects that may have preceded it. Be sure not to be critical of other projects that are competitive or have preceded this proposal. Show collaboration where possible. This characteristic is frequently viewed as a strength by grantmakers.
6. Avoid circular reasoning, where the absence of a problem is presented as a problem. For example, "The problem is we have no community center in our community. Building a community center will resolve that prob-

lem." It is better to focus on what a community center would mean to the community. "The problem is the lack of available facilities for community members to use, and especially youth-at-risk and gang-related issues."

### Project Description

The project description should contain three subsections: (a) goals and objectives, (b) methodology, and (c) staffing and administration. The proposal has already dealt with need. This section describes how the proposal, when funded, will operate and solve the problem. It provides sufficient detail, facilitating a clear understanding of the process and how the project will meet the described need. Goals and objectives establish a basis for measuring outcomes of the project. Each provides a clear level of distinction. Goals separate the problem or need into achievable work units. For example, a problem statement that reads, "How can we reduce the rise in juvenile crime and its impact upon at-risk youth in our neighborhood?" might generate several goals that could read:

1. To determine the at-risk youth population and who among the population has the greatest potential to engage in criminal behavior.
2. To establish an outreach program to reach targeted youth.
3. To establish a collaborative program of after-school activities and neighborhood resources meeting the needs of targeted youth.

Goals provide a general direction. They take the broader problem or need statement and divide it into workable units. For the grantmaker, it shows that the organization has established a direction and a plan leading to a solution. Objectives are a natural subdivision of goals and more clearly delineate how the goal will be established. Objectives are more specific, are based on a goal, and are measurable. There are four common types of objectives. *Behavioral objectives* suggest some type of human behavioral impact. An example would be, "Over a period of nine months, targeted youth will exhibit a more positive feeling about themselves." Objectives should address a single outcome. An objective stating, "Over a period of nine months, targeted youth will have a more positive feeling about themselves and about their families" should be written as two separate objectives. *Performance objectives* deal with proficiency or skill development. For example, "At-risk youth participating in the program over a six-month period will develop and exhibit study skills resulting in improved school performance." The objective may appear to have two outcomes, but the actual outcome is improved school performance. This is a measurable outcome. The development and exhibiting of study skills are processes that facilitate the measurable outcome. *Product objectives* suggest a deliverable item or hands-on product that other people can use or that is used by the grantseeker. An example is the statement, "To develop a manual for outreach workers that provides proven approaches to reaching at-risk youth." Both the product and the users of the product are clearly defined. A *process objective* looks at how a methodology was implemented and modified. It suggests, in many cases, an assessment process (e.g., "Methods used in the outreach program will be documented and assessed to determine which are most effective").

Methodology describes how the problem will be solved once the grant is awarded. This section provides a description of the grant administration. Smith and McLean (1988) suggest that several items should be considered:

1.  The overall design of the project should include an overview of how the project will be administered from start to finish. This is a narrative beginning with a restatement of the problem followed by a summary of the entire design process.
2.  Specific activities that are planned, and the sequencing of the activities within the project.
3.  The relationship between planned activities and the stated goals and objectives. Linking the activities with the goals and objectives is essential to the grantmaker's understanding of how outcomes are achieved. Goals and objectives do not stand alone. They must always be tied to process.
4.  Identify the specific procedures used to implement the program. A discussion of how the procedures will operate, as well as when they will be implemented. This may include a discussion of the sequencing of actions occurring before planned activities are implemented.
5.  Explain how program participants are selected.
6.  Identify project completion timelines for each phase of the grant.
7.  Discuss plans for collaborations with other organizations.
8.  Describe the project "deliverables," such as newsletters, process manuals, training materials, publications, seminars, and workshops.

Staffing and administration are important parts of any grant proposal. This section explains the competence of the organization's members who will be administering the grant. One of its purposes is to convey to the grantmaker confidence in the organization's capability to successfully carry the project to completion. Included are key people involved in the project, their experience, education, and training as related to the project. Résumés for existing staff should be included in the appendix with a narrative summary in the text.

When new staff are proposed as part of the grant project, it is necessary to justify the positions and demonstrate how the staff will have adequate responsibilities related to the project. Projects that propose new positions but fail to provide for continuation of the positions after the conclusion of the grant may find it a detriment to successful grantseeking. Finally, a project relying primarily on new staff will be less attractive than a mix of permanent and new staff.

## Organizational Information

The introduction to this section is a description of the grantseeker's qualifications or evidence of credibility for the proposed project. The introduction tells the grantmaker about the organization, its mission, its purpose, a brief history, and its general goals and objectives. There is a discussion about the organization's current programs, activities, service statistics, strengths, and accomplishments. This section needs to focus on the strategic plan and progress toward achieving it. Also included is a discussion about the function and size of the governing board and its involvement in the organization. The grantmaker should be able to get a feel for the composition, commitment, and involvement of that governing board. Any special constituent groups serving as volunteers are identified and it is stated how they support the project's goals. How the staff will be involved in the proposed project and in the variety of activities focusing on the organization's mission will

also be articulated. Finally, a description of the organizational activities and the identification of the services provided to the various constituencies should help to emphasize the appropriateness of the expertise of the organization as it fits with the proposal.

## Budget

The budget can be a key factor in successful grantseeking. Convincing the grantmaker that the budget effectively and efficiently responds to the needs related to the grant is important. A well-constructed budget with a strong supporting narrative is a positive reinforcement to the grant proposal. Budgets normally identiify two primary sources of funds: those requested from the grantmaker, and those provided by the grantseeker. The grantmaker normally provides money, but may also provide other types of resources. The grantseeker can provide a variety of different types of resources. These include money from the operating budget, in-kind services (such as staff or secretarial assistance), or external resources (such as sponsors or volunteers). In-kind donations are services rendered by individuals who are members of the organization, the cost of their services, and contributions of services such as office space, utilities, telephone service and so forth. The total in-kind contribution is determined and added to the budget as part of the grantseeker's contribution. For example, a secretary who makes $30,000 a year and has 10 percent of her time assigned to the project would represent $3,000 in in-kind services. Office space might be priced at $500 month with utilities adding another $30 monthly for an annual in-kind contribution of $6,360. The budget should clearly reflect the types of in-kind services provided. The budget process follows the budget procedures explained in Chapter 14. As a guide, the budget should:

- Address (in financial terms) exactly what the narrative of the grant has proposed;
- Provide complete compensation information about each staff position, including rate of pay, percent of time allocated to the project, fringe benefits, mileage rate, per diem rates, honorariums, and so forth;
- Include actual costs for supplies and services related to the project; and
- Include items paid for by other sources.

Figure 10.6 shows how a sample budget for a project might be formatted. A supporting budget narrative would only be necessary to explain unusual or unclear costs. A budget narrative is framed in one of two ways: a footnote style providing a description of different budget items, or the budget narrative could be written as part of the document. In some cases, grantmakers provide a budget form for grantseekers to complete.

## Evaluation Process

The evaluation section of the proposal explains how project outcomes are assessed. It provides the grantmaker with measures of effectiveness for grant dollars awarded. Grantmakers increasingly demand accountability. Evaluation is integrated throughout the project. The evaluation process should include an assessment of the process and continuous progress toward intermediate and final outcomes. A well-prepared evaluation process is an important criterion in their decision making. A checklist for the evaluation narrative, at a minimum, includes the following:

| Item | Number | Item Cost | Total Cost |
|---|---|---|---|
| Printing of envelopes & stationery | 300 | $80.00 | $24,000.00 |
| Questionnaire printing | 150 | $3.00 | $450.00 |
| Postage for questionnaire | 150 | $2.75 | $412.50 |
| Data input (student hours) | 40 | $8.50 | $340.00 |
| Data analysis (student hours) | 40 | $8.50 | $340.00 |
| Telephone interview | 60 | $10.25 | $615.00 |
| Qualitative date analysis | 120 | $15.00 | $1,800.00 |
| Travel | | | $0.00 |
| Dissemination of data - conference | partial | $1,500.00 | $1,500.00 |
| Dissemniation of data - conference | partial | $1,500.00 | $1,500.00 |
| Sub-total | | | $30,957.50 |
| Overhead | 40% | $12,383.00 | $12,383.00 |
| Total Requested | | | $43,340.50 |
| In-kind Contributions | | | |
| Co-primary research time | 12% | $72,000.00 | $8,640.00 |
| Co-primary research time | 8% | $65,000.00 | $5,200.00 |
| Benefits | 28.70% | $13,840.00 | $3,972.08 |
| Clerical | 23.10% | $732.00 | $169.09 |
| Total In-Kind Contributions | | | $18,713.17 |

**Figure 10.6**
**Sample grant budget**

- Explain how the evaluator and the process will be selected.
- Include an evaluation procedure for each goal and objective.
- Identify interim outcomes and match them to timelines for the project and reporting periods.
- Describe data-gathering methodology and connect it to goals, objectives, and timelines.
- Describe any instruments or tools used and how they support the project.
- Explain how evaluation data are used and disseminated to stakeholders.
- Describe the evaluation reports.
- Explain how evaluation is used to enhance the project's progress and outcomes.

### Commitment and Capability

The grantmaker appropriately asks, "What is the potential for success of the project?" The answer to this question comes only after a careful review of the grant proposal reveals soundness in conceptualization, effectiveness in design, and confidence in delivery. Confidence in delivery comes, in part, from demonstration of the grantseeker's commitment to

---

**CASE STUDY (part 3):**
**Building the Grant Proposal**

Following the meeting with the foundation executive director, the recreation director returned and met with the aquatics supervisor and assistant director. The director described the process that the department needed to follow. It would involve a letter describing the program, how much money was requested, how it would be used, and how the program would achieve sustainability.

The working group of three created a strategy for acquiring the grant. The aquatics supervisor provided information about all agencies currently providing recreation programs for people with disabilities. The assistant director began to gather information about operating costs for the program, available department facilities, program adaptations, etc. The director focused on funding strategies and gaining city council support.

For the director, the first step was to determine a strategy leading to sustainability. After conversations with a number of colleagues and the city council member responsible for parks and recreation, a strategy was formulated. Selling the strategy to the city council was the next step for the recreation director.

This small but committed project team met at least weekly to discuss what was learned, identify new issues, and refine strategies. For example, the aquatics supervisor felt that, if the grant was successful, other agencies might expect the city to provide all services and discontinue their current involvements. It was determined that 11 agencies were currently providing services. A meeting was scheduled with individual agencies, and the aquatics supervisor and director met with each agency's manager. Two questions were asked. First, each organization was asked to write a letter of support for the grant. Second, each organization was asked to commit to its existing level of service for at least five years. Every agency agreed. This could not have occurred without the groundwork that the aquatics supervisor had done over a four-year period of working with these groups.

Next the director and assistant director organized the budget. It required them to look five years into the future to anticipate costs. They arrived at a $100,000 first year costs for salaries, travel, and supplies. Then, working with the city comptroller, a 5.5

---

**CASE STUDY (part 3):**
**Building the Grant Proposal (continued)**

percent annual growth was projected. Detailed costs were developed for the first year, and years two through five depicted the adjusted growth.

Next, the director focused on funding the grant. The foundation executive director suggested that strategic partnerships and creative financing would enhance the grant's potential for funding. The recreation director proposed a six-year model of cost sharing. The proposal called for 100% funding by the foundation in year one and a 20% reduction in the foundation's commitment in years two through five. The city would make no contribution in the first year, but beginning in the second year would contribute 20% to the cost of the program and an additional 20% each year until, in year six, the city would cover the cost of the program. The recreation director also committed the department to actively seek out additional grant sources with a goal of meeting 50% of the cost of the program by year six.

The director met with each city council member individually to secure their support. It was forthcoming in a letter signed by the mayor and committing the city's funds to the project.

The director put a packet together under an appropriate a cover letter. The packet included the request, nature of the project, funding level requested, explanation of the city commitment, and the timeline. The letter from the Mayor was attached, as were the 11 support letters from the not-for-profit agencies. The letter was submitted to the foundation's executive director.

---

and capability of achieving success. The grantseeker explains how similarly funded projects have been successful, how the presence of staff, facilities, and other resources all contribute to the potential success of the proposed project. A concise discussion of strengths, resources, and successes allows the grantmaker to gain a clearer picture of the grantseeker's capability. This section of the proposal is not long, but provides critical support to the preceding sections.

### Step 4: Submitting the Grant Proposal

The culmination of the grantwriting process is the submission of the grant proposal to a grantmaker. All of the components described in Step 3 are included in the proposal. The submitted proposal must have a professional look. It should be bound if it is large, should conform to

good grammar, and be easy to read. Before sealing the package for delivery to the grantmaker, the grantseeker should complete one final review, ensuring that all materials are included and in the requested/intended order.

### Step 5: Grantmaker's Decision

The grantmaker can make one of several decisions regarding a proposal. The grantmaker may (1) award the grant in full, (2) make a partial grant award, (3) defer consideration of the proposal to a later date, or (4) deny the grant request. If the final option is taken, the grantmaker is under no obligation to explain why the proposal was rejected. In the same regard, the grantseeker should not read a lack of worthiness or value into a rejection. A grant rejection may be due to a lack of available funds, an overabundance of similar proposals, or it may have fallen outside the guidelines of the grantmaker. In some cases, the grantmaker will ask for changes in the proposal with a resubmission. Regardless of whether the grant proposal is rejected, funded in part, or needs modification, the grantseeker should call the grantmaker and ask how the proposal might be strengthened. This feedback may be important in strengthening the grant proposal for future submissions.

In cases where only portions of the grant were funded or where there was a decision to defer to a later time, the grantseeker must decide whether to accept the decision of the grantmaker or to withdraw the proposal and seek another grantmaker. This can be a difficult decision, as the grantseeker has invested considerable energy in the process. If the grantseeker determines that it may have a better opportunity elsewhere, then it may be appropriate to seek another grantmaker.

Even when full funding is awarded, the grantseeker still must choose to accept the grant. A grantmaker may attach conditions to the funds, and the grantseeker will have to determine if they are appropriate. An important deciding factor in the acceptance of a grant is whether the project can be accomplished and whether it remains consistent with the values and mission of the organization.

### Step 6: Grant Administration

Grant administration involves managing the project for which the grant was awarded, along with maintaining appropriate communications with the grantmaker. Some grantmakers choose to have little contact with the organization after an award is made, but most require some type of ongoing contact. The grant administrators should consider the following:

---

## CASE STUDY (part 4):
### Administration of the Grant

The funding proposal was successful and it was awarded in February, with a July 1 starting date to conform to the city's budget calendar. Several tasks occurred simultaneously. The department set up a separate account to administer the program from money received from the foundation. Later, two accounts were established, one tracking city contributions and expenses and the original to track expenses and revenue received from the foundation, or other anticipated gratuitous income sources. The city established a relatively seamless approach for the administration of funds and determination of cost centers.

The aquatics director was charged with preparing a job description for the new staff person (funded by the grant), and to conduct the search process (working with human resources and coordinating with the not-for-profit agencies). A few not-for-profit organizations were invited to participate in the interview process.

The assistant director, working with a local university, established an assessment process to begin with the receipt of grant funds on July 1 and continuing beyond the life of the grant. The director committed to quarterly progress reports with distribution to the foundation, city council, and the park and recreation board.

Several years later, the program was working well, meeting the defined outcomes, jointly funded by the city and the foundation and by several local individual and organizations. Some not-for-profit organizations made efforts to reduce their services, but were reminded of their commitment.

- Where feasible, have a single point of contact from the grantseeking organization to the grantmaking organization. This simplification enhances communication and reduces the potential for confusion.
- Don't leave questions about the grant unanswered. Make contact with the grantmaker to resolve issues before they become problems.
- Always make contact with an individual, and not with an organization.
- Include the project name and grant identification number on all correspondence.
- All correspondence should be clear and specific. Do not assume people know the issue being discussed.
- Always seek permission before making changes in the budget.
- Make regular progress reports to the grantmaker. Any deliverables such as news letters, reports, brochures, and annual reports should be provided.
- Stick to the timeline. If changes are required, seek approval from the grantmaker.
- At the conclusion of the report, submit all required information in a timely and complete manner.

Knowledge of all the requirements of the grantmaking organization, as well as the criteria of the grant, will ensure a more effective administration process.

## Summary

Grantseeking is neither a complicated nor a mystical process, but it can be a time-consuming process. Successful organizations have implemented the steps outlined in this chapter. Identifying potential grantmakers, paying careful attention to detail, and taking time to learn the grantseeking process frequently results in successful receipt of grants. Thankfully, most worthy ideas can be matched to the interests of generous, willing grantmakers. The decision to award a grant is based on the sustained efforts of the grantseeker to find a grantmaker that is a good match for a proposed project.

## References

Foundation Center. (2006) *Foundation Growth and Giving Estimates*. Foundation Center: New York, NY.

Smith, S. H., & McLean, D. D. (1988). *ABC's of Grantsmanship*. Reston, VA: American Alliance for Health, Physical Education, Recreation and Dance.

# NOTES

# CHAPTER 11

# Philanthropy and Fundraising

## Introduction

In contemporary government enterprises and among not-for-profit organizations, the traditional reliance upon
support from the general fund is waning.
Although the expectations for meeting social needs placed on many sport,
tourism, and leisure service and other
not-for-profit organizations are increasing, budgetary resources are stagnant in
many organizations and declining in others. Partnering with philanthropic and
not-for-profit organizations and individuals is increasingly becoming an attractive
and necessary approach to securing additional resources. It is not unusual in
forums conducted by the National Association of State Park Directors, for
example, to have as much as 60 percent
of all presentations focused on partnering, friends' groups, and philanthropy.
One state reported the simultaneous creation of almost 200 friends' groups with

not-for-profit fundraising. Furthermore,
many and varied training programs on
fundraising designed for sport, tourism,
and leisure service professionals are offered by major fundraising organizations
and universities. This chapter looks at the
concept of philanthropy and the process
of fundraising as it applies to sport, tourism, and leisure service organizations.

## Philanthropy

A charitable act is a social exchange
that occurs each time a gift is made.
The decision to make a gift comes after
someone trusted by the donor asks. A
gift implies a considerable level of confidence and trust in both the asker and
the charitable organization's ability (and
faithfulness) to do what is "right" with
the donation.

Philanthropy is synonymous with
charitable giving. While charitable giving

is perceived as giving for the social good, the social good is increasingly being interpreted in a broader context of issues. In the narrowest sense, charitable giving is giving resources to those in need or to organizations that assist them. This perspective of giving has been broadened to include all types of philanthropy, which can be defined as an act of trust on the part of a donor toward the organization that will receive and use the donation.

The philanthropic process is uniquely American. No other region in the world has the same level of giving, nor the social and governmental structure to allow such massive levels of giving. In 2004, over $248 billion were donated to charitable causes. Of that amount, $187 billion were donated by individuals, and the balance was donated by foundations and corporations.

Philanthropy is an activity of and resource to individuals and not-for-profit organizations. It is not-for-profit organizations working in conjunction with individuals and public and private organizations that secure donations from individuals and other not-for-profit organizations and foundations. Sometimes referred to as *the third sector*, philanthropic organizations focus on meeting social needs that are neglected by other sectors. In public park and recreation organizations, for example, there has been a steady decline in financial resources made available from the public purse to fulfill the public recreation mission. To counteract this, public agencies have turned to the philanthropic sector. The National Park Service is probably the leader in this movement, although other federal land-managing agencies, state park agencies, public recreation departments, and many not-for-profit sport organizations are close behind. The Florida Park Service produces a Citizen Support

Organization Handbook for the express purpose of extending the resources of the Florida Park Service. Hundreds of American cities have developed foundations to support their social service programs. Many state sport corporations are highly dependent on charitable giving for their support. Philanthropy has become intertwined with daily services and programs provided by sports and sport, tourism, and leisure service organizations.

Both independence and volunteerism characterize philanthropy. Independence is a characteristic in the sense that individuals and organizations making donations give independently of conditions that could have been associated with the gift. In philanthropy, the gift is given voluntarily; that is, the donor does so of his or her free will with the intent of promoting a particular purpose or meeting a particular need.

## Why Fundraising is Important

There are many good reasons to use fundraising to develop and sustain public and not-for-profit sport, tourism, and leisure service organizations. The Philanthropy and American Outdoors Workshop (Ross, 1997) suggests 10 reasons why organizations should include fundraising in their revenue structure plan:

1. There is growing evidence that public agencies at all levels of government are becoming increasingly dependent upon external philanthropic support. Traditional services offered by public agencies are either dwindling or being replaced by for-profit enterprises.

2. Philanthropy is one of America's most distinctive virtues. Giving to public/society benefit purposes and

giving to leisure, sport, and environment and wildlife has experienced significant increases in recent years.

3. The "Greening of America:" Contributions to environmental causes, including our parks, forests, open spaces, and wildlife, is big business—almost $7 billion annually. The numerous not-for-profit environmental and park support organizations hope to benefit as current generations pass unprecedented wealth to the baby boomer generation—an estimated $12 trillion by 2015.

4. Tax-law changes are having an impact on the amounts and kinds of gifts Americans make today. Capital gains, appreciated property, estate planning, charitable trusts, endowments, gift annuities, bequests, etc., are becoming part of our everyday language in the public and private not-for-profit community.

5. Sport, tourism, and leisure service organizations are well positioned to make the case for philanthropic support. They are in the quality-of-life and resources business.

6. Socially and environmentally oriented public service professionals have those desired qualities to make fundraising a success: a dedication to fulfilling a public trust; a desire to work with both the general public and those with affluence or influence (hopefully, both); a willingness to ask the hard questions; and an ability to communicate a sense of urgency.

7. Partnership building is here to stay and is critical in obtaining the diverse philanthropic support available.

8. Individual citizen donors and volunteers are marching to a different drummer today, demanding accountability, ownership in what they give to, and a direct voice in how the philanthropic dollars are spent.

9. We are faced with what Andrew Carnegie called "the proper administration of wealth." He formulated three alternative ways of disposing of wealth: bequest it to one's relatives, endow it to the public good, and administer it during one's lifetime for public benefits. Carnegie preferred and practiced the third alternative.

10. From fundraising to the stewardship of gifts received, sport, tourism, and leisure service organization professionals demonstrate their public trust.

## The Role of Fund Development

The roles of fund development can be many. Regardless of how the organization is structured, it is how the philanthropy dollar is used and how effectively the donor or potential donor perceives that use that is of most importance. Some of the roles include the following:

- Building community: Sport, tourism, and leisure service organizations have long been involved in building communities. They are seen as contributing to the quality of life of communities. The Riverwalk Foundation in Naperville, Illinois, focuses on securing funding that will build the quality of life along the community's river that runs through the downtown. Other community foundations have focused on improving the community.

- Funding opportunities to invest in human capital: This is a frequent source of giving. Sport, tourism, and leisure service organizations have their foundations in human capital and continue to strengthen their involvement in this area.

- Seeking a design to allow the accomplishment of objectives: The City of Baltimore, Maryland, when faced with a $500,000 annual deficit in its golf course operations, reorganized them under an independent not-for-profit corporation. The not-for-profit corporation was able to receive gifts, but more importantly, it reorganized golf operations in such a way as to relieve the public from a significant tax burden.

- Offering a means for donors to fulfill their aspirations: Friends of the outdoors, friends of parks, friends of wildlife, sports corporations, state tourism bureaus, and similar types of friends groups provide donors with the opportunity to give of both their time and money. These are among the most popular approaches to giving in the United States.

## Why People Give

Understanding why people give is as important as knowing how to ask for money. Not all people are motivated to give for the same reasons. Several reasons have been suggested for giving. For some, it fulfills social, religious, or philosophical convictions. Religious organizations receive the largest amounts of charitable contributions. Social and philosophical reasons are inherent in society as motivations for giving. When Ted Turner, founder of the Cable News Network and other major cable television channels, pledged $1 billion to the United Nations' efforts, it was for philosophical and social reasons.

The government has made charitable giving an obvious tax advantage, both at the federal and state levels. Every phil-anthropic organization makes sure its potential and actual donors understand the tax advantages of giving. Another reason for giving is for gratitude or for a commitment to public service that will lead to a better society. Some individuals hope to gain appreciation and public recognition for their efforts. In some cases, givers may hope for redemption. Some give out influence in the form of guilt or competitiveness by challenging others to give at the same level or by offering a matching grant as an incentive. Other philanthropists want to create a memorial to themselves or others who are dear to them. Many buildings, parks, monuments, and tourist attractions are created as memorials to an individual or a family (e.g., Rockefeller Center, Carnegie Hall). An observant walker on any college campus or public park will note the names on benches, fountains, and buildings that were made possible by the generosity of a successful alumnus, family, or friends. Finally, some donors want to keep their life's work in the family and make sure it is perpetuated for future generations through the creation of foundations.

## Charitable Organizations

Most charitable organizations are organized under the Internal Revenue Service (IRS) tax code as 501(c)(3) classification. In order to qualify for 501(c)(3) status, an organization must meet certain requirements. Included for foundations (which are the most common in support of sport, tourism, and leisure service organizations) are articles of incorporation that have been filed with the appropriate state authorities. Requirements for incorporation vary in each state. The IRS also requires that the organization provide a detailed narrative of all of the activities of the organization—past, present, and future. The Florida Park Service has provided the following narrative as an example to consider:

### Activities of a Charitable Organization Established to Support the Park System

- Development of Educational Media: The development of at least five educational videos relating to the resources, management practices, and recreational opportunities in Florida state parks.
- Promotion of Florida State Parks: Undertake a program to promote Florida state parks through the production of three driving tours of three representative Florida ecosystems. Also, help sponsor traveling exhibits on Florida state parks.
- Development of Endowment Fund: Commence the establishment of a dedicated endowment fund for the support of major needs in Florida state parks. The fund will be established and administered by a committee of the board of directors.

The charitable organization also needs to identify its sources of income, describe its actual and planned fundraising program in detail, and provide the names, addresses, and titles of the officers of the board of directors. If public officials are involved in the organization, they must be mentioned by title. Many of these organizations receive all or part of their administrative support from the organizations they serve. If so, this must be noted in the IRS submission. Additional information requested by the IRS includes activities and operational functions focusing on the assets of the organization, as well as financial data for the current year and the three previous years.

## Fund Development

Fund development is a planned process that involves promotion of understanding, participation, and support. It is a process of encouraging the public to give of its time, talent, and resources to play an active part in achieving the organization's goals. Figure 11.1 illustrates a perspective of the development of donors. The development process involves the three stages shown to the left in Figure 11.1. They include the contact phase, the growth phase, and the commitment phase. Fund development is a process of finding and nurturing potential contacts until they become donors committed to the cause of the organization. Such a process can take years to accomplish.

Fund development is a strategic marketing process designed to bring together potential donors with the not-for-profit organization in such a way that both benefit from an exchange. The donor may be giving for altruistic reasons or for financial benefit. The marketing process is different from the type of marketing that a commercial organization practices. While there are some similarities, there are also some significant differences. The product that a commercial organization sells is a tangible benefit or commodity to the customer. In some sense, charitable organizations provide the same advantages, in terms of tax benefits, but as previously discussed, they also provide some philosophical, social, and cultural benefits that commercial organizations are not well suited to provide. The marketing campaign of the charitable organization focuses on securing committed donors. The three phases depicted in Figure 11.1 are further divided into eight levels within the pyramid. The initial contact phase is important for maintaining a base of new and committed donors. The universe of

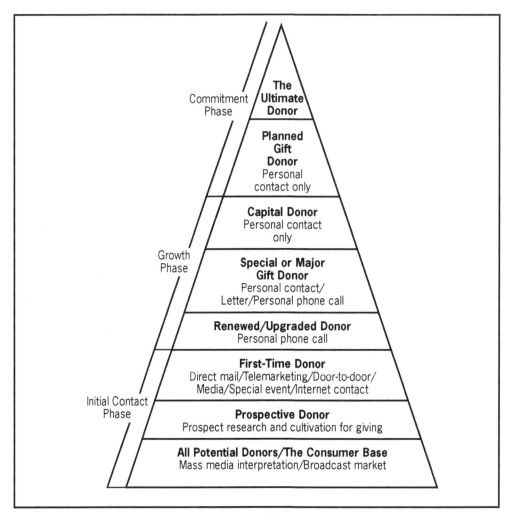

**Figure 11.1**
**The donor pyramid**

suspects, or consumer base, is seen as all individuals who might be contacted. This is a global population of potential donors from which the organization could potentially draw. In reality, only a small part of the population is going to become actual donors. With limited funds available for the search for new donors, the charitable organization must begin to narrow its list of potential donors. Some organizations maintain profiles of donors to assist in efforts to target the most re-

sponsive prospects. Table 11.1 illustrates three characteristics for segmenting the population by a cultural organization. The elitist group was seen as its primary long-term benefactors, while the other two groups were seen as less promising sources of donors.

First-time contributors are the lifeblood of an expanding donor pool. Not only does this group represent a new source of money, but also a new contact. The charitable organization immediately

### Table 11.1
### Population titles and characteristics as donors (Golan, 1998)

| Sociodemographic title | Population characteristic | Targeted nonprofits |
|---|---|---|
| Elitist | Socio-economically top tier individualists. Provide cutting edge corporate and foundation support. Targeted for planned gifts. | Arts and culture International affairs Environmental issues Political and social issues |
| Elite and Democratic Access | All of the above, plus mass appeal and special events. | Higher education Environment Social services |
| Mass Appeal | Some of the above. Direct mail approach. Some advertising campaigns will reach. | Health care Education Social services |

moves the new donor to the growth phase. The narrowing of the population of donors to those who might give is critical. Whether the winnowing is done through a mass mailing, telephone calls, or individual contact, the charitable organization needs to maximize the efficiency and effectiveness of the contact. Researching and knowing potential donor sources is critical and discussed in more detail in the section on annual campaigns.

In the growth phase, the donor begins to receive more frequent or sustained contact from the charitable organization. The intent is to encourage the donor to change from a once a year minimal contributor to one who makes multiple annual donations. The goal is to create a commitment to the charitable organization's goals and mission that will continue to grow, along with donation size. As depicted in Figure 11.1, there are three levels of contact and giving used in this phase, each one requiring a higher level of involvement on the part of the charitable organization and resulting in a higher level of giving by the donor.

The growth phase typically occurs over several to many years. In the growth phase, matching of donors' desires with organizational needs is the greatest importance. Growth in this phase comes when the donors see their gift as something that meets their desires. They have become committed to the charitable organization or some aspect of its operations and are willing to commit some of their financial resources to it. At this level, personal contact becomes more and more important to the success of the effort.

A few donors will move from the growth phase to the commitment phase, and, as might be expected, the size of their gifts will increase. The frequency of gifts may decrease, although this is not always the case, but the size of their gift and its impact on the charitable organization will be significant. These are the donors who will give $1 million or more to endow a chair, or $500,000 to build a community structure, or $200,000 to endow a scholarship fund.

Finally, as illustrated in Figure 11.1, the once-large pool of donors continues to get smaller as the charitable organization moves toward securing the ultimate donor. The willingness of the donor to give is a function of both economics and commitment to the charitable cause. An individual with a desire to give much, but whose economic resources are limited, may always be a special or major gift donor. The ultimate donor has the economic resources to make a gift that has a major impact on the charitable organization's ability to achieve its mission. As each organization strives to develop the ultimate donor, it would be unwise for it to focus all of its energies on this limited field of donors. It must rely on diverse, multitiered fundraising and donor development efforts.

## Fundraising Sources

A successful fundraising program draws upon at least seven different potential sources of funds. These include *individuals, boards and board members, corporations and industry councils, foundations, special events, government,* and *planned giving.*

*Individuals* constitute the most significant source of all philanthropic dollars available to charitable organizations. Major donors are cultivated over a period of time and provide the core of success to many charitable organizations. These individuals are important because they generate an enduring personal loyalty to the charitable organization. Typically, these individuals have the interest and wealth necessary to act on their enthusiasm for the benefit of the charitable organization. Major donors have become benefactors for risky projects, providing necessary capital to successfully undertake a project that the charitable organization might not otherwise fund. Finally, these individuals have extensive contacts and can bring others (and their money) to the charitable organization. Although they will be few, the major individual donors should be recruited and nurtured with great care. Individuals are drawn to charitable organizations because they believe that they have the ability to make a difference. For example, the Riley Foundation has supported Bradford Woods summer camp programs for individuals with disabilities for over 50 years, during which time it has funded many major capital improvements. The Riley family established and made the initial investment in a foundation that supports the Bradford Woods summer camp program, along with many other programs for children with disabilities. Cultivating major donors requires a long-term commitment on the part of the board and the chief executive officer (CEO) of the charitable organization. It requires personal communication from peers, prompt acknowledgment of communication and gifts, and the dissemination of advanced news of the charitable organization's activities.

*Corporate and industry councils* have been consistent givers to philanthropic causes. Since 1950, they have given about five percent of total contributions (about $12 billion annually). Many corporations restrict their giving to local communities where they have operations. They do so for many reasons, including strengthening the community, enhancing board connections, stimulating economic development, and providing educational outreach. Most corporations have a separate corporate foundation into which they make donations and from which they award grants. Gaining access to corporate foundation grants is facilitated by continuous nurturing of a relationship between the foundation and the sport, tourism, and leisure service organization. The Battle Creek, Michigan, Parks and Recreation Department, for example, has consistently worked with the Kellogg Foundation to ensure a steady source of capital income for park and recreation facilities.

*Boards and board members* are an important source of income and prospective donors. Board members of charitable organizations have usually made large donations or are expected to contribute during their tenure on the board. In addition, board members identify and work with potential major gift givers.

Charitable organizations and support foundations occasionally reach out to other *foundations* as sources of funds. Many foundations only give to intermediary foundations or charitable organizations. The search for and use of foundations as a major income source requires considerable effort, but can result in sizable contributions.

*Special events* can be a major source of income for some charitable organizations. The extent to which special-event fundraising is used depends upon the purpose and focus of the charitable organization. Sports organizations, cultural groups, and symphonies are a few examples of groups that use special events extensively. Whether it is a "run for youth" or a "jazz festival in the park" or a "riverwalk festival," the purpose is the same: to raise community awareness about the charitable organization and its function and purpose, and to raise money. Special events bring in diverse donor groups that might not otherwise be interested in the charitable organization. A positive spin-off of special events is the publicity it generates and the potential it offers for board development. On the negative side, the cost-benefit ratio of a special event is sometimes quite low. Special-event fundraising is not always an effective long-term single-focus strategy, but it does serve as an important ingredient in the mix of effective fundraising.

*Government* at all levels is perceived as a potential supporter for charitable causes. Such support frequently comes in the form of grants to sport, tourism, and leisure service organizations, but may also include special supportive legislation. The value of the latter is well understood by the Miami–Dade County Parks and Recreation Department, which maintains a full-time liaison with the state legislature. This person's assignment is to lobby for the department's interests. Government is an especially important source of funds for capital projects. However, capital development funds from the government are not usually forthcoming without an intense amount of lobbying and preliminary work. The cost and uncertainty associated with seeking government funding may sometimes be too great. Many small communities have learned not to hold out too much hope for the government to provide them with money that may not be forthcoming, or have found that, when government funding does come, it is too little to support what was planned.

*Planned giving* is discussed later in this chapter. It is a core process that helps to make a charitable organization self-sustaining and also allows it to grow.

## Goal Setting, Relationships, and the Gift Pyramid

Any successful fundraising effort is grounded in goal setting. Figure 11.2 illustrates the relationship of organization goals to gift-giving potential, as well as to the organization's mission statement, to the board, and to the staff. A sport, tourism, and leisure service organization's mission statement answers the following: (1) who is served, (2) what services are provided, and (3) how the services are delivered. The mission statement is a starting point for the charitable organization's fundraising efforts. Some charitable

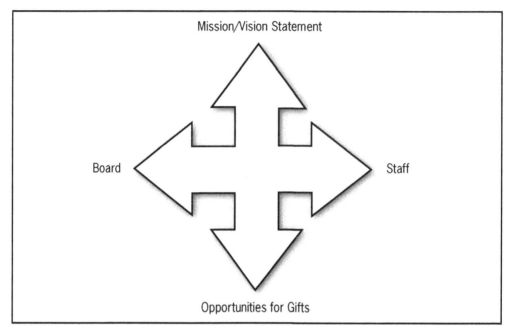

**Figure 11.2**
**Goal relationships in fundraising**

organizations call their mission state- ment a "statement of purpose." The Parks and Wildlife Foundation of Texas, Inc., identifies its purpose as being "to provide private support for the efforts of Texas Parks and Wildlife Department." It fur- ther states that the department and the foundation play a leading role in ensur- ing both the protection of Texas' unique heritage and the provision of full outdoor opportunities for future generations.

The *staff* plays an important and on- going support role in fundraising. The annual giving program is a major focus of the charitable organization's employees and volunteers. They are the behind-the- scenes workforce ensuring the success of the campaign without becoming directly involved in the publicly visible parts of the process. Public appeals are reserved for the CEO, members of the board of di- rectors, or honorary spokespersons. The activities of the staff will vary according

to the size and nature of the organization, their level of expertise in fundraising, and the expectations of the board when it comes to staff involvement.

*Opportunities for gifts* represents the range of potential program areas and services to which donors might give. They are defined by the charitable orga- nization and represent the development and accomplishment of their mission. The leaders of the organization develop and implement strategies that build on their individual and collective strengths. Such strategies might include signing let- ters, attending top-level meetings with potential donors, making strategic calls, attending media opportunities with do- nors, attending receptions, and generally creating a high level of public visibility. The board defines the opportunities for gifts with the help of significant input from the chief executive officer and the support staff. The strategy to actually receive the proposed gifts is part of organizational goal development.

Each charitable organization has a unique perspective on its expectations of the board's role in fundraising. All boards of directors have multiple responsibilities. They have a general responsibility to govern the organization in such a way as to ensure the success of its mission—which also assumes a fiduciary, programmatic, and capital responsibility. Secondly, the board is responsible for the recruitment and selection of board members who agree with the mission of the organization and can potentially give to the organization. Most boards have some type of annual retreat, where they discuss the charitable organization's mission and functions, build board relationships, and strengthen staff and board relationships. Board members are expected to make major efforts in securing funds for the charitable organization. These efforts may include an expectation for them to personally make donations. One major symphony, for example, expects each board member to make a minimum annual contribution of $650,000. Failure to do so means removal from the board. While not all boards have this same type of requirement, almost all expect contributions and fundraising efforts from their members.

## Goal Setting

The annual campaign involves the establishment of fundraising goals. The goals should be realistic and designed to meet the charitable organization's identified needs. Goal setting begins by examining the charitable organization's financial needs for the coming year. This examination involves constructing an operating budget that shows all committed and desired services and programs. If the charitable organization is committed to providing funds to another organization, this is taken into account as part of the committed funds. Another goal-setting activity is the identification of which programs and functions will require external funding and which can be supported either by internal funding sources or through direct cost recovery from sales, fees, etc.

The act of setting an achievable goal for contributed income is based on several factors, such as the history of giving to the charitable organization, the level of current giving, current economic conditions, the frequency of past appeals and their effectiveness, and the attractiveness of the programs.

Table 11.2 illustrates a budget that defines a gift goal. In general, projected contributed income should be set at 90 percent of the previous year's donation level. This practice allows for the incidence of donors who may not continue contributing to this charitable organization. The remaining 10 percent of the gift goal must be met through the contributions of new donors, or else the need projection should be reduced.

## The Gift Pyramid

The rule of thirds (see Table 11.3) represents a commonly accepted standard for planning levels of giving. It is a useful tool in goal setting. The rule of thirds suggests that a third of the funding goal will come from 10 to 15 gifts; the next third will come from the next 25 donors; and the final third will come from all other gifts. The rule of thirds reminds fundraisers not only where their potential donors are coming from, but also where to concentrate their energies. Obviously, the rule of thirds is to be used as a guide and not as a formal expectation.

**Table 11.2**
**Example goal setting using a budget**

| Budget | Amount | Totals | Goal |
|---|---|---|---|
| Expenditures | | | |
| Committed funding | $750,000 | | |
| Desired funding | $450,000 | $1,200,000 | |
| Income | | | |
| Earned income | $350,000 | | |
| Deferred income/Investment income | $600,000 | | |
| Special events | $50,000 | $1,000,000 | |
| Desired contributed income (Goal) | | | $200,000 |

## Fundraising Strategies

A successful fundraising process requires a variety of strategies designed to take advantage of different donor levels. A fundraising campaign recognizes different types and levels of donors and makes appropriate overtures. While direct mail or telephone solicitation will secure a first-time donor and may retain a donor in the early stages of commitment, it will not likely entice individuals at the top of the gift pyramid. Diversifying fundraising strategies is essential. This section looks at annual campaigns, planned giving, special events, and sup-

**Table 11.3**
**Rule of thirds—example of gifts/prospects needed for a $2,500,000 capital or endowment campaign**

| | Gift Level | Gifts Needed | Prospects Needed | Total Dollars |
|---|---|---|---|---|
| Top Third | $250,000 | 1 | 1 | $250,000 |
| | $150,000 | 1 | 2 | $150,000 |
| | $100,000 | 3 | 6 | $300,000 |
| | $75,000 | 4 | 8 | $300,000 |
| | | | Subtotal | **$1,000,000** |
| Middle Third | $50,000 | 10 | 16 | $500,000 |
| | $25,000 | 15 | 45 | $375,000 |
| | | | Subtotal | **$875,000** |
| Bottom Third | $10,000 | 20 | 75 | $200,000 |
| | $5,000 | 40 | 100 | $200,000 |
| | $2,500 | 50 | 125 | $125,000 |
| | Under $1,000 | Many | Many | $100,000 |
| | | | Subtotal | **$625,000** |
| | | | Grand Total | **$2,500,000** |

port organizations as differing strategies. The strategies do not represent all those available, but constitute effective strategies organizations utilize.

There are four types of fundraising campaigns. The *annual campaign* focuses on raising funds for annual operating expenses. *Planned giving* takes a longer-term perspective and focuses on different types of gifts that may not be available for years. *Special events* are a less effective way of securing income, but raise the level of community awareness. *Capital campaigns* (which are described elsewhere in this book) reflect the need for not-for-profit organizations to invest in construction, land acquisition, or other major purchases.

## Annual Campaigns

*Annual campaigns* are the primary source of income for annual operating funds for many organizations. An annual campaign is an organized process that raises a specific amount of money over a specified period of time. Examples include the United Way, public radio and television stations, the Red Cross, Boys and Girls Clubs, and the Girl Scouts. The development of a well-planned annual campaign requires considerable effort on the part of the not-for-profit organization's staff, its board, and volunteers. The annual giving campaign has two primary functions: (1) to acquire new donors; and (2) to retain donors and upgrade their level of giving.

The annual giving campaign generally results in low levels of donations ($1 to $50), but this is more than offset by the number of donations made. Annual giving campaigns are seen as a predictable source of income because income tends to fluctuate minimally. The donations received are intended to provide a short-term benefit to the organization focusing

on ongoing operations. These donations are typically unrestricted, allowing the organization's managers to determine how to best use the money.

The two most common methods of conducting an annual campaign are mail and telephone solicitations. Direct mail is the least expensive annual campaign fundraising methodology. Most annual campaigns use some type of direct mail strategy. The development of a successful mailing list requires considerable effort. Returns from cold, or untested, lists can be as low as one percent, while on a more predictable, or tested, list, as high as 66 percent. The more refined the list, the higher the expected return. Greater accuracy and currency in the mailing leads to a higher rate of return. Another factor affecting the rate of return is how well those who receive the mailing know the charitable organization. This factor is termed "name recognition." Organizations with greater name recognition can expect a higher rate of return from direct mailings.

When retention is the goal of the mailed message, additional strategies are developed. The strategies should include multiple (two or more) mailings (or contacts requesting donations) per year, thank-you notes, newsletters, and other methods of communication. Effective direct mail campaigns should:

- Raise funds cost-effectively.
- Dramatically increase the number of donors to an organization.
- Increase the visibility of the organization among the general public.
- Help identify better prospects for other giving strategies.
- Identify potential volunteers and new workers for the organization.
- Reach a greater number of those you want to reach in the way you want to

reach them.
- Give more control to the development aspect.
- Provide instant gratification.
- Give the not-for-profit organization the opportunity to tell the full story.
- Be individualized/personalized and segmented to a specific audience.

Telephone solicitations have a higher rate of return, but are more difficult to conduct. They are usually reserved for those individuals from whom a donation is realistically anticipated. Often a letter to the potential donor precedes the telephone campaign. Telephone campaigns are more costly and time-consuming than direct mail campaigns and are therefore expected to result in larger donations and provide a greater percentage of revenue. Staff, volunteers, and board members should all be involved in telephone campaigns.

### Planned Giving

Planned giving is an inclusive term addressing a scope of philanthropic giving. It may involve the annual campaign, but more frequently, planned giving is associated with other major fund drives. Planned giving is an effort by the organization to ensure its future through a program where donors are identified, contacted, nurtured, and made part of a giving program that benefits the organization and the individual. In many instances, the results of the planned giving are deferred, with the actual donation occurring years in the future.

Table 11.4 identifies six different types of planned giving approaches.

*Outright gifts* are gifts of money or other tangible property given with an immediate benefit to the not-for-profit sport, tourism, or leisure service organization. Such gifts may be given without regard to how they will be used, or the donor may choose to put specific conditions on the gift. The larger the gift, the more likely some parameters will be established.

*Bequests*, by contrast, are made available to the charitable organization only after the donor dies and the will has gone through probate. Bequests are the single most important source of income for charitable organizations. Bequests allow the donor to retain control of the donation throughout his lifetime while simultaneously reducing the estate tax for the donor's heirs. Bequests come in many forms. They may include a fixed amount of money, a percentage of the total estate or a part thereof, or a specific item in estate (e.g., land, stock).

A *life income gift* is given to the charitable organization as an irrevocable gift. The asset is invested by the organization, with all or part of the income earnings paid either to a single beneficiary or to multiple beneficiaries for a specified period of time. The charitable organization can use that part of the investment income from the gift not given to the beneficiary. Once the beneficiary dies or the predetermined period of income to the beneficiary expires, the full benefit of the gift is made available to the organization. A pooled income fund can be compared to a mutual fund in the sense that the contributions of multiple donors are pooled together and managed as a single investment. The obvious advantage is the size of the fund, allowing for a greater return and broader investment opportunities. The investment generated from the principal provides support to the charitable organization after the donor's death.

The *charitable remainder annuity trust* provides income to both the charitable organization and the donor. The donor makes a fixed contribution to the

## Table 11.4
### Overview of some planned giving instruments

| Type of Gift | Form of Gift | Benefit to Donor | Benefit to Nonprofit |
|---|---|---|---|
| **1. Outright Gift** | Cash<br>Securities<br>Real securities<br>Insurance<br>Personal<br>property | Deductible for income<br>tax purposes | Funds available for<br>immediate use by the<br>organization<br>Frequently without<br>restrictions or terms of<br>trust |
| **2. Bequest:** Anything one owns at the time of the death may be passed on to an organization or person through one's last will and testament. Moreover, all forms of life income gifts may be in testamentary form to benefit family or friends and will then become available for use by named organizations. | | | |
| **3. Life Income Gifts** | | | |
| A. Pooled income | Appreciated<br>securities<br>Cash | Variable income that may<br>provide hedge against inflation<br>No capital gains tax on<br>appreciated gift | Ensures future funding |
| B. Charitable remainder unitrust | Real estate<br>Securities<br>Cash | Same as pooled income funds, *plus*<br>can be tailored to donor's situation<br>Permits deferred income<br>Includes real estate | Ensures substantial future<br>funding |
| C. Charitable remainder annunity trust | Cash<br>Securities | Fixed income<br>Tax deduction in year the gift is made<br>No capital gains on appreciated gift;<br>alternative mimimum tax may apply | Ensures substantial future<br>funding |
| D. Charitable | Cash<br>Securities | Fixed income for a lifetime<br>Tax deduction early years of gift | Portion of funds are<br>available to organization<br>Ensures future financing<br>Upon death of insured,<br>remaining payable to the<br>organization |
| **4. Charitable Lead Trust** | Real estate<br>Securities<br>Cash | Allows property to be passed<br>to other with little or no<br>shrinkage due to taxes | Provides organization with<br>current income for the<br>length of the trust for a<br>period of 10 years |
| **5. Revocable Charitable Trust** | Real estate<br>Securities<br>Cash | All or part of amount placed in trusts<br>is available if needed by donor<br>Removed burden of managing<br>assets | Very high percentage of<br>revocable trusts are not<br>revoked and thus provide<br>future funding |
| **6. Insurance Policies** | | | |
| A. Organization is made owner and beneficiary of policy current in force | Life insurance | Donor gets income tax deduction<br>for value of policy when transferred<br>Future premium payments may be<br>deducted as gift<br>Donor can make large future<br>gift at small present cost | Organization may borrow<br>on policy<br>Organization may cash in<br>policy<br>Organization may receive<br>full face value of policy at<br>insured's death |
| B. Paid-up policy is given to an organization | Life insurance | Tax deduction based on current<br>value of policy | Organization may keep<br>policy and receive face<br>value upon death of insured |
| C. Organization is named benefi-ciary of policy, but not owner | Life insurance | Enables donor to make large future<br>gift at small present cost<br>Donor may change beneficiary later<br>Donor may borrow on policy | Upon death of insured,<br>organization will receive<br>face value of policy |

Source: KPMG Peat Marwick, *Management Issues*
Note: This table was revised by the AAFRC Trust for Philanthropy. The trust gratefully acknowledges the advice of the National Committee on Planned Giving. The contents of the table are the responsibility of that trust. This table is for information purposes only and is not a substitute for legal or professional advice.

not-for-profit with the opportunity to add additional funds. The charitable organization manages the contribution, and the donor receives a guaranteed return on the contribution annually. The donor can determine when the return begins (e.g., after retirement) or can set it for a fixed length of time (e.g., 20 years). This is known as deferring income. If the return on the investment is greater than the amount promised the donor, then the charitable organization retains it as earnings. The charitable organization eventually receives the returns. *Charitable remainder unitrusts* are very similar to a charitable remainder annuity trust, except instead of a fixed amount, the return to the donor will vary, depending on the market.

The final type of life income gift is a *charitable gift annuity*. This is a combination gift and investment, and it is among the oldest and most popular of the methods of making a life income gift. While similar to the others previously presented, the charitable gift annuity immediately becomes the property of the charitable organization, which then guarantees the donor a lifetime income.

A *charitable lead trust* provides assets to the charitable organization for a specified period of time, but not indefinitely. It allows the donor to preserve assets for himself while providing income for a charitable organization. The income received by the charitable organization is either a percentage of the trust assets as annually revalued or a fixed dollar amount. A charitable lead trust can be in the form of property, securities, or cash.

A *revocable charitable trust* puts the resources (real estate, cash, or securities) in control of the charitable organization, but allows the donor to access the trust. The donation is placed in a trust so it might be available to the donor, if

desired. Not only does this type of trust remove the burden of the donor managing assets, but in many cases, the trust ultimately is given to the charitable organization.

When *insurance policies* are given, they are placed wholly or partially in the control of the charitable organization. There are three methods of providing life insurance proceeds to such an organization. The first is to make the charitable organization the owner and beneficiary of a policy currently in force. The donor secures an income tax deduction for the value of the policy when transferred, and all future insurance premiums are treated as charitable donations by the IRS. The charitable organization has the option of cashing in the policy for its current value, borrowing on the policy, or waiting until the death of the benefactor to receive its value. The second method is for a benefactor to give a paid-up policy to a charitable organization. To the donor, the advantage is a tax deduction based on the market value of the policy. The charitable organization benefits immediately by knowing, upon the death of the donor, it has a certain level of income. The third method is for the charitable organization to be the owner and the beneficiary of the policy. In this instance, the benefactor can make a large future gift at a small present cost. The charitable organization receives the face value of the policy upon the death of the benefactor. One problem with this, however, is the possibility that the donor will borrow against the policy or change the beneficiary at any time.

### Special Events

Special events provide a unique opportunity for an organization to put its mission forward to the public, to secure new potential donors, and to generate a profit. Special events come in many forms and might include runs, festivals, dinners, social outings, golf tournaments, dances, and other types of creative approaches to raising money. Special events are seen as an attractive and relatively easy method of raising money. However, they are time consuming, require considerable effort to be successful, can be financially risky, and may not generate a profit. The easiest way to ensure the financial success of a special event is to have someone underwrite it. When this occurs, all the proceeds become profit. An underwritten special event can also put a higher level of pressure on the organization to be successful.

### Support Organizations

Support organizations are increasingly popular among sport, tourism, and leisure service organizations. At the federal, state, and local levels, "Friends of the Park" or "Friends of the Zoo" or "Friends of the Botanical Garden" or "Friends of the Sports Club" have grown dramatically. The National Park Service has 64 co-operating associations. In Ohio, the state park system has over 4,000 volunteers who annually contribute over two million hours of service. In Oregon, a state parks trust program has been established and has grown from four to 16 organizations since the mid-1970s. The trusts receive financial donations, land, and gifts for the state park system. In Maryland, friends groups have operated two smaller parks and purchased cabins for rental by the state park as a revenue source. In Indiana, the state park division of the government cooperated with a private foundation to develop a new state park. The state purchased the land, and the foundation undertook a major development.

The Florida Park Service views support groups, or citizen support organizations, as valuable sources of volunteers to support ongoing operations. These support organizations may provide guides, as well as brochures, exhibits, interpretive areas, and conduct tours or special programs. All support groups are member based and may or may not have a membership fee. Members of the support groups can provide special educational needs, serve as a communication liaison to the community, develop special exhibits, and help in other ways. In addition, most support groups are organized in such a way that they are able to receive funds, seek grants, and accept gifts and bequests of money or tangible property.

Support groups are usually organized as tax-exempt organizations under the umbrella of the parent public or private not-for-profit organization. Each support group must operate according to rules and procedures approved by the parent organization. Funds, volunteers, members, and potential partners are directed to the parent organization in order for it to fulfill its mission. Generally, the parent organization has developed a set of priorities and has identified needs to be met (such as volunteers for special events, funding for capital and interpretive projects, operation of concessions areas, etc.). Priorities are generally agreed upon in advance by the support group and the parent organization. A well-organized support group has a board of directors and a variety of committees who focus on meeting the needs of the parent organization. The committees work interdependently and independently on different projects. The committees become highly engaged in the process and meet the needs of individual members, as well those of the support group and the parent organization.

Support groups require the same care and nurturing that annual campaigns and planned giving programs require. Members of support groups are donors and often give considerably more than just their time. The parent organization should find effective ways of nurturing support group members. These can include member-only lectures, special recognition, newsletters, group travel tours, estate planning seminars, and others—all designed to keep members active.

Although support groups are formed to support the parent organization, they require a certain level of independence and autonomy. The delicate balance between independence and interdependence is an ideal that parent and support organizations need to achieve. Some parent organizations have complained they have lost control of their support groups, and some support groups protest they are just "rubber stamp" organizations. Not only should there be sufficient independence to allow the support group to make decisions and be flexible enough to respond to changing demands and economic conditions, but there should also be accountability and shared vision.

## Selecting Fundraising Strategies

At some point an organization must select a fundraising strategy. The challenge is to determine the most appropriate strategy for the needs. For example, should the annual campaign be used for the purchase of new land or for the board to secure operating dollars for day-to-day support. While there are no formal rules, there are suggestions for the use of various kinds of fundraising strategies presented in this chapter. Table 11.5 identifies 18 approaches to fundraising and six scenarios to use the strategies.

The questions posed by River Network (a not-for-profit organization supporting the development of clean rivers) can be very helpful in selecting an appropriate fundraising strategy:

1. Does this strategy fit with the vision and mission of the organization?
2. Is this strategy cost effective (as a general rule, will it bring in at least twice what it will cost)?
3. Will our target constituencies (those we are asking for donations from) respond well to this strategy?
4. Do we have the organizational skill and expertise we need to carry out this strategy?
5. Do we have the resources (money, people) to carry it out?
6. Does this strategy build or strengthen our organization and its staff/board/volunteers?
7. Does this strategy represent a stable (repeatable) source of income? Does the strategy strive to build repeat donations, even for one-time activities?
8. Can this strategy be integrated into program activities already planned? If there is an ongoing fundraising program, how does this strategy fit into the existing program?
9. Has this strategy worked well for us or groups like ours in the past?
10. Does this strategy take advantage of our special fundraising assets (a celebrity on the board, a member who owns a restaurant, a large group of volunteers, etc.)?
11. Timing: does this strategy fit well with other activities we have planned?
12. Are there other benefits accruing from this strategy beside money (media exposure, good will, etc.)?

## Summary

Philanthropy and fundraising are an increasing part of the budget and fiscal

**Table 11.5**
**Suggestions for utilization of fundraising strategies (adapted from the River Network's "River Fundraising Alert" 11(2))**

| Best Strategies | Start-up | General Operating Support | Projects | Building/ Equipment Purchase | Crises | Reserve Fund /Endowment |
|---|---|---|---|---|---|---|
| Bank loan/line | | | | X | | |
| Bequests | | | | | | X |
| Board requests | X | X | | X | X | X |
| Annual campaign | | X | X | | X | X |
| Capital campaigns | | | | X | | X |
| Corporate proposals | | | X | X | | |
| Earned income | | X | | | | |
| Foundation proposals | X | | X | X | X | |
| Government proposals | | | X | | | |
| In-kind requests | X | X | X | X | | |
| Local business memberships | X | X | | | | |
| Major donor requests | X | X | X | X | X | X |
| (Employee) matching gifts | | X | | | | |
| New members and renewals | | X | | | | |
| Organizational memberships | | X | | | | |
| Special appeals | | X | X | X | | X |
| Special events | X | X | | | X | |
| Workplace campaigns | | X | | | | |

operations of sport, tourism, and leisure service organizations. Managers of these organizations must be well versed in the different strategies and methodologies of fundraising and know how philanthropy can assist their organizations. Sport, tourism, and leisure service organizations have been among the recent beneficiaries of support groups and philanthropic efforts. Sport, tourism, and leisure service organization managers who ignore the impact of philanthropy will find their organizations left out of a key source of income.

# References

Golan, J. (1998.) Comments on fundraising: Winning strategies and practices with a special eye to Carnegie Hall. From notes of November 10, 1998, lecture notes given to a graduate philanthropy course at Indiana University.

Greenfield, J. M. (1994.) *Fundraising fundamentals.* New York: John Wiley & Sons.

River Network. (2004.) Choosing your fundraising strategies. *River Fundraising Alert 11*(1 & 2). http:www2.rivernetwork.org/library/fra2004_v11n2.htm.

Ross, J. R. (Ed.). (1997.) *Philanthropy and Americans outdoors: Fundraising and partnering workshop.* Bloomington, IN: Indiana University.

# NOTES

# CHAPTER 12

# Sponsorship

## Introduction

Sponsorship as a communication vehicle for companies to reach targeted consumers has been growing rapidly for the last 25 years. Global spending for sponsorship contracts has increased from $2 billion in 1984 to an approximately $37.7 billion in 2007; that reflects an increase of 11.6 percent from the $33.7 billion spent in the previous year. According to the IEG Sponsorship report, U.S.-based companies increased sponsorship expenditures in 2007 by 11.7 percent, to approximately $15 billion. European companies had plans to spend $10.6 billion in 2007, an increase of 11.6 percent from the $9.5 billion spent in 2006. Similar trends are also evident in other parts of the world; Asian Pacific companies estimated sponsorship spending to hit $7.4 billion in 2007 (+15.6 %), Central and South American companies were expected to spend $3 billion (+11.1%), and companies from all other regions combined undertook approximately $1.8 billion (+5.9%) worth

of sponsorship. The IEG Report also predicted sport-related sponsorship agreements in the U.S. alone to hit a record amount of $9.9 billion in 2007 (+10.8%), (*Sport Business News,* 2007).

Sponsorship can be described as a "mute" or "non-verbal" medium that targets active sport participants, spectators, and media followers in order to enhance the sponsors' brand awareness and image, and consequently, increase the sponsor's product or services sales (Cornwell & Maignan, 1998). It is formally defined as "a cash and/or in-kind fee paid to a property (typically sports, arts, entertainment, or causes) in return for access to the exploitable commercial potential associated with that property" (Uckman 1995). It is, in other words, the acquisition of rights to affiliate or directly associate with a product or event for the purpose of deriving benefits related to that affiliation or association. These benefits may take the form of brand image enhancement, retailing opportunities through point-of-sales and various promotional activities, naming rights for a sport facility and/or sporting event, acquisition of media time for direct advertising, signage, and hospitality. Specifically, sponsorship agreements provide the legal foundation for:

- The right to use the sport property's brand associations (name, logos, trademarks, mottos) in order to accentuate the sponsor's direct association with the property (exclusive association within a product or service category, official sponsor/supplier/ product, etc.) through advertising spots, promotional activities, publicity opportunities, or any desired means of communication.
- Naming rights for the sporting event, or the facility.
- The right for the sponsor to execute promotional happenings (e.g. contests), direct advertising, and sales-focused activities in conjunction with the sporting event, the facility and/or the web presence of the property.
- Hospitality benefits for the sponsor's customers and/or employees.

Sport sponsorship has its roots in ancient Greece, where cultural and religious events (often games to honor the deities) were financed from *Chorigia* (sponsorship) by wealthy citizens of the City-Republic. This practice was also observed in ancient Rome, where Roman aristocrats (patriarchs) sponsored gladiator games and spectacles to attract public support and recognition. In modern times, and until the early 1980s, corporate sponsorship had the form of donations to various cultural and sporting events with no specific expectations, on behalf of the sponsoring company, of taking anything in return for their support. However, after the financial success of the 1984 Olympics in

Los Angeles, and the wide acceptance of tobacco corporate sponsorship in motorsports events worldwide (due mainly to U.S. government regulations against cigarette advertising on radio and television), the nature of sponsorship has dramatically changed. A market-driven approach has replaced the previous philanthropic nature of sponsorship activities, and involvement in sponsorship agreements and relations is now considered as business-related behavior (Uckman 1995). Corporations can utilize sponsorship as a strategic marketing tool to reach their targeted markets of consumers, helping the organization in its quest for a sustainable competitive advantage (Amis, Slack, & Berrett, 1999). As more management executives become aware of the numerous advantages of sponsorship over the traditional forms of direct advertising, approaches to sponsorship from sponsors, sport properties and consultants are becoming more professional, research, and results-oriented.

In an era of escalating advertising fees around mega sport events, where a 30-second ad during the Super Bowl half-time period has a price tag of $2.6 million, sponsorship advantages are very difficult to ignore. Sponsorship offers higher levels of visibility for the sponsor, extensive media coverage, and increased publicity opportunities (all of them leading to brand awareness). However, the greatest of all advantages is the potential for brand image enhancement, and as a result of this, fan loyalty to the sponsor's products and/or services.

Product loyalty is a sought-after marketing objective for corporations because it is easily transformed into repeated sales and increased revenues. Sports are often associated with fan engagement and loyalty. As sport spectators are exposed to corporate messages under the favorable conditions of excitement and enjoyment that sporting events generate, they are more receptive to those messages (Dolphin, 2003). In addition, fans tend to appreciate and reward with their loyalty corporations that financially support their favorite club, team, or athlete, thereby securing their success in and out of the sport arena. The NASCAR case, where racing fans not only are highly associated with the league, but also fanatically support a specific driver (and the products he endorses), is the desired outcome all corporations wish to achieve through their sponsorship agreements.

## Causes of Sport Sponsorship Growth

There are several factors contributing to the growth of sport sponsorship for the last 25-30 years (Hardy, Mully, & Sutton, 2007). A list of the most significant factors follows:

1. *The U.S. government ban on tobacco and alcohol advertising:* The ban of tobacco advertising on TV in the early 1970s forced tobacco firms to redirect marketing budgets and brand-building efforts in promotional methods other than direct advertising. In the late 1990s, the tobacco industry spent approximately $200 million in sport sponsorship, most of it in motorsport-related events (Furlong, 1994).

2. *Excessive "noise" in the print and electronic media:* With the increase of channel availability through cable television, the expansion of the Internet and world wide web, and the growing number of special-purpose magazines and newspapers, direct advertising in recent years has ex-

perienced a substantial growth. As a result of the plethora of print and electronic media, the average consumer is bombarded with thousands of messages for commercial products and services every day. That situation creates "noise" in the consumer's mind, which does not allow advertising messages to achieve their full potential. In such noisy environments ,advertising dollars are almost wasted. Today, companies try to identify methods that overcome these noise obstacles and allow their messages to reach the targeted consumers with as little noise as possible. Sponsorship is a great alternative because, under certain circumstances, it can minimize the noise effects observed in direct advertising (i.e., exclusivity clause in sponsorship agreements, purchase of naming rights, designation of the company as the official sponsor/provider of a product/service, etc.).

3. *Rising advertising costs for television exposure:* Advertising costs for companies that want to secure exposure in media with national appeal continue to rise. The cost of a 30-second advertisement in the 2007 NFL Super Bowl was $2.6 million, an increase of 15 percent from the 2004 Super Bowl. This situation led corporations to the realization that advertising may not be the cost-effective proposition that it was in years before. Involvement in sponsorship partnerships with sport properties has been proven to achieve a higher level of exposure for corporate partners and, in most cases, at lower costs compared to exposure gained through traditional advertising campaigns.

4. *The increasing commercialization of sport:* Sponsorship became an ac-

ceptable form of support for amateur sports as their National Governing Bodies found in corporations the ideal partner to help them realize their organizational goals and growth plans. The financial success of the 1984 Summer Olympics held in Los Angeles was the very first successful example of the tremendous potential this partnership might have for sport properties all over the world. Until then, mega sporting events like the Olympics were mainly financed by public subsidies and by the International Olympic Committee (which, at that time, was at the verge of bankruptcy). The 1976 Olympics in Montreal is a vivid example of financial failure; it took the city of Montreal more than 30 years to pay off the debts generated to stage those games. Peter Ueberroth, President of the Los Angeles Olympics Organizing Committee (LAOOC), faced the resulting reluctance of public authorities to financially support the Games and developed a different vision for the event. His vision called for corporations to become partners by developing a mutually beneficial relationship. One of his actions was to limit the number of Olympic sponsors to 30 in order to reduce the clutter (noise effect) of advertising. He also established category exclusivity, where a corporation could buy the right to become the only sponsor within that product/service category. The adoption of these actions allowed Ueberroth to significantly increase the sponsorship fees that corporate sponsors had to pay, thereby securing the viability and financial success of the Games. At the same time, sponsors realized the increased benefits that Olympic sponsorship had to of-

fer, as sponsors and property worked together to achieve common goals (e.g., securing Games exposure, increase in sponsors' brand awareness and positive image, prevention of ambush marketing, success of hospitality events, achievement of outstanding event management etc.). The realization of corporations that sponsorship is the desired platform of corporate exposure was given another boost after the IOC president's decision to allow professional athletes to participate at the 1992 Olympics in Barcelona, Spain. The participation of high-caliber professional players for the first time in history was received with much enthusiasm and positive feelings from the public, and subsequently from major corporations, which saw in this action, a unique opportunity for exposure to greater consumer masses all over the world.

5. *The increasing media interest in sport programming:* The public interest in sports has been growing steadily for the last 30 years as a result of changing lifestyles, availability of leisure time, and increasing participation in fitness and sporting activities (e.g., the fitness boom in the 1970s). This interest is also translated into interest for additional sport programming. The advent of cable television as well as the growth of new media sources (the Internet, subscription services via satellite, pay-per-view channels) were instrumental in satisfying the public's desire for more sports programming, and, at the same time, the needs of sponsors for additional means of exposure through them. These reasons, along with the fact that networks find sporting event broadcasting less costly to produce

compared to sitcoms, shows, or documentaries, create a formula of success that media outlets find difficult to ignore. The example of the X Games, created by ESPN in 1995, demonstrates how a non-traditional sporting event, influenced by the alternative lifestyles characterizing Generation X, found viewership success in mainstream media surrounded by devoted fans and major corporations and brands sponsoring its activities, with a loyalty that is admirable in the sponsorship business (Puchan, 2004).

6.  *Changes in governmental policies related to sport activity around the world:* Although in the United States funding for the national governing bodies (NGBs) of various sports is coming from private sources (through fundraising events, institutional grants, and other various activities), in other parts of the world government funding for the development of grassroots programs is the primary source of support. In Greece and China, two of countries that have recently accepted the responsibility for organizing Olympic Games, government funding was behind every action that the NGBs undertook. In difficult financial times, where public sources are scarce, NGBs felt the need to look for other sources of funding in order to cover their budgetary deficits (DeSchriver & Jensen, 2003). Corporations and private institutions were then targeted to contribute financially in exchange for media exposure. Companies were, through sponsorship, also able to improve their public image by demonstrating good corporate citizenship.

7.  *The globalization of sports, and corporate desires to successfully penetrate foreign markets:* Doing business in a foreign country is a challenging experience for many corporations, since they have to overcome cultural and language barriers, and adapt their production, employment, and marketing practices to the local customs and traditions. The global appeal of sports has presented a unique opportunity to those corporations operating in foreign markets. Sport sponsor partnerships enable corporations to use sport properties as promotional vehicles in their attempts to successfully penetrate foreign markets. The 2008 Olympic Games in China, for example, were viewed by many international companies as the golden opportunity to promote, through sponsorship partnerships, their products in an emerging marketplace. The same purpose was served by the $400 million sponsorship of the national soccer team of Brazil by NIKE. The company accomplished a number of goals by signing a 10-year sponsorship agreement: (a) it established NIKE as a reputable manufacturer of soccer equipment, a reputation the company's rivals, ADIDAS and PUMA, have enjoyed for years; (b) it allowed the company to penetrate (through joint promotions, grass roots tournaments, charity events) not only the Latin American market, but also the global market due to the international appeal of the sport property-partner; and (c) it enhanced the company's brand image through the association with one of the most beloved and successful teams in this very popular international sport.

## Setting Sponsorship Objectives

When clear objectives for involvement in sponsorship have been articulated, potential sponsors are better able to assess the value of their direct financial participation in a sponsored event. The selection of a sponsored activity requires that sponsoring companies first decide which objectives they desire to achieve through the partnership. Sponsors then choose the activity that is most likely to enable them to achieve their predetermined objectives. Setting clear objectives beforehand enables sponsoring companies and sport properties to evaluate all related activities and actions more easily and more effectively (Farrelly, Quester, & Mavondo, 2003).

It is obvious that one of the key objectives for any sponsoring company is to increase its ability to reach, influence, and involve existing and/or potential customers in something that excites them and attracts them to the company's brands (or services) and thereby establish a competitive advantage. Another key objective is to provide the sponsor with a desired return on their investment. This return on investment (ROI) may be expressed in monetary terms (e.g., increase of quarterly sales and revenues) or in a variety of other ways (e.g., quantity and quality of broadcast coverage). Sponsoring companies need to attach great importance to objective quantification in order to be able (during the postevent evaluation) to assess ROI. Sponsors may need the sport property's assistance in undertaking that task. Each objective should be as clear and as specific as possible. Generalizations and/or ambiguities will almost guarantee that the primary results of a sponsorship will be unquantifiable (Kolah, 2003). Even if the event or property performed well in terms of attendance, etc., it may be impossible to prove that the sport property has delivered on the objectives of most interest to the sponsor.

As an example, consider an international company like SAMSUNG that manufactures electronics. If one of its sponsorship objectives is to increase sales for the brand, then that objective needs quantification. The company needs to determine the expected or desired impact of sponsorship using the following measures:

(a) Type of sales/markets affected (new customer, repeat, extended);
(b) Distribution channels enhanced (retail, web, catalogue);
(c) Time frame (duration of the sponsorship);
(d) Benchmarks (successes of comparable activities); and
(e) Other critical success factors.

Determining the corporate objectives to be accomplished through sponsorship is a challenging, time-consuming, and strenuous situation. Every corporation, based on its size, resources, and appeal to regional, state, national, or global markets, has different marketing issues to address through sponsorship. Researchers agree that there is an integrated and complex set of objectives that potential sponsors consider when deciding if and how much sponsorship to extend.

Ukman (2003) divided sponsorship objectives into three major categories: (a) image objectives, (b) sales objectives, and (c) media/promotional objectives.

By meeting *image objectives,* sponsors expect to:

- increase awareness of their brand;
- showcase their social responsibility;
- change or enhance their corporate image;

- build relations with external communities and public policy makers;
- build relations with employees, their unions and other stakeholders;
- increase the relevance of their brand to specific markets; and
- increase brand loyalty.

Through meeting *sales objectives*, sponsors expect to:

- stimulate retail and distribution channels;
- expand their customer database and generate new leads;
- find new/incremental business opportunities from major clients;
- display products or services;
- build business with co-sponsors;
- stimulate their sales force; and
- increase sales to end customers.

Finally, companies set *media/promotional* objectives in order to garner promotions in new distribution channels, and to reduce marketing costs (Ukman, 2003).

Tripodi (2001) further suggested that sponsorship objectives can be grouped into two major categories: (a) corporation-related, and (b) product/brand-related. *Corporate-related* objectives refer to increasing public awareness of the corporation and its products/services, enhancing company image, altering public's perceptions, fostering community involvement, building business/trade relations and goodwill, and enhancing staff/employees' relations and motivation. *Product/Brand-related* objectives serve the purposes of increasing target market awareness, building brand image within the target market (positioning), increasing sales and market share, and blocking/preventing competition from being successful within that target market

(Cornwell, Roy, & Steinard, 2001). These objectives might be used for positioning or re-positioning products and/or services for a targeted market (Tripodi, 2001).

Sponsorship research identifies the following list of corporate objectives that most influence management's decisions to enter into a sponsorship relationship with a sport property (Clark, Cornwell, & Pruitt, 2002):

a. To increase public awareness of the product (brand), the company, or both;

b. To change or enhance product (brand) and/or company image and reputation by fostering favorable associations with the sporting event;

c. To improve the company's community relations (demonstrating good corporate citizenship);

d. To identify the company with the targeted consumer segments;

e. To create promotional opportunities for the company's products and/or services;

f. To stimulate sales of products and/or services;

g. To enhance employee motivation, involvement, and loyalty, and to facilitate staff recruitment;

h. To generate media exposure through publicity;

i. To create opportunities for hospitality and entertainment for the company's business partners, clients, and workforce, thereby influencing key contacts;

j. To develop business-to-business relationships (networking, cross-promotions) with other sponsoring companies that support the same sport property;

k. To create and sustain a competitive advantage through exclusive association with a sport property;

l.  To demonstrate unique product features, advantages, and innovations;
m.  To develop a database of prospective customers and leads for the company's sales executives; and
n.  To build a new customer base.

## Sponsorship: The Corporate Perspective

When corporations consider sponsorship activities, they look for sport properties that can make a significant, valuable, and measurable contribution to current and future brand communications. They believe that:

(a) the property (team, athlete, facility, or event) should demonstrate a good fit with the brand (or company) image and, ideally, be unique to that brand so that there is no confusion in the minds of the consumers (Meenaghan, 2002; Sports Sponsorship, 2007);

(b) the geographic reach of the sponsored activity should cover an appropriately matched target market; and

(c) the timing and duration of the sponsorship (multiyear contract, seasonal event, etc.) should fit in with the company's overall promotional campaign (Simpson, 1999).

Taking the above noted factors into consideration, sponsoring companies normally apply the following process in selecting the right property, event, or organization for their anticipated "win-win partnership" (Martin, 1996):

*Phase 1:*
(a) Assess customers' perceptions and attitudes (through survey instruments, informal interviewing, or focus groups).

(b) Management team agrees on the desired image of the brand and/or company that is to be promoted through the sponsorship partnership.

*Phase 2:*
(a) Identify all potential sponsorship partners.

(b) 'Short list' the sport property/events that have an image that most nearly fits the desired image of the company/brand.

*Phase 3:*
Meet with the most promising partnership candidate(s) and closely examine:
(a) Communication objectives
•  What does the company want to accomplish through that sponsorship agreement?
•  What communication outcomes (brand awareness, brand image enhancement, hospitality opportunities, etc.) does the company seek?
•  Does the existing image of the sport property best fit the desired image of the brand/company? (Jobber, 2001)

(b) The targeted consumers
•  What target group of consumers is the company trying to reach?
•  Where are these customers located?
•  Does the audience/fan base for the sponsored event match the company's customer base?

(c) The inherent risks associated with the sponsorship partnership
•  What are the associated risks for either the sport property or the sponsoring company?

- Are there any image-related risks associated with the termination of the sponsorship agreement?

(d) Promotional opportunities
- What are the promotional opportunities for the company's products and/or services?
- What are the promotional opportunities for the sport property/event?

(e) The sport property's past record in sponsorship success
- What does the property's record with past sponsors look like? If sponsoring companies had withdrawn in the past, what were the reasons behind that development?
- What were the results of previous sponsorship partnerships with that property? Did the sponsors meet their desired objectives?

(f) The overall cost of this partnership
- Does the cost of entering into and participating in the sponsorship agreement justify the expected return on investment (ROI)?

*Phase 4:*
Undertake a formal sponsorship agreement. Be sure to include a statement of purpose, objectives, terms and conditions, and a description of the process by which the partnership will be evaluated.

## Sponsorship Acquisition: The Sport Organization's Perspective

Before looking for a sponsorship deal, the sport property needs to evaluate what it has to offer to prospective sponsorship partners. It must be realistic in determining what it can deliver and what market it can reach.

The sport organization will need to know how many events will be held, how many people will be involved as participants and spectators, and how extensively participation is shared through broadcast media. Not only is it important to know how many people can be reached by the corporate sponsor through the sport organization, but relevant details about those people must also be understood. Age, gender, family stage, income, and education are just a few of the demographic characteristics that might be of interest to a potential sponsor.

In addition to knowing what markets can be offered to the sponsor, an inventory of all marketable assets, such as signage, media opportunities, naming rights, hospitality events, promotions, etc., should be compiled.

The sport organization must then find potential sponsors. Begin by looking at existing sponsorship activity in order to get a sense of what types of corporations are involved in sponsorship. Note the type of organization, not just the specific company. Sometimes a company will extend its sponsorship activity, and sometimes a currently involved sponsor's competitor will be eager to get involved in sport sponsorship. Never offer sponsorship opportunities for the same event to competing corporations!

All of the information that the sport organization collects in determining its sponsorship offering and potential sponsors is used in developing the sponsorship package. The sponsorship package is a top-quality presentation that outlines the sport organization's offer of benefits to sponsors, and a set of proposed partnership actions. Sponsorship packages "may be tiered to reflect levels of expenditure that would just 'make it happen', to more sophisticated versions that reach more people with extensive publicity" (Sports Sponsorship, 2007).

## Selling the Sponsorship Opportunity

When it is time for the provider of a sponsorship opportunity and the potential sponsor to get together and make a deal, the matter of 'selling' the sponsorship should be relatively simple. After all, the advance work and preparation should have served to bring together partners with reciprocal interests and mutually beneficial resources, and the sponsorship agreement is just the expression of details of how those interests will be satisfied.

Not all potential sponsors, however, readily see the benefits being offered to them through sponsorship opportunities. The sponsorship sales strategy that a sport organization develops must account for this, and the individual who presents the proposal to enter into a sponsorship agreement will have to be very well prepared. Proper preparation includes thinking of ways in which the sponsorship partnership would be integrated in the marketing campaigns of the targeted companies, as well as reading annual reports, company newsletters, trade organizations, media reports, etc. in order to more fully understand the target corporation's objectives, activities, priorities, and circumstances. Preparation also includes deciding what products may be sponsored (collectively or exclusively), finding out who to contact, and estimating the level of sales to be realized.

After the sport property has decided the sales strategy it will follow in order to successfully attract sponsors, it is time to initiate the sales process. Typically, the sport property will begin by approach-

ing major companies first in order to sell its best (and most expensive) inventory (naming rights, exclusivity packages, event TV rights, etc.). In addition to securing large sponsorship contracts early in the sales process, selling to major sponsors first has the advantage of momentum and example. That is, the property can take advantage of name recognition of major corporate sponsors and more easily convince smaller companies of the good business practice of being part of its sponsorship program.

The sales process usually involves the following:

- Soliciting interest in a face-to-face meeting with prospective sponsors using a proposal brief (a one-page document that contains basic information about the sponsorship opportunities with the sport property).
- After the prospective sponsor expresses an interest, scheduling a meeting with management executives who have decision power over sponsorship partnerships. At this first meeting, it is imperative for the seller of sponsorship opportunities to spend most of the time listening to what the prospective sponsor has to say.
- Preparing for the meeting by learning about the prospective sponsor. Answers to the following questions should be known:
  (a) Where does the sponsoring company spend its marketing budget at that point in time?
  (b) Does the company have sponsorship partnerships with other sport properties?
  (c) What does the sponsoring company think about these relationships? Have they been satisfied with the

outcomes/met their sponsorship objectives?

- After the initial meeting is over, assessing the situation and examining if the property can realistically deliver what the sponsor wants. If the assessment is positive, a follow-up meeting is scheduled (usually within the next 7-10 days following the first meeting).
- Returning to the second meeting with a detailed sponsorship proposal; this is a multipage document that includes the offer letter with all supporting information. Sponsoring companies use this document to facilitate their internal decision-making process.
- Allowing the prospective sponsors to intervene and modify the "draft" proposal in order to meet their organizational needs.
- Negotiating the final terms of the agreement and closing the deal.

## The Sponsorship Proposal Document

A sponsorship proposal may address various issues depending on the needs of the sponsorship company and the complexity of the agreement (multiyear contract, parties involved, etc.). The following elements are usually included in a sponsorship proposal document:

- Property facts (i.e., history of the organization, organizational chart, contact info, etc.)
- Event(s) schedule
- Photographic displays
- Audience demographics, purchase behavior, and loyalty studies
- List of existing sponsors
- Sponsor case histories and clients'

testimonials
- Naming rights and/or exclusivity categories
- Sponsorship packages
- Post sponsorship evaluation processes
- Summary of rights and benefits for the sponsor
- Sponsorship fee information

The proposal should be written in such a way that it captures the attention of the audience. Use of irrelevant data in order to impress the audience will have a negative effect. Judicious use of attractive graphics is encouraged, and care should be taken to incorporate only the information that is necessary for the sponsor to assess the value of the sponsorship deal. Descriptions of activities and benefits should be precise and related to the interests and uniqueness of the prospective sponsor. The proposal also needs to be so thorough that the prospective sponsor is left with very few or no unanswered questions.

## Marketing Benefits of Sponsorship

The main motivation for corporations to sponsor a sport, tourism, or recreation event or facility is to gain access to the vast number of individuals that are exposed to the events being sponsored and, by association, to the corporation or its products. The most common ways of promoting corporations through sponsorships include the following:

- Stadium signage (score boards, advertisement boards, etc.)
- Branding opportunities (logo placement, promotional giveaways, uniforms, etc.)

- Corporate hospitality opportunities (luxury suites, premium-level season tickets, ticket discounts, etc.)
- Naming rights
- Advertising (and virtual advertising)
- Publicity opportunities (radio, television, print media)
- Promotional events and contests
- Cross promotions
- Direct marketing, personal selling, and retail promotions

All these methods are used by most properties to maximize the marketing benefits of sponsorship. Three of the above noted methods are deserving of further discussion.

### Cross Promotions

Promotion is the critical mechanism for positioning a product or service in the minds and the hearts of the consumers. Cross promotions is where two or more sponsoring companies develop a business relationship with the sole purpose of creating a joint-promotion themed around the sponsored property. This mutually beneficial solution allows sponsors to exchange their resources, so that they both efficiently advance their business objectives (Kolah, 2003).

### Virtual Advertising

In virtual advertising, virtual images can be projected and broadcast on top of existing inventory (ads, posters, and signs) or digitally inserted into previously untouchable areas, such as the playing field. This type of advertising allows a sport property to carve up its international TV footprints and sell multiple narrowcast advertising packages worldwide. It also allows a sport property to remove all in-stadium advertising and provide its TV partners with "advertisement-free" stadiums and arenas. In this instance, virtual advertisements can be superimposed onto blank advertising boards, allowing for animated messages and, more importantly, the same space to be sold many times over. Virtual advertising technology allows a sport property and its TV broadcast partners to define advertising on the same board according to the needs of advertising companies across different regions in the country. Virtual advertisement digital boards are actually less costly than rotating boards, and are much more versatile (ibid).

### Hospitality

Hospitality benefits provide sponsors with unique opportunities to get to know clients in a relatively informal atmosphere and develop a relationship that may otherwise have taken a significant amount of time and resources to nurture. The opportunity to impress clients while they are attending a sporting event (especially when the event has a wide appeal, like the Super Bowl or the Olympic Games) can be substantially increased. Hospitality deals also allow a large number of people (clients and sponsors' employees) to be invited to an event for which tickets may be scarce and interest high. The appeal of hospitality benefits is significant for both the property (low cost of offering) and the sponsor (high return on investment through nurturing business relationships or improving management-employee relations).

## Evaluation

The effectiveness and value of a sponsorship partnership should be regularly evaluated. Evaluations should generate formal reports that are studied by the sponsoring company and the sport property. Evaluation reports can be highly effective not only in securing the sponsor for the following year, but also can be used as a marketing tool in recruiting new sponsors. In times when sponsoring companies are forced to look closer at the cost effectiveness of their investments, it is imperative that sport properties are fully engaged in post event evaluation activities (D'Astous. & Bitz, 1995).

A meaningful sponsorship evaluation begins with the decision about what is to be measured and against what criteria those measurements will be assessed. Jiffer and Ross (1999) suggest the following as essential elements in an event sponsorship evaluation:

1. Exposure—How well was the sponsors' brand positioned in the mind of the consumer?
2. Attention—What level of customer attention was given to the company's products and/or services?
3. Knowledge/Awareness—What is the level of customers' basic or extensive knowledge regarding the company's products and/or services?
4. Attitudes—How well did the sponsorship enhance the sponsor's ability to influence customers' perceptions regarding its products?
6. Behavior—Did the sponsored event stimulate positive changes in the consumers' consumption patterns?

Several methods can be employed in measuring the success of a sponsorship agreement. These include:

*Print Press Monitoring:* monitoring the press media and collecting any press clippings that refer to the sponsored event and the sponsoring company.

*Photographic Record:* recording all activity related to sponsors exposure using digital photography and/or even video clips with participant and spectator comments regarding the event and the affiliated sponsoring company.

*Television Exposure:* measuring and reporting the amount of broadcast time given to the event, the number and reach of the channels that carry the event, and the estimated number of viewers watching the event.

*Telephone Interviews:* assessing the awareness level for a sponsor in a very quick and inexpensive way.

*Mailed Survey Instruments:* using surveys to measure consumers' knowledge and attitudes regarding the sponsor's products.

*In-depth Interviews and Focus Groups:* qualitative research involving samples of target markets and highly focused discussion about the desired outcomes of the sponsorship arrangement. The discussion is focused on generating new ideas to be used in future sponsorship partnerships through open-ended questions, and circulation of opinions and suggestions from participants.

SPINDEX *Method:* a method that is used in measuring the exposure time obtained by each of the sponsors in all TV broadcasts and on all broadcasting channels. SPINDEX values are calculated by employing four measures: advertising time obtained throughout the television broadcast; the number of times that an advertisement was shown; the duration of the broadcast; and the number of viewers watching the broadcast. The resulting SPINDEX scores provide the sponsoring company with an accurate idea of the cost per advertising second, the cost per television viewer, and the cost per SPINDEX point (i.e., the cost per 30-second TV spot).

Evaluation reports are a tool to gauge what the sponsorship has actually done for a sponsor. However, some sport properties have been reluctant to get involved in the post-sponsorship evaluation measurements in fear of losing the sponsor if the research shows that the partnership has not generated the hoped-for benefits. In addition, some sponsoring companies are reluctant to undertake evaluation research because of the monetary cost and time factors involved in this process. Other concerns are the danger of getting conflicting data through the surveys and the challenge of deciding what information is relevant.

The drawbacks to sponsorship evaluation are outweighed by its positive aspects. The formal report of the evaluation is "hard copy" evidence that the sponsorship agreement between the two parties either did or did not meet the original objectives. It serves as evidence of the property's commitment to the sponsorship partnership, and it shows the sponsoring company that the property cares how the relationship is affecting the company's bottom line.

## Summary

Sponsorship in sport, tourism, and leisure service organizations is an effective way to generate revenues and create synergistic relationships within the community. Sport sponsorship, in particular, has made millions of dollars available for sport properties and provided corporations with additional marketing opportunities. The objectives of both the sponsor and the sport property should be clearly articulated before entering into a formal sponsorship agreement. Those objectives should also be understood early in the process of identifying and securing potential sponsors and sponsorship situations. That process involves many steps.

Sponsorship can manifest itself in many ways, but it always includes providing the sponsor with unique opportunities to promote its corporate image or product line. How well the company or its products are promoted is the main question to be answered in the formal sponsorship evaluation process.

## References

Amis, J., Slack, T., & Berrett, T. (1999). Sport sponsorship as distinctive competence. *European Journal of Marketing, 33* (3/4), 250-272.

Clark, J., Cornwell, T. B., & Pruitt, S. (2002). Corporate stadium sponsorships, signaling theory, agency conflicts, and shareholder wealth. *Journal of Advertising Research,* 16-32.

Cornwell, B. T., & Maignan, I. (1998). An international review of sponsorship research. *Journal of Advertising (27)*1.

Cornwell, B., Roy, D., & Steinard, E. (2001). Exploring managers' perceptions of the impact of sponsorship on brand equity. *Journal of Advertising, 30* (2), 41-51.

D'Astous, A., & Bitz, P. (1995). Consumer evaluations of sponsorship programmes. *European Journal of Marketing, 29* (12), 6-22.

DeSchriver, T., & Jensen, P. (2003). What's in a name? Price variation is sport facility naming rights. *Eastern Economic Journal, 29* (3), 359-376.

Dolphin, R. (2003). Sponsorship: Perspectives on its strategic role. *Corporate Communications: An International Journal, 8* (3), 173-186.

Farrelly, F., Quester, P., & Mavondo F. (2003). Collaborative communication in sponsor relations. *Corporate Communications, 8* (2). 128-138.

Furlong, R. (1994). Tobacco advertising legislation and the sponsorship of sport. *Australian Business Law Review, 22* (3), 159-189.

Hardy, S., Mullin, B. J., & Sutton, W. A. (2007). *Sport marketing.* Champaign-Urbana: Human Kinetics.

Jiffer, M., & Roos, M. (1999). *Sponsorship – A way of communicating.* Stockholm

Jobber, D. (2001). *Principles & practice of marketing* (3rd ed.). Berkshire: McGraw-Hill Publishing Company.

Martin, J. H. (1996). Is the athlete's sport important when picking an athlete to endorse a nonsport product? *Journal of Consumer Marketing, 13* (6) 28-43.

Meenaghan, T. (2002). From sponsorship to marketing partnership: The Guinness sponsorship of the GAA all-Ireland hurling championship. *Irish Marketing Review, 15* (1), 3-23.

Kolah, A. (2003). *Maximizing the value of sponsorship.* London: SportBusiness Group Ltd.

Puchan, H. (2004). Living 'extreme:' Adventure sports, media and commercialization. *Journal of Communication Management, 9* (2), 171-178.

Simpson, C. (1999). A sporting try. *NZ Marketing Magazine, 18* (8), 34-37.

Sports Sponsorship. Retrieved in April 7, 2007 from http://www.sports-sponsorship.co.uk/sponsorship.htm

SportBusiness. Retrieved in April 7, 2007 from http://sportbusiness.com.news/161115/sponsorship-spending-to-rise-and-rise.

Tripodi, J. A. (2001). Sponsorship: A confirmed weapon in the promotional armory. *International Journal of Sports Marketing & Sponsorship*, 1-20.

Ukman, L. (1995). *IEG's complete guide to sponsorship.* Chicago: International Events Group.

Ukman, L. (2003). *Measuring the result of sponsorship.* Chicago, IL: IEG Valuation Services.

# NOTES

# SECTION E

# Expenditure Management

Budgets are important financial management tools, and the chapters in this section describe how budgets are prepared and managed. Operating and capital budgets are contrasted, and a description of the budget styles or formats that are most frequently used by sport, tourism, and leisure service organizations is presented. This discussion emphasizes the need for detailed attention to all aspects of planning to receive and spend financial resources. This section also provides helpful guidance in presenting a budget proposal.

Management of revenue includes accounting for all income received by the sport, tourism, and leisure service organization. In addition to personal integrity, the financial manager needs skills in bookkeeping, accounting, and financial reporting in order to deal with another very important management concern—that of managing expenditures (covered in the next section). Chapter 13 is not intended to serve as an all-encompassing treatment of the very complex world of business accounting, but it does provide an introduction to and overview of the most commonly used accounting and reporting tools, along with a discussion of the basic principles and generally accepted accounting practices.

# Budgeting Basics

## Introduction

Individuals who are new to budgeting are sometimes overwhelmed with the expectation of putting numbers together to create meaning. As fewer people balance their own checkbooks, and more rely on computer programs, or pay others to manage their finances for them, the idea of taking on a task that requires even the most basic budgeting skills can seem daunting. Putting together a budget for a program, profit center, or an entire organization can be a challenging activity when budgeting skills and experience are lacking. This chapter addresses budgeting basics. It discusses simple budgets, articulates some rules for developing program and activity budgets, and provides direction for structuring a larger budget document.

Most budgeting is a process of gathering, organizing, and reporting financial facts and plans in a format that is understandable to other individuals. Every professional skill area has its own unique terminology and so does budgeting. However, budgeting crosses professional disciplinary boundaries; that is, everyone has to do it! All organizations deal with budgeting, and thankfully, the basic concepts are common. Unique terms may be present within different industries, but the process of budgeting is much the same, whether for a small summer recreation program, a community festival, or the operation of a $26 million multisport complex.

## Budget Construction Guidelines

There are some general rules that individuals, new or experienced, must follow when constructing budgets. Those who are new to budgeting would do well to apply these rules strictly.

One of the problems with budgeting is that the individual constructing the budget rarely has all the information needed to complete the process. Budgeting then, is a process that begins with gathering what information is readily available and seeking out the additional required information. Some of this information may be simple to acquire, other information may be more challenging. It is important to involve as many individuals in the budgeting process as possible. If budgeting for a recreation center, for example, it would be prudent to have all the staff who have budget respónsibility involved in the process. This might include the snack bar manager, the office manager, the facility maintenance manager, the program directors, and others. The staff should gather information related to their areas of responsibility, such as the number of employees, their schedules, total hours worked, supplies consumed, unique expenditure needs, and other budget facts for the previous year, along with anticipated revenue and expenditure activities for the next budget period.

### Gathering Information

All of the budget information should be organized and kept where it is readily available for use. Budget information may be gathered from previous budgets used for the same activity or program, from similar budgets available from other sources, or created by gathering information from previously unused sources. For example, salaries may be required, but how much to pay per hour may not be known. The organization may have a standardized pay scale for part-time and full-time salaries along with descriptions of how the salaries are to be applied. A budget for purchasing T-shirts could be based on an existing standing contract with a manufacturer, an outstanding purchase order, or a list of preferred vendors. There is almost always a source of information for gathering budget data.

The challenge is to get the most correct source.

The organization of the budget data is structured around common categories. For instance, the most common categories for all budgeting include salaries, small cost equipment, supplies, rental, utilities, charges and services, and operations. Each of these categories might be subdivided. Salaries can be subdivided into full-time, permanent part-time, part-time, seasonal, contract, or others. They can be subdivided again by type of function, such as a department or operating unit. An aquatics program may have the following seasonal or part-time employees: life guard, head life guard, junior life guard, learn-to-swim instructor, assistant manager, manager, cashier, concession operator, concession manager, and so on. Each position most likely has a separate rate of pay that may include pay ranges. For example, the life guard might earn from $8.50 per hour to $12.50 per hour based on experience, number of years with the program, training, and so forth. Figure 13.1 illustrates three levels of categorization of life guards for the aquatic program described above.

Anticipating costs associated with equipment can also be challenging. Equipment falls into two different categories for purchasing. Some equipment, typically below a specific cost (such as $500) is considered operational (see chapter 15) and appears in the *operational* budget. Equipment that is more expensive and may have a multiyear life-span is considered to be *capital* (see Chapter 16). Money for the operational and capital budgets comes from different income sources as suggested in Chapter 8. For a softball complex, chalk for lining the base paths, bases, pitching rubbers, light bulbs for the field lighting, grass for the field, fertilizer, trash cans, trash bags, and

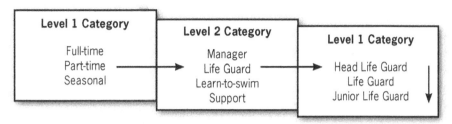

**Figure 13.1**
**Example of Employee Classification for Life Guards**

concession supplies are expendable (used up in a short time, such as one year) and appear in the operating budget. Bleachers, benches, special soil for the field, and field drying agents are longer lasting and appear in the capital budget. For the same softball complex, utilities may include electricity, water, sewer, telephone, and cable or satellite television and are part of the operating budget.

### Identify the Budget Goal

It is important to identify what the end product should include and how it will be presented. If it is a budget for a program, then the budget may include salaries, supplies, equipment, room rental, marketing, and other items. Most of the time the agency will define in advance what the budget should include. By following the prescribed format and understanding what goes in each category, the budget will be consistent across different departments. Finally, there should be a consistent effort to improve the budgeting process as experience with it grows.

### Essential Information

Invariably, after all the information has been collected, the individual preparing the budget has more information than immediately seems necessary. It is important to then ask, "What information is essential?" Essential information is that which allows the program manager

to reasonably predict financial needs and set defensible expectations in areas where not much is known.

### Gathering New Information

Gathering and organizing information into categories is the starting point. Organized information can be put together to create new information, such as the total cost of a program. Here's a simple illustration:

Unknown: The cost of Program A
Known: The program is going to meet for 6 weeks, 3 hours a week, and has 1 instructor at a cost of $8.50 per hour.
Calculation:
total cost = 6 weeks x 3 hours x 1
    instructor x $8.50 per hour
total cost = 6 x 3 x 1 x $8.50
total cost = $153

### Organizing the Data

Getting the answer is only part of the budget process. It must also be organized so others can understand it. This is typically accomplished using a spreadsheet. The data labels should be short and descriptive of the information contained in the cells below the labels. These may be prescribed by the organization. It is also appropriate to provide detailed footnotes to explain the data in the spreadsheet. In Figure 13.2 note how the data labels represent the information known. It is the same information in the shaded area above, except it is listed so someone else looking at the data sees a snapshot of how the total cost was determined. In row 2, the data row, the precise information required was placed in the cells. A formula was used to arrive at the total cost in cell F2. In the examples in this chapter, all information will be depicted on the spreadsheets.

In the following sections, the budget examples become increasingly complex. Each example is based on the guidelines previously discussed. Reference is made to the appropriate guidelines.

## Determining Costs

The classes in Example 1 (Program B) meet once a week. In Example 2 (Program C), most of the classes meet once a week, but some meet three times a week. Example 3 (Program D) provides a more complex budget for an aquatics center program.

Example 1 (Program B):
Simple Class Budget

*Known Information:*
1. There are 12 classes.

all of the classes meet once a week for 8 weeks;
each class period is 1 hour long.
2. The salary (rate of pay) for the instructor is $9.00 per hour;
for the dance coordinator, $2.50 per class;
for the room, $5.00 per hour.
3. There are 15 participants per class.
4. The program fee is designed to recover costs (it should neither lose nor make money).

*Determining the Cost of the Program:*
1. Total number of hours classes meet. This is determined by taking 3 known items (number of classes, number of weeks, and length of individual classes) and multiplying them, as shown below:
12 classes x 8 weeks x 1 hour per class = 96 hours
2. Total cost of instructors, dance coordinator, and room rental. Multiply the cost of each by the total number of hours:
1 instructor x $9.00 per hour x 96 hours = $864
1 coordinator x $2.50 per hour x 96 hours = $240

| ◇ | A | B | C | D | E | F |
|---|---|---|---|---|---|---|
| 1 | Position | number | program length in weeks | hours per week | rate of pay | total cost |
| 2 | Instructor | I | 6 | 3 | $8.50 | $153.00 |

**Figure 13.2**
**Example Spreadsheet**

1 room rental x $5.00 per hour x 96 hours = $480

3. Total cost of program is determined by adding together the cost figures above. In each case, new information was generated that was used to answer the next question:
total cost = $864 + $240 + $480 = $1,584

### Organizing the Data

The data in Figure 13.3 are organized similarly to Figure 13.2. One column was added to include the number of classes. Inclusion of the number of classes was an important new variable in this example.

Example 2 (Program C):
Expanded Class Budget

*Known information:*
1. There are 12 classes:
   7 of the classes meet 1 time a week for 8 weeks;
   5 classes meet 3 times a week for 8 weeks;
   all class periods are one hour in duration.
2. The rate of pay for the instructor is $9.00 per hour;

for the dance coordinator, $2.50 per class;
for the room rental, $5.00 per hour.

3. The agency has determined that indirect costs (or costs the agency has that the program needs to help pay for even though they don't appear as direct program costs) should be charged at a rate of 12.5% and added to the total cost of the program.
4. There are 15 participants per class.
5. The program fee is designed to re-cover costs (it should neither lose nor make money).

Items 4 and 5 are not essential information for this budget example. The purpose is only to determine the cost of the program. If supplies were being purchased based on the number of participants, then item 4 would be essential information. In item 3, above, the only information that is essential is the indirect costs at 12.5%.

*Determining the Program Cost*
Again, the first question that the program manager needs to ask is, "What

| ◇ | A | B | C | D | E | F | G |
|---|---|---|---|---|---|---|---|
| 1 | Position | number | number of classes | program length in weeks | hours per week | rate of pay | total cost |
| 2 | Instructor | 1 | 12 | 8 | 1 | $9.00 | $864.00 |
| 3 | Dance Coordinator | 1 | 12 | 8 | 1 | $2.50 | $240.00 |
| 4 | Room Rental | 1 | 12 | 8 | 1 | $5.00 | $480.00 |
| 5 | Total Cost | | | | | | $1,584.00 |

**Figure 13.3**
**Data Organized for Example 1 on a Spreadsheet**

information is essential?" There may be information related to the program that is not essential. Essential information allows the program manager to determine the answer to each unknown piece of information. In this case, the essential and unknown information are as follows:

1. Total number of hours classes meet.
   7 classes meet 1 time a week
   5 classes meet 3 times a week (for those meeting 3 times a week, include the "3" as new variable:
   total hours for 1 meeting per week classes = 7 classes x 8 weeks x 1 hour per class
   total hours = 56 hours
   total hours for 3 meetings per week classes = 5 classes x 8 weeks x 3 times per week x 1 hour per class
   total hours = 120 hours
   total program hours (classes in both formats) = 56 hours + 120 hours = 176 hours

2. Total cost of instructors, dance coordinator, and room rental. Multiply the cost of each by the total number of hours:
   instructor cost = 1 instructor x $9.00 per hour x 176 hours
   instructor cost = $1,584
   coordinator cost = 1 coordinator x $2.50 per hour x 176 hours
   coordinator cost = $440
   room rental cost = 1 hour room rental x $5.00 per hour x 176 hours
   room rental cost = $880

3. Total cost of the program is determined by adding together the cost figures above. In each case, new information was generated that was used to answer the next question:
   total program cost = $1,584 + $440 + $880
   total program cost = $2,904

4. The indirect cost of the program is figured by multiplying the program cost by the indirect fee:
   indirect costs = $2,904 x .125
   indirect cost = $363

5. Total cost of program is arrived at by adding the indirect costs and program costs:
   total program cost = $2,904 + $363
   total program cost = $3,267

### Organizing the Data

The data in Figure 13.4 added a new column to include the number of meetings per week. In addition, the spreadsheet was divided into two groups, one identifying the classes meeting one time per week and a second for those meeting three times per week. Organizing the spreadsheet to show the two different class structures (meeting times) allows a clearer depiction of the data. The indirect costs were determined for each of the class meeting alternatives individually. Another approach would be to add the total costs and then multiply by 12.5 percent. The final total was calculated by adding the subtotals and the indirect costs for each program group.

Example 3 (Program D):
A Program Budget

*Known Information:*
The public aquatic center is an outdoor facility operating five major programs during the summer over a 12 week period (June 5 to August

| ◇ | A | B | C | D | E | F | G | H |
|---|---|---|---|---|---|---|---|---|
| 1 | Position | number | number of classes | program length in weeks | meetings per week | hours per class | rate of pay | total cost |
| 2 | 1-Time a Week Class Meeting | | | | | | | |
| 3 | Instructor | 1 | 7 | 8 | 1 | 1 | $9.00 | $504.00 |
| 4 | Dance Coordinator | 1 | 7 | 8 | 1 | 1 | $2.50 | $140.00 |
| 5 | Room Rental | 1 | 7 | 8 | 1 | 1 | $5.00 | $280.00 |
| 6 | Sub Total | | | | | | | $924.00 |
| 7 | Indirect Costs | | | | | | 12.50% | $115.50 |
| 9 | 3-Times a Week Class Meeting | | | | | | | |
| 10 | Instructor | 1 | 5 | 8 | 3 | 1 | $9.00 | $1,080.00 |
| 11 | Dance Coordinator | 1 | 5 | 8 | 3 | 1 | $2.50 | $300.00 |
| 12 | Room Rental | 1 | 5 | 8 | 3 | 1 | $5.00 | $600.00 |
| 13 | Sub Total | | | | | | | $1,980.00 |
| 14 | Indirect Costs | | | | | | 12.50% | $247.50 |
| 16 | Total Cost | | | | | | | $3,267.00 |

**Figure 13.4**
**Data Organized for Example 2 on a Spreadsheet**

27). The program areas and management information are provided below.

1. The open swim program operates 7 days a week for 8 hours a day.
   Six lifeguards are on duty at all times at a rate of $8.70 per hour.
   Two concession staff are on duty at all times at a rate of $6.00 per hour.
   One cashier is on duty at all times at a rate of $6.00 per hour.

2. The family swim program operates 3 days a week for 3 hours a day.
   Two lifeguards are on duty at all times at a rate of $8.70 per hour.
   Two concession staff are on duty at all times at a rate of $6.00 per hour.
   One cashier is on duty at all times at a rate of $6.00 per hour.

3. Lane swim operates 6 days a week for 3 hours a day.
   One lifeguard is on duty at all times at a rate of $8.70 per hour.

4. The Learn-to-Swim program operates 4 days a week for 4 hours a day
   One lifeguard is on duty at all times at a rate of $8.70 per hour.
   Six learn-to-swim instructors are on duty at all times at a rate of $9.50 per hour.

5. The swim team meets 6 times a week for 3 hours a day.
   Two coaches are on staff for 4 hours each day (6 days) at a rate of $12.50 per hour.
   Two assistant coaches are on duty 3 hours each day (6 days) at a rate of $9.00 per hour.

6. The management team consists of the following:
   an aquatics supervisor who is full-time and has a salary of $35,600 and has benefits charged at a rate of 27 percent of the base salary;

a maintenance worker who is full-time and has a salary of $23,000 and has benefits charged at a rate of 27 percent of the base salary; a pool manager position works 5 days a week, 8 hours a day, at a rate of $16.50 per hour; a head lifeguard position works 5 days a week, 8 hours a day, at a rate of $14.50 per hour; an assistant head lifeguard position works 5 days a week, 8 hours a day, at a rate of $12.00 per hour; benefits for all employees not receiving 27 percent (there are only 2) are set at 9 percent.

*Determining Salary Costs:*

The information above provides detail about positions, rate of pay, hours per week, and number of staff. The information that is still required includes how many hours per season each person works, what the total cost is of each position for the season, what the cost of benefits is, and what the total cost is of the salaries for the program.

The aquatic supervisor has 100 percent of her salary assessed to the pool, plus 27 percent of her benefits. The maintenance worker has his $23,000 salary and 27 percent benefits assigned to the aquatics program. Following the process discussed previously, the known information is the annual salary and the annual benefit percentage. The desired information is the cost of benefits and the total cost of the position. The formula for determining cost would be as follows:

total cost = (salary x benefit percent = benefit cost) + salary

a)  salary = $35,600 + $23,000
b)  benefit percentage = 27%

resulting in a completed formula that looks like:

total    cost    =    $58,600    x .27($58,600)%
total cost = $74,422

In example 2 the budget was organized around class meetings. In this example the logical approach is to organize around a program area. Figure 13.5, at the end of this section, depicts such a structure. The benefits are determined after all other salaries are determined. Using the program approach, the first area budgeted was open swim. The following formula is used throughout the example. The first instance applies to lifeguards:

total cost = number of employees per hour x number of weeks in season x days per week x hours per day x salary

a)  number of employees per hour = 6
b)  number of weeks in the season = 12
c)  days per week = 7
d)  hours per day = 8
e)  salary = $8.70 per hour

Placing the known information in the formula, the total cost can be calculated:

total cost = 6 x 12 x 7 x 8 x $8.70
total cost = $35,078.40

In each case, known information is used to generate needed information. Pausing to reflect on how to set up the formula is essential. This would be repeated for each position until all costs were determined.

The formula for computing the cost of the concession staff during open swim would look like:

total cost for concession staff = number of employees per hour x number of weeks in season x days per week x hours per day x salary

a) number of employees per hour = 2
b) number of weeks in the season = 12
c) days per week = 7
d) hours per day = 8
e) salary = $6.00 per hour

   total cost = 2 x 12 x 7 x 8 x $6.00
   total cost = $8,064.00

The same formula applied to the cashier looks like:

   total cost = 1 x 12 x 7 x 8 x $6.00
   total cost = $4,032.00

The same processes are applied for each program area. The total cost for full-time staff is $58,600 and for part-time and seasonal staff is $101,928. Benefits are applied below:

   Full-time benefits = full-time total salaries x 27%
   Part-time benefits = part-time salaries x 9%
or
   full-time benefits = $58,600 x 27% = $15,822
   part-time benefits = $101,928 x 9% = $9,173.52

### *Organizing the Data*

The data are organized by individual program area, followed by management staff, and then benefits. The total cost of the program is $136,720 and is shown in Figure 13.5.

## Budgeting for Contingencies

Every good budget preparer knows that the budget is an educated guess and that unexpected changes are going to occur. The budget should include some flexibility to accommodate such contingencies. Contingency costs should be included in the budget at five percent or 10 percent of the total of the budget. When, for example, utility costs go up and the increase was not expected or provided for in the budget, the needed extra funds will be available in the contingency account. Contingency funds allow for emergencies, mistakes in the budget, and cost overruns. They should not be used as justification for poor planning, inadequate research, or whimsical spending.

## Summary

Basic skills of budget preparation were discussed in this chapter. The principles of moving from known information to new information will allow any individual working on a budget process a logical and systematic approach to successfully developing a budget. Some budgets will be more complex than those demonstrated here. Nonetheless, the principles discussed and illustrated here provide a foundation for all budgeting processes.

| ◇ | A | B | C | D | E | F | G | H |
|---|---|---|---|---|---|---|---|---|
| 1 | Position | number | number of classes | program length in weeks | meetings per week | hours per class | rate of pay | total cost |
| 2 | **Open Swim** | | | | | | | |
| 3 | Lifeguard | 6 | 1 | 12 | 7 | 8 | $8.70 | $35,078.40 |
| 4 | Concession staff | 2 | 1 | 12 | 7 | 8 | $6.00 | $8,064.00 |
| 5 | Cashier | 1 | 1 | 12 | 7 | 8 | $6.00 | $4,032.00 |
| 6 | Sub Total | | | | | | | $47,174.40 |
| 7 | | | | | | | | |
| 8 | **Family Swim** | | | | | | | |
| 9 | Lifeguard | 4 | 1 | 12 | 3 | 3 | $8.70 | $3,758.40 |
| 10 | Concession staff | 2 | 1 | 12 | 3 | 3 | $6.00 | $1,296.00 |
| 11 | Cashier | 1 | 1 | 12 | 3 | 3 | $6.00 | $648.00 |
| 12 | Sub Total | | | | | | | $5,702.40 |
| 13 | | | | | | | | |
| 14 | **Lap Swim** | | | | | | | |
| 15 | Lifeguard | 2 | 1 | 12 | 6 | 3 | $8.70 | $3,758.40 |
| 16 | Sub Total | | | | | | | $3,758.40 |
| 17 | | | | | | | | |
| 18 | **Learn-to-Swim** | | | | | | | |
| 19 | Lifeguard | 1 | 1 | 12 | 4 | 3 | $8.70 | $1,252.80 |
| 20 | Instructor | 6 | 1 | 12 | 6 | 3 | $9.50 | $12,312.00 |
| 21 | Sub Total | | | | | | | $13,564.80 |
| 22 | | | | | | | | |
| 23 | **Swim Team** | | | | | | | |
| 24 | Coaches | 2 | 1 | 12 | 6 | 4 | $12.50 | $7,200.00 |
| 25 | Asst. Coaches | 2 | 1 | 12 | 6 | 3 | $9.00 | $3,888.00 |
| 26 | Sub Total | | | | | | | $11,088.00 |
| 27 | | | | | | | | |
| 28 | **Management** | | | | days / wk | hrs / day | | |
| 29 | Aquatic Supervisor | 1 | 1 | 1 | 1 | 1 | $35,600.00 | $35,600.00 |
| 30 | Maintenance Wrk 1 | 1 | 1 | 1 | 1 | 1 | $23,000.00 | $23,000.00 |
| 31 | Pool Manager | 1 | 1 | 12 | 5 | 8 | $16.50 | $7,920.00 |
| 32 | Head Lifeguard | 1 | 1 | 12 | 5 | 8 | $14.50 | $6,960.00 |
| 33 | Assistant Head Lifeguard | 1 | 1 | 12 | 5 | 8 | $12.00 | $5,760.00 |
| 34 | Sub Total | | | | | | | $66,520.00 |
| 35 | | | | | | | | |
| 36 | **Benefits** | | | | | benefit | total salary | |
| 37 | Full time employees | | | | | 27% | $58,600.00 | $15,822.00 |
| 38 | Part-time & Seasonal | | | | | 9% | $101,928.00 | $9,173.52 |
| 39 | Sub-Total | | | | | | | $24,995.52 |
| 40 | Total Cost | | | | | | | $136,720.00 |

**Figure 13.5**
**Data Organized for Example 3 on a spreadsheet**

NOTES

# CHAPTER 14

# Budget Preparation

## Introduction

Budgeting is a process that focuses on providing managers with information and tools to manage fiscal resources and operations. Well-constructed and readable budgets ultimately allow managers to make more informed decisions. Budgeting is linked to organizational goals and objectives. It is a tool to help achieve them. Furthermore, budgeting allows sport, tourism, and leisure service organizations to translate their organizational visions into realities. Budgeting is clearly an essential component of the larger management processes of any organization. In today's competitive and changing society, sport, tourism, and leisure service organizations cannot function effectively without a clear understanding of how good fiscal management contributes to their day-to-day success. Few decisions facing sport, tourism, and leisure service organization managers are more daunting than those made concerning how to allocate limited fiscal resources. Yet, the decision making involving the allocation of human and fiscal resources is that which affects the organization's ability to achieve its vision.

## Budget Processes

### What is a Budget?

Budgeting is one of the most important tasks in which a sport, tourism, and leisure service manager can be engaged. The budget is a financial plan and frequently translates the operational and strategic plans of the organization into achievable activities over a period of time. *A budget is a document depicting the anticipated revenues and expenditures of an organization* (most often over a one-year period). Budgets anticipate expenditures and revenue and are linked to organizational and individual work plans. Edginton and Williams (1978) originally described ten benefits resulting from the budgeting process. Modified for today's fiscal environment, nine are presented here:

1. Budgeting is a systematic process that brings structure to the organization.
2. Budgeting requires the manager to do advance planning for the organization, which reinforces strategic and long-range planning.
3. Budgeting provides a starting point for building organizational and individual work plans.
4. Budgeting moves the organization toward measurable and quantifiable outcomes in both human and material terms.
5. Budgeting encourages standardization in fiscal operations, encouraging an efficiency that unifies approaches to spending and revenue accounting. It allows an organization to be more efficient.
6. Budgeting, in the absence of other measures, allows managers and subordinates to communicate on a common level. It reinforces other measures of effectiveness in the organization.
7. The budget is an essential part of a complex decision-making process in most organizations.
8. The budget provides policy-setting bodies with a measurement tool used in formal evaluation.
9. The budget serves as a policy body's mechanism for control.

Budgets are classified as two types: *operating budgets* and *capital budgets.* Operating budgets deal with current expenditures for a specified period of time, while capital budgets cover longer periods of time in attempting to address major projects requiring significant investments of dollars. Capital budgets are funded for more than one year at a time and are adjusted on an annual basis. Capital budgeting is discussed in detail in Chapter 16. Almost all managers work with operating budgets. Fewer work with capital budgets, yet they contribute to the construction of capital budgets in important ways.

### The Budget Cycle

Budgets usually span a one-year period, called a fiscal year. A fiscal year is not always the same as the calendar year. The most common fiscal year period is from July 1 through June 30 of the ensuing year. The U.S. Government's fiscal year is October 1 through September 30. Many private not-for-profit and commercial sport, tourism, and leisure service organizations use January 1 through December 31 as their fiscal year. It is acceptable and common to refer to a fiscal year by the year in which it ends. If a fiscal year begins July 1, 2007, and ends June 30, 2008, the fiscal year is referred to as FY2008 (fiscal year 2008).

The importance of a fiscal year lies in the spending and accounting process. Money is allocated, encumbered, and expended within a given fiscal year. Allocated funds are those dollars that the legislative/policy body approves for use by the sport, tourism, and leisure service organization. _Encumbered funds_ are those dollars that have been committed for purchases, but have yet to be paid by the organization to the vendor. As an example, a municipal parks and recreation department, which purchased new playground equipment for $34,000 in March, issued a purchase order for the purchase. The department recorded the money as being committed or encumbered, but not spent. Sixty days after the purchase order was issued the vendor installed the playground equipment. Shortly thereafter an invoice was received, the department issued a check to the vendor, and the money was no longer encumbered, but expended. *Expended funds*, then, are those funds paid out for services and items purchased, leased, and rented and for which invoices have been received and checks issued.

A fiscal year provides a fixed starting and stopping point for budget administration. Policy-setting or legislative bodies and managers need to be able to establish budgetary guidelines for their organizations. The fiscal year is recognized as an accounting standard. It allows organizations to accomplish fiscal planning for a fixed period of time. It allows government organizations to match anticipated tax revenues against projected expenditures. It allows commercial and not-for-profit enterprises to plan for revenues and expenditures.

Budget cycles can take up to 24 months, and some organizations have longer planning cycles. Figure 14.1 illustrates three fiscal years and includes the budget preparation time and the budget

closeout period. The length of time required to construct a budget will vary from organization to organization–it is mandated by the organization's governing body. Accounting bodies prefer to finalize or close out an organization's end-of-the-year budget within 30 to 90 days. Even when some funds remain encumbered, budgets can be closed out with the knowledge that encumbered funds remain to be expended.

## Budget Preparation Cycle

A typical budget preparation cycle includes four tasks, as depicted in Figure 14.2. In a government agency, the budget cycle is usually prescribed by the legislative authority, such as a city council, a park board, a county council, or a state or provincial government. For not-for-profit organizations, a board of directors defines the budget process. Not-for-profit organizations that depend on the United Way for part of their operating budget may be required to follow a United Way budget presentation process in full or in part. Commercial enterprises may have

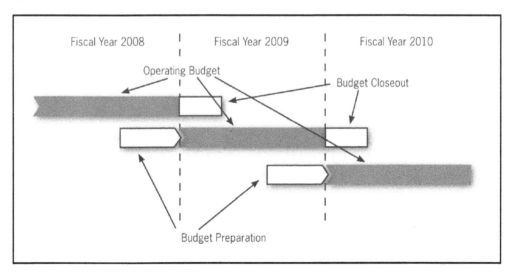

**Figure 14.1**
**Three-year budget calendar**

a specified set of instructions and procedures to follow, or they may be flexible in their approach to budget development. Regardless of the type of sport, tourism, and leisure service organization, there are some commonalities that each type of organization can follow in the development of a budget.

An example of a municipal budget cycle (Figure 14.2) includes activities and deadlines. A budget preparation document includes such items as specific directives from the legislative body, any restrictions on budget growth, identification of budget deadlines, budget formats, budget decision guidelines, and specific instructions that either may be applicable only to this budget period or may be new to the organization. The guidelines are typically transmitted in a letter, with supporting documentation from the head of the legislative body or the designated

administrative officer. The organization is expected to comply with all of the guidelines prescribed by the legislative authority.

The budget guidelines include a budget calendar, which is an orderly timetable showing the dates when necessary action must be taken in preparing the budget. A budget calendar frequently initiates the process 12 months in advance of the start date of the budget. (The example in Table 14.1 begins six months in advance.) The budget guidelines and calendar are provided so the legislative, executive, and departmental entities will avoid encroachment on one another, and give order to the budget preparation. This development phase is the most critical phase of the budgeting process and realistic completion dates should be articulated. Completion dates should be established for the following:

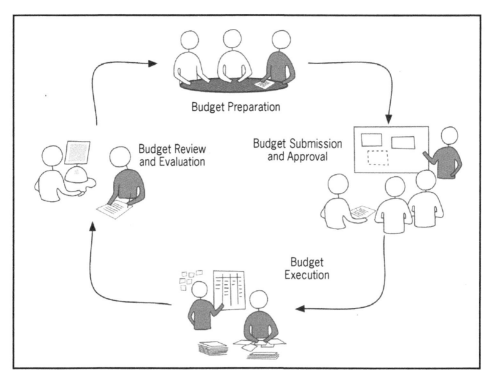

**Figure 14.2**
**Budget preparation cycle**

| Date | Actions to be Completed |
|------|-------------------------|
| 2 January (-180) | Mayor's budget policy letter requesting department heads to submit proposed work program and budget estimates for ensuing fiscal year. Necessary forms and revisions to budget manual are transmitted with the letter. |
| 1 February (-150) | City administrative officer (CAO) approves staff budget assignments, which are thereafter distributed to the staff. |
| 1 March (-120) | Service betterment budget estimates, if any, received from department heads. |
| 10 April (-80) | CAO reviews tentative Capital Improvement Expenditure Program (CIP) and, upon approval, transmits it to the Public Works Priority Committee. |
| 10 April (-80) | CAO submits annual salary recommendations to City Council. |
| 10–30 April (-80 to -60) | Hearings conducted by the Public Works Priority Committee to determine final priority of capital projects to be included in CIP for ensuing year. |
| 10–17 April (-80 to -73) | Preliminary budget hearing held by CAO and Budget Coordinator with the Assistant Budget Coordinator and staff analyst for each department. |
| 18–28 April (-74 to -92) | CAO, assisted by Budget Coordinator, conducts departmental budget hearing with each department head, at which time the staff analysts' recommendations for that departmental budget are presented and the department head is given an opportunity to express his or her viewpoint. |
| 1 May (-60) | Final date for submission by City Controller of the official estimates of revenue from all sources (other than general property taxes). |
| 1 May (-60) | CAO submits official estimate of revenue from general property taxes. |
| 1–5 May (-60 to -55) | Mayor, assisted by CAO, conducts budget conferences with each department head. Attended by council members, press, and taxpayer groups. |
| 5–12 May (-55 to -48) | Final budget decisions made by Mayor, who is assisted by CAO. |
| 12–31 May (-48 to -30) | Budget printed under supervision of CAO. |
| 1 June (-29) | Mayor submits budget to City Council. |
| 1–20 June (-29 to -10) | Council considers Mayor's budget and makes modifications as it deems necessary. |
| 20–25 June (-10 to -5) | Mayor considers any modifications made by City Council and may veto such changes. |
| 25–28 June (-5 to -2) | Council considers Mayor's veto of any items and may vote to override Mayor's veto by a two-thirds' majority. |
| 1 July (0) | Beginning of fiscal year—budget takes effect. |

**Table 14.1**
**A detailed example of a public budget preparation cycle**

- Distribution of instructions and forms.
- Preparation of revenue estimates.
- Return of the completed budget request forms.
- Completion of review and preliminary preparation of work assigned to the central budget agency.
- Completion of executive review and executive determination of final budget content.
- Submission of the budget to the approving body.
- Completion of public or shareholder hearings (if required).
- Final action by the approving body
- Executive approval or veto of the adopted budget and legislative action thereon.
- Completion of administrative action, if any, needed to actuate budget appropriations.
- Beginning of the fiscal year.

The calendar should also include the following:

- Schedule showing responsibilities of the various officials and departments to specific items.
- Excerpts of legal and administrative rules that govern budget formulation and execution.

It is recommended that each sport, tourism, and leisure service organization develop its own budget calendar using the policy and administrative bodies' calendars as a guide. The calendar should provide information similar to that found in the policy body's calendar, although it should be specific to the organization.

## Funds

Budgets are constructed around account-based funds. Funds come from any of the five income sources discussed in

---

## CASE STUDY
### Portland Area Metro Parks Budget Process

The Portland Area Metro Parks is part of the metro government and follows a budget cycle identified by the government. Figure 14.3 depicts the current budget cycle for creating a budget. The following description of the budget process is abstracted from the 2006-2007 Metro budget:

*Review of prior year.* Each fiscal year begins with a review of the previous year's budget cycle, determining what was successful and where there were problems. The process is refined for the next year. Budget parameters are developed, setting out basic assumptions for departments to follow, along with policies and priorities.

*Budget Manual.* The budget manual provides departments with detailed instructions for preparing and submitting their budgets. The submitted budgets are initially reviewed by the chief operating officer and staff. The manual covers how to increase/decrease the number of employees, changes in personnel costs, capital budget preparation, and so forth.

*Parks Requests.* The department staff reads the instructions and prepares the budget based on guidelines provided by the chief operating officer. The budget is a forecast of program activities and financial needs for the next fiscal year. The forecasts provide the foundation for the department's budget requests.

*Review and Analysis by the Chief Operating Officer.* The Finance Department and financial planning division review all budget requests and share the results with the

## CASE STUDY
### *Portland Area Metro Parks Budget Process (continued)*

submitting department and the chief operating officer. The chief operating officer and chief financial officer meet with the department to discuss identified issues and program changes.

*Review and Analysis by the Metro Council.* The Metro Council is composed of community members and serves as the policy-setting board for the Metro government. It ultimately approves the budget after review and discussion.

*Changes to the Budget after Adoption.* There are several ways a budget can be modified after adopted and these are prescribed in the Oregon Local Budget Law.

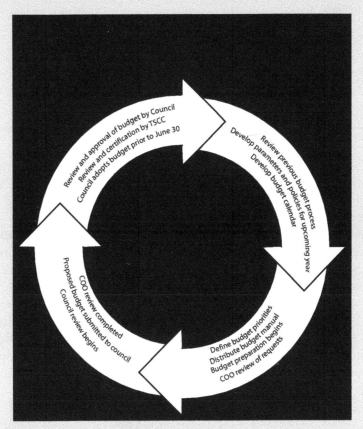

**Figure 14.3**
**Portland Metro budget cycle**

from: http://www.metro-region.org/article.cfm?ArticleID=19522

### Metro Parks - Budget Preparation Calendar

The annual budget cycle includes these primary steps:
*July-August*
- Review previous budget process
- Develop parameters and policies for upcoming year
- Develop budget calendar

---

### CASE STUDY
#### Portland Area Metro Parks Budget Process (continued)

*September-January*
- Define budget assumptions and priorities
- Distribute budget instructions
- Budget and five-year capital budget preparation
- Council President review of requests

*February-March*
- Council President review completed
- Proposed budget prepared
- Council briefings

*April-June*
- Proposed budget submitted to Council
- Review and approval of budget by Council
- Review and certification by Tax Supervising and Conservation Commission
- Council adopts budget prior to June 30

Source: http://www.metro-region.org/article.cfm?ArticleID=9467

---

Chapter 8. They are segregated from the regular operating budget for the purpose of carrying on specific activities. Funds are unique to government and not-for-profit organizations. Funds are a separate group of accounts that are managed independently of each other. They have come about because government organizations have legal restrictions placed on them regarding how specific revenue may be expended. A local option hotel/motel tax may be restricted by state or city code for use to support greenways, greenbelts, or convention and meeting facilities. These funds can be divided into three categories:

governmental funds, proprietary funds, and fiduciary funds. Each is described below and depicted in Table 14.2.

### Government Funds

Included within the three types of funds are sub-funds that are common to most public sport, tourism, and leisure service organizations. Most government fiscal operations are conducted through four types of funds: (1) general fund, (2) special revenue fund, (3) capital projects fund, and (4) debt service fund.

The *general fund* is most common to all public organizations. It supports all

---

Table 14.2
Types of government-based funds

| Governmental Funds | Proprietary Funds | Fiduciary Funds |
|---|---|---|
| General Fund | Enterprise Funds | Expendable Trust Funds |
| Special Revenue Fund | Internal Service Funds | Nonexpendable Trust Funds |
| Capital Projects Fund | | Agency Funds |
| General Obligation Fund | | |
| Debt Service Funds | | |
| Special Assessment Funds | | |

operations not assigned to other funds. In public park and recreation agencies, this fund will vary from less than 30 percent to more than 90 percent of the operating budget. Included in it might be personnel services, maintenance operations, supplies, contractual services, etc. Sources of revenue for the general fund are most frequently property taxes, but they also may include sales taxes, special taxes, intergovernmental grants, and licenses and permits.

The *special revenue fund* is used for specific services and is usually legally restricted for that purpose. User fees and charges are the primary source of revenue for special revenue funds. Fees collected from recreation programs and services are a common source of revenue. These fees are deposited in a special revenue fund and used to pay for recreation programs and services. The fund can also be used to partially defray or wholly pay for operating expenses, personnel services, supplies and materials, etc.

A *capital projects fund* focuses on the acquisition, design, and construction of capital facilities or major projects that have an economic life of greater than one year. These projects include aquatic complexes, recreation centers, conference centers, sport complexes, ice arenas, public parks, and other major buildings and structures. It also includes the purchase of large or expensive pieces of equipment. Money for a capital projects fund can come from a variety of sources, including special taxes, intergovernmental grants, and proceeds from the sale of revenue or general obligation bonds.

A *debt service fund* is used to pay the organization's long-term debt and, in the case of government, the general obligation debt from the sale of bonds. Any organization involved in capital projects of significant size has probably engaged in long-term debt. Revenue for the debt service fund comes primarily from taxes, grants, special assessments, and intergovernmental grants.

Public parks and open spaces provide important opportunities for recreation activities.

A *special assessment fund* consists of money targeted for a specific project or task. Assessments are made to specific individuals or organizations for an identified service or benefit to be received.

### Proprietary Funds

A proprietary fund has a profit and loss component and is designed to provide for ongoing activities as a self-sustaining operation.

An *enterprise fund* receives most of its revenue from user charges and typically supports a major operation or enterprise. Examples of enterprise fund operations include civic centers, aquatic complexes, and major parks, zoos, and sport complexes.

*Internal service funds* transfer money between different departments within the same organization for services rendered. For example, if the YMCA program division needs 8,500 brochures, and their printing services division provides the brochures, the program division would be billed internally by the printing division for their costs. This fund allows organizations to track the cost of services provided internally and serves as a way to charge the services of internal support services and measure their utilization by other internal organizations.

### Fiduciary Funds

Fiduciary funds are used to account for assets received and held in trust by either a government or a not-for-profit organization. The organization is perceived as a trustee, custodian, or agent for the funds. Three types of funds are common to fiduciary funds: nonexpendable trust fund, expendable trust fund, and an agency fund.

The *nonexpendable trust fund* requires that the principal remain unspent, but allows the expenditure of income generated from an investment of the principal. The income may be spent in the general fund or assigned to specific programs or other funds. A nonexpendable trust fund may accrue income to the principal from a variety of sources, such as accrued interest, donations, grants, and bequests.

An *expendable trust* allows spending from the principal. Art endowment and zoo endowment programs are common examples of expendable trusts. Individuals are encouraged to contribute to a specific endowment, and the agency uses the money contributed for day-to-day operations or for special projects.

An *agency fund* allows an agency control over a set of designated funds. Examples might include lottery funds used to finance parks and recreation, or a hotel and motel tax for a convention center operation or sport complex operation.

Less common funds include annuity funds, endowment funds, loan funds, and operating funds.

An *annuity fund* holds money that remains after an annuity contract has expired. These funds can be used in any manner that the organization chooses unless specific restrictions are placed upon them.

An *endowment fund* is most frequently used by not-for-profit organizations, but has the same characteristics as a nonexpendable trust.

A *loan fund* is a separate fund set aside with the constituent funds available for loan for specific functions or services. One example of a loan fund is the provision of loans to faculty, students, and staff at a university.

An *operating fund* is made up of all those funds that are available for use by the board of a not-for-profit organization. The operating fund fulfills the same role as the general fund in a government.

## Budget Preparation Format

There are many different ways to format and prepare a budget. Table 14.3 provides a summary of 12 of the more common budget formats. Each budget format provides decision makers with different kinds of information. Depending on the goals of the sport, tourism, or leisure service organization, one or more appropriate budget formats are selected.

The object classification budget is the most common format for public, not-for-profit, and commercial organizations. It is a budget format that allows managers to use the budget as a tool to accomplish goals and objectives. Expenditures are classified into a specific category (called a code). However, as government and not-for-profit organizations become more entrepreneurial and develop revenue-generating operations, the object classification budget format cannot meet all of their information requirements and is frequently paired with another budget type, such as the program budget. (Chapter 15 discusses selected budget formats in detail.)

## Budget Preparation Activities

Budget preparation is the responsibility of the chief executive officer (CEO) of the sport, tourism, or leisure service organization. This person may be the director, the executive director, the superintendent, the manager, or the owner. The CEO sets the agenda and the tone for budget preparation for all members of the organization. Budget preparation should be a co-operative endeavor among the organization's members and the external budget agency, if one is present. Cooperation among participants in the budget process is a key element in the success of the organization. It should be viewed as a shared process rather than a competitive process.

Effective budget preparation engages all members of the organization. Budget preparation should be taken to the lowest levels of the organization, thus fostering understanding, input, and commitment from organization members. This process may necessitate training for members of the organization, as well as an enhanced level of trust. Decentralizing budget decision-making to the lowest possible levels results in an increased commitment to the budget and to the organization's purpose and direction. Ultimately, the CEO defines each member's role in the budget's preparation and sets the tone for budget operations. A single individual should be designated as the budget preparation officer (BPO). The BPO ensures conformity in the budget preparation, collects and collates all of the data submitted by different budget managers, identifies discrepancies, and resolves disputes. The BPO also ensures that the budget conforms to the guidelines proposed by both the CEO and the policy body and is linked to the department's strategic or long-range plans. The department BPO briefs each member of the organization who has contributed to the budget, coordinates closely with the department executive officer, and prepares the final budget document for submission to the legislative or policy body.

### The Relationship of Strategic Planning to Budget Preparation

The budgeting process is linked to strategic planning. An organization, during the process of development of the strategic plan, should engage in aligning the budget with the strategic plan. Budget preparation decisions should help to achieve key tasks identified in the stra-

Table 14.3
Comparison of commonly used budget formats

| Type of Budget | Description | Purpose/When Used | Advantages | Disadvantages |
|---|---|---|---|---|
| Object classification budget | Looks at operations as categories (objects) and classifies expenditures into those categories | Most common of budget types in use by government, nonprofits, and corporations. Provides ease of budget classification and management. | • Relatively easy to establish<br>• Process is uniform and follows standardized procedures<br>• Category development is predetermined | • Does not provide flexibility to meet changing issues<br>• Requires detailed cost estimates at the program level<br>• Categories sometimes too generalized to provide budget detail |
| Line item budget | Similar to object classification except items replace specific categories for classification | As common as object classification and provides similar ease of budget classification and management. | • Allows some flexibility<br>• Allows for multiple system utilization<br>• Allows for budget adjustments with minimal difficulty | • Requires detailed planning and preparation<br>• Some loss of reporting accuracy because expenditures collapsed into broader categories or lines |
| Activity budget | Budget areas are divided into "activity areas" and focus on the cost to perform a specific function | Allows agencies to have a clearer delineation of the costs associated with different functional activities | • Clearly defines services as activities<br>• Allows for comparisons between activities<br>• Provides a clear picture of where budget funds are allocated | • Can be difficult to set up and requires detailed accounting system<br>• Some activities don't fit easily<br>• Reduces some levels of flexibility |
| Function budget | Similar to the activity budget and allows agencies to group activities under major functions | Grouped activity budgets are tracked and administrators are able to view their change in expenses over a period of time | • Comparison of functional costs<br>• Improves knowledge of where funds are allocated | • Budgets may not lend themselves to easy comparison<br>• Uses object classification approach and retains similar disadvantages |
| Performance budget | Used to measure end results of activities based on performance outcome measures | Similar to the program budget and more frequently used with operations with repetitive measures, such as maintenance and food service | • Highly standardized units of measurement and cost<br>• Provides for high control and detailed accuracy<br>• Effectively integrates with computer-based operations management | • Requires reporting sophistication<br>• Not particularly useful in non-repetitive situations<br>• Fixed approach to management and decision making |
| Planning, programming, budgeting system | Identifies the relationship between costs and end results (or outcomes) of programs | Used to measure the outcome of budget expenditures on programs. Focus is on the impact of expenditures rather than the cost of the program | • Focuses on service goals<br>• End results most important<br>• Provides for comparative analysis of programs and services | • Requires establishment of an equitable measurement system<br>• Difficult to determine importance of need and value<br>• Comparisons not always possible across entire organization |

**Table 14.3**

**Comparison of commonly used budget formats (continued)**

| Type of Budget | Description | Purpose/When Used | Advantages | Disadvantages |
|---|---|---|---|---|
| Zero based budgeting | Focus on actual costs of programs requiring all programs regularly justify existence | When an agency needs to assess for decision makers operations and justify which operations are worthy of retention | • Encourages regular review of value and importance of programs<br>• Provids for increased flexibility<br>• Enhances decision making when focusing on essential services<br>• Facilitates an orderly review | • Increased justification and reporting<br>• May increase internal competition<br>• Increases organizational tension |
| Program budget | Explains and justifies expenditure in the context of organizational goals | Used when fuller explanation of programs and costs are identifiable and linked to outcomes | • Provides narrative justification<br>• Focuses on values of programs and services, not just costs<br>• Creativity and flexibility enhanced | • Requires increased sophistication in analysis and reporting<br>• Limited budget/cost detail provided |
| Fee budget | Determines actual cost of service and operations and allocates to specific categories | When budget requires a detailed accounting of specific areas | • Provides a more detailed account of actual cost<br>• Shows per-participant costs | • Use restricted to appropriate areas<br>• Requires detailed knowledge of needs before initiating<br>• May not include all actual costs |
| Unit budget | Used frequently in large organizations, groups costs by subunit and allows for use of different budgeting approaches within subunit | Useful for viewing costs across entire organization, does not suggest commonality among units; rather, depicts where expenditures are | • Clear description of unit expenses<br>• Simple to present and comprehend<br>• Opens budget process to public | • Not a stand-alone system<br>• No budget detail available<br>• Requires top down policies |
| Increment/decrement budgeting | Traditional approach of increasing or decreasing budget by fixed percentages, done without regard to levels of importance | Makes the budge process relatively simple by addressing issues of increase with a fixed percentage | • Provides for hassle-free predictable growth<br>• Reduces decision making<br>• Simplifies the budget process | • Demand and need not addressed<br>• Encourages status quo<br>• Discourages creativity and flexibility |
| Running budget | Developed and modified based on income and expenses, driven by income and limiting income | Organizations without stable income can adjust budget accordingly throughout the fiscal year | • Based on daily accounting<br>• Real-time budget accountability<br>• Revenues tied to income | • Not a stand-alone system<br>• Budget administration process<br>• Time consuming to administer |

tegic plan. Strategic planning is about achieving organizational futures. Linking the budget to strategic planning becomes a visible method of moving from planning to action. Budget decisions should focus on the organization's values, vision, mission, and action plan. A strategic plan is not intended to address all operations of the organization, but rather its emphasis is upon those action items deemed necessary to achieve the organization's vision. Strategic planning complements, but does not replace, effective evaluation of day-to-day operations, special initiatives, capital projects, etc. Strategic planning is another budget preparation component that the BPO and budget manager must consider.

### Budget Preparation Philosophies

How budget needs are estimated depends on the type of preparation philosophy the organization adopts.

An *open-ended budget* allows for the optimum program operation for the organization. The budget is not hindered by restrictions on spending; rather, it requires decision makers to adjust the budget to meet the organization's budget capabilities. This adjustment is typically accomplished through reductions in proposed expenditures. Open-ended budgeting has fallen into disfavor in an era of accountability and limited budget growth.

A *fixed ceiling budget* typically places a limit on the growth of a budget. A fixed ceiling budget assumes previous budgets were adequate and minimal growth will continue to meet organizational needs. A fixed ceiling budget fits a mature organization focusing on minimal change. It is also a politically safe budget. However, such budgets often fail to take into account changing needs of the organization. The format reacts to available in-

come, suggesting that either politics or an attitude of sharing proportionately among competing groups is an equitable approach to budgeting. A fixed ceiling budget remains an acceptable model.

A budget based on *workload measurement and unit costing* seeks to devise units of work and to determine unit costs. This budget approach attempts to quantify work as performance and output. In sport, tourism, and leisure service organizations, workload measurement budgets work best for units with repetitive types of activities.

An *increase/decrease analysis* is a form of fixed ceiling budget depicting changes from the previous year's expenditure lines. An item-by-item control looks at each budget item and asks if it is essential, desirable, or justified. Alternative budget proposals ask staff members to prepare a basic budget supplemented by an outline for alternative budget levels (such as a budget that is called base, then an alternative budget with an increase of 15 percent and another alternative budget with a decrease of 15 percent). Alternative budgets provide rationales for different budget proposals and detailed budget information. Almost all budget preparations go through some form of alternative budget preparation, but rarely in a formally requested manner. Such an approach requires a considerable amount of time and effort on the part of the budget preparers and usually yields little return for the additional work.

*Factorial estimating* looks at past expenditures and factors what it believes will be future expenditures. More specifically, it looks at operating expenses and revenues in a detailed format over a period of years and attempts to estimate or forecast future expenditures. The reliance upon historical data is appropriate for most sport, tourism, and leisure service organizations, but those organizations that rely wholly upon the past to predict the future will find that they are ill prepared to meet the demands and needs of their constituents or legislative body.

*Historical analysis* is an almost identical approach to factorial estimating, except that it typically leaves out personnel-related services.

A variety of philosophies can be applied in preparing a budget. Historically based, open-ended, measurement, or work measurement philosophies have been the most commonly applied to budgeting processes that determine work program requirements. Personnel need oriented budget preparation has used work measurement and historical analysis, and a budget focusing on estimation of the cost of supplies, materials, and equipment usually relies upon historical analysis. Equipment needs have used a fixed ceiling format as the primary method, although in some instances, an open-ended budget is utilized effectively.

### Preparing the Departmental Work Plan

The departmental work plan is an integral part of the budget preparation process. It involves identifying the work of the sport, tourism, or leisure service organization for the planned fiscal year and then matching the proposed budget with the desired work. It usually requires a series of trade-offs between what the organization would like to do and what it can realistically accomplish within the constraints of its budget. The department work plan involves at least three components: (1) ongoing functions of the park and recreation organization, (2) new or proposed functions of the organization, and (3) special one-time or infrequently reoccurring functions of the organization.

Preparing an annual work plan requires in-depth knowledge of the organization's work processes and their relationships to the vision and mission. Delegating budget preparation and management to the lowest possible level in the organization assumes that those who do the work are best prepared to estimate its costs and outputs. The delegation of budget preparation does not eliminate the need for constant oversight and justification at each step of the process.

To facilitate the process of budgeting for annual work plans, the financial manager of the sport, tourism, or leisure service organization should do the following:

- Conduct an annual review of each program or service and assess consistency with the organization's vision and mission.
- Annually assess the effectiveness of each program and service in relation to the organization's goals and objectives, the standards established for the program or service, and customer satisfaction.
- Initiate a level-of-performance review to determine if the program or service meets agreed-upon levels of service or satisfaction.

### Estimating Personnel Service Requirements

In most sport, tourism, and leisure service organizations, personnel costs are the single largest expenditure item. The costs will range from 50 percent to 90 percent of the organization's operating costs. Given this level of funding, the importance of determining personnel costs cannot be underestimated. In the budgeting process, the purpose of the personnel functions is to determine the type, quantity, and quality of personnel needed to accomplish the work plan of the organization during the fiscal period.

Personnel costs are most frequently figured on a fixed growth, as opposed to a fixed ceiling, budget. An organization should take several approaches to determining personnel costs. First, it should determine the costs for full-time personnel. Since the bulk of these individuals are already on a fixed salary, the annual allowable percentage of growth is frequently determined by the policy body. In government and not-for-profit organizations, it may be a fixed percentage of a salary base (e.g., cost-of-living raises will be 3.5 percent for the next fiscal year). This has been and continues to be the most common approach taken to salary adjustments. The fixed growth may be based on anticipated available funds, government-determined cost-of-living increases, inflation, or what the policy body negotiates with the employees or their representatives.

Most full-time, salaried employees are compensated within a fixed salary range. Employees are hired at a particular salary within the existing range, and salary adjustments can occur every year. Table 14.4 illustrates sample salary ranges for different positions.

The salary ranges, or steps, as shown in Table 14.4, represent the salary increases an employee will receive after a specified period of time with the organization. A person starting at step one of position code 87456 will receive $27,456 in annual wages. Each period, usually one year, the person can anticipate a salary increase to the next range. In addition, there may be annual cost-of-living increases, essentially increasing the value of the next step. The steps in Table 14.4 are based on a 4.5 percent increase. If the legislative body determined that a 3.0 percent cost-of-living increase was appropriate, then the entire step range would increase by three percent. An individual at step two would receive an increase of three percent and have a new annual salary of $29,552. At step five, the individual has achieved the highest pay possible in that position. Future increases would come from cost-of-living adjustments or a redefinition of the salary range. The number of steps in a salary range will vary from organization to organization. It could consist of as many as 20 or more steps.

Permanent part-time positions are usually determined in the same way. Seasonal or temporary part-time positions are determined in any number of ways. Most organizations begin with a minimum wage approach and then value each position on the basis of its contribution to the organization, the prevailing wage for a similar position, and the availability of qualified individuals. In one community, when the indoor pool began its fall and winter season, the parks and recreation department could not hire a sufficient number of qualified lifeguards. An

### Table 14.4
### Example salary ranges

| Position Code | Position Title | Step 1 | Step 2 | Step 3 | Step 4 | Step 5 | Step 6 |
|---|---|---|---|---|---|---|---|
| 87456 | Program Supervisor | $27,456.00 | $28,691.52 | $29,982.64 | $31,331.86 | $32,741.79 | $34,215.17 |
| 85543 | Assistant Director | $33,663.00 | $35,177.84 | $36,760.84 | $38,415.08 | $40,143.75 | $41,950.22 |

Budget preparation is often a process of shared decision making.

analysis of the job market showed that the number of available lifeguards was far diminished from the summer. The agency had erroneously assumed the summer lifeguard wage would be adequate for the indoor season. What it had failed to take into account was the fact that college students, who made up the core of the summer lifeguards, returned to school, thus reducing the market availability by over 60 percent. The parks and recreation agency ultimately increased the wage by $2.00 per hour to attract other qualified lifeguards.

### Staffing Issues

Determining staffing needs for programs is a function of budget managers. Information pertaining to the number of personnel, the rate of pay, the length of time to be employed, and the justification for the position are provided to the budget preparation officer for inclusion in the budget. An important tool that is used by budget preparation officers and CEOs to determine staffing needs and reviewing staffing patterns is the detailed organization charts, table of organization, or manning table. Additionally, the budget preparation officer needs to look at workload trends in the organization. Organizations should be involved in some type of workload analysis that provides this information. Included in workload trends are new or amended legal requirements affecting the organization's programs and services, newly initiated policies or changes in existing policy regulations, planned changes in the organization, changes in systems and/or procedures, and approved workload consolidations. The CEO attempts to balance workload demands with available personnel and match demands with existing commitments. At the disposal of the CEO is his or her experience over a period of years with staffing patterns. This experience quotient, although not scientifically quantifiable, is an important component of the budgeting process. Finally, the CEO has to make certain assumptions about the future. These assumptions are based on existing facts, past history, knowledge of the organization and its members, political implications and realities, and stakeholder expectations.

Personnel costs are collected for all positions and placed in the department's operating budget. If the personnel costs are assigned to different funds within the organization, the positions are appropriately categorized. This process can become complicated, but when properly organized and cross-referenced, it becomes an organized and understandable document. In most organizations, there will be some salary savings every year. A salary savings occurs when one or more positions in the organization remain empty for any period of time. For example, a position paying $2,000 a month that is vacant for three months results in a $6,000 salary savings for the organization. Over a period of time, these vacancies can produce a significant financial savings for the organization. In some cases, the BPO may know about these vacancies in advance; in other cases, they will occur during the fiscal year, and adjustments will have to be made in the operating budget. Most budget preparation officers anticipate salary savings and figure them in as part of the budget.

For some organizations, overtime is a significant issue. The Fair Labor Standards Act (FLSA) prescribes overtime rules for most organizations. Employees can be identified as exempt from overtime, depending on their positions and responsibilities, but most employees will more likely be affected by the FLSA overtime rules. Public organizations are particularly challenged by the overtime costs. In a northern states community, for example, the parks and recreation department may be assigned to be part of the snow removal process—a responsibility whose cost is almost impossible to predict, but which will always involve overtime. Most organizations set aside a certain amount of the personnel costs for overtime. The organization must determine what is an acceptable level of overtime and how the organization will fund the overtime. In some cases, organizations have adjusted work hours to overcome anticipated overtime costs. In one community, the recreation maintenance crew members modified their hours from mid-December through mid-February to accommodate a six-day week for maintaining outdoor ice rinks.

### Contractual Service Requirements

A growing option in public, private not-for-profit, and commercial organizations is contractual services. The growth of contractual services is base in part on the belief that some functions can be done more effectively and efficiently at a lower cost by outside vendors. Whole communities have embraced the concept of contracting out services. The City of Indianapolis, Indiana, leases its golf courses to independent contractors. Every organization has some form of contractual arrangement, even if it is only with the copy machine repair person. The level and extent of contractual management is not typically an issue in the budget process. At some policy level, the decision (and action) to become involved in contractual management was made. If the organization has not made the decision about contracting for services, then the budget preparation process provides an opportunity to make a determination. Issues needing resolution include the following: comparative costs between the sport, tourism, leisure service organization accomplishing the task versus a commercial contractor; presence of qualified contractor personnel; actual cost, impact upon the organization's productivity; and quality of work. Some of the common types of services privatized or contracted out include park

---

## Partnerships Provide Income for Capital Improvements in New York City Parks

New York City has over 27,000 acres of parks, but for 20 years has seen a steady decline in park employees, operating budgets, and capital budgets. A number of support groups are actively engaged in supporting public parks.

The parks department has actively sought out partners to alleviate reduced funding levels. In late 2006, the parks department announced a cooperative agreement with a local sports foundation for a near-exclusive use of Randall's Island park and its ball fields for 20 private schools. The sports foundation, working on behalf of the private schools, is contributing $85.5 million over 30 years to help upgrade and maintain the fields.

The sports foundation, organized in 1992, has previously contributed $42 million for a track and field stadium and run free summer and weekend programs for thousands of children in the communities of East Harlem and the South Bronx. The foundation is one of 20 such groups the parks department works with on an annual basis, and it is projected that the department receives $60 to $70 million annually.

The New York example, while large, is typical of what public agencies are doing across the Untied States.

---

maintenance, golf course management, landscape maintenance, tree trimming, fleet (trucks and vehicles) maintenance, animal and pest control, building maintenance, janitorial services, refuse collection, and security services.

In San Jose, California, the decision to become involved in public-private competition began in late 1996. The argument for public-private competition is that the public sector should be competitive with the private sector in both cost and quality. It does not necessarily involve the replacement of public workers with private workers. In San Jose, the effort focused on "maximizing the value of services for the public, rather than on deciding which sector ultimately delivers the service" (San Jose, 1997). The process includes contracting in, as well as contracting out. In fiscal year 1996, San Jose contracted to external contractors about 25 percent of its operating budget, or $250 million. In establishing the public-private competition, the city also established criteria for each service that it considered for competition. An important part of the competitive model was to ensure that employees were not threatened by the new process and that they had the opportunity to bid on privatized projects.

### Materials, Supplies, and Equipment Costs

Materials and supplies that are not part of the capital budget comprise the second most costly item in most operating budgets. Budget managers determine the type, quantity, and quality of material required to carry out annual work plans. Organizations take into account issues such as present inventories, cost, annual use levels, any patterns in changing use or provision of services, new programs and services, etc. The organization usually begins with an assessment of what was purchased during the previous year and whether it was sufficient to accomplish the required tasks. Program reports, year-end reports, and inventories provide some of this information. Proposed work plans are compared with the previous year's work plans to determine changes in anticipated needs. If standards have been established for programs or services, or if they exist and are modified, those standards may affect the need for materials and supplies.

Projected inventories assist in providing another picture of material and supply needs. Many organizations have adopted a just-in-time delivery process in which the supplier provides storage and delivers on call. For example, one park district determined it needed 30,000 pounds of seed for the entire year. In previous years, it had purchased seed on three separate occasions. Consolidating into a single purchase and requiring the supplier to maintain the inventory reduced the cost significantly and eliminated the need for the park district to provide long-term storage requirements. The purchase was negotiated so payment was made only when seed was delivered. Thirty thousand pounds was the guaranteed purchase at a guaranteed price.

Where purchasing departments are nonexistent, it is incumbent upon the sport, tourism, or leisure service organization to participate in well-formulated purchasing. The establishment of standing purchase orders with local vendors is a common strategy for maintenance operations. Larger purchases are typically bid to a number of potential vendors and may or may not be a part of the capital budget. A set of specifications is established for each purchase item and used as a guide for the vendor to make a bid. Careful development of the specifications is essential, as well as an effort to ensure that bias is removed from the purchasing process. There is rarely a requirement that an organization take the low bid, but when not taking the low bid, the organization must demonstrate that the higher bid more closely conforms to the advertised specifications. When the organization must go to bid is typically determined by statute and also by the legislative/policy body.

Equipment purchases defined as capital equipment include items with a longer life span (greater than one year) including fitness equipment, pitching machines, computers, lawn mowers, trucks, sailboats, rental bicycles, and cars. In almost every situation, the equipment has a specific life span, after which it requires replacement. In preparing the equipment portion of the budget, the sport, tourism, or leisure service organization needs to ensure there is an inventory of all equipment. The inventory should include date of purchase, classification code of the equipment, description of the item, purchase price, its current location, current condition (which may require an annual or more frequent inspection), and life expectancy. For some pieces of equipment, the BPO may desire to establish a replacement schedule. A re-placement schedule allows the budget preparation officer to look forward and anticipate major equipment costs for the organization. Some organizations set aside money every year for replacement of equipment into a capital replacement fund. This strategy reduces the impact on the annual budgets for major purchases occurring during one fiscal year. Equally important is the spreading of major purchases over several years, rather than trying to make all purchases in a single year.

### Reviewing Budget Estimates at the Departmental Level

While the CEO must ultimately accept responsibility for the final budget document, it is the formal and informal processes that contribute to development of the final submitted document. Throughout the process, there is a continuous flow of information up and down the organization, exchanges of detailed data, analyses of decisions regarding the budget, etc. Each budget manager should meet with the BPO and the CEO and brief them on his or her section of the budget document. The CEO should provide a completed budget presentation for the sport, tourism, or leisure service organization's budget managers and then answer questions. This final review assures that all of the issues associated with the budget's preparation have been discussed and the document is ready to be submitted to the legislative or policy-setting body.

## Summary

Budgeting is an essential management tool in any sport, tourism, and park and recreation organization and requires an understanding of how budgets work, of basic budgeting processes, and of how managers use budgets. The budget cycle, budget calendar, and budget guidelines drive the budgeting process for sport, tourism, and leisure service organization

administrators. A knowledge of funds and how they operate contributes to the ability of managers to allocate appropriate resources. Budget formats are prescribed by the legislative or policy body and determine how they choose to look at budgets. Corresponding budget preparation philosophies suggest an approach to budgeting ranging from fixed ceiling to alternative budget proposals. The 18-month to two-year planning cycle for any budget allows a sport, tourism, or leisure service organization to plan, approve, implement, and close a budget. A manager's ability to estimate budget costs increases with experience, but knowing how to prepare an activity budget is the critical foundation for all budget processes in sport, tourism, and leisure service organizations.

## References

Edginton, C., & Williams, J. (1978.) *Productive management of leisure service organizations.* Hoboken, NJ: John Wiley & Sons Inc.

City of San Jose. (1997.) http://www.sanjoseca. gov/quest/sjpolicy.htm

## NOTES

# CHAPTER 15

# Budget Formats

## Introduction

Budget preparation is a two-stage process. Establishing budget guidelines and determining the budget format are essential tasks. There are multiple budget formats that an organization can select. Each sport, tourism, or leisure service organization must determine the format that is appropriate for its needs. A commercial or not-for-profit organization may select a format that meets its unique needs, but the format for public organizations is more likely dictated by legislation. A board of directors or a legislative/policy board may establish a different format consistent with its own needs, and a large organization may specify multiple budget formats, each with a different purpose and linked by a unit budget. This chapter looks at the most common budget formats that organizations use.

## Common Budget Formats

Budgets can be presented in a variety of formats, but the choice is typically dependent upon the organization's CEO's view of how a budget is organized. The purpose of budgeting is to secure financial control and to achieve the goals, mission, and vision for the organization. Additionally, managerial productivity is seen as an important outcome of budgeting. The type of approach adopted by a sport, tourism, or leisure service organization is a reflection of how the legislative or policy body best feels the organization should achieve its goals. Different types of budget formats reflect an emphasis upon different goals. For example, an object classification or line item budget focuses on financial control. Program and performance budgets focus on goal attainment. Zero-based budgeting and planning-programming budgeting systems focus on managerial productivity. The CEO and the budget preparation officer should determine the level of detail necessary in any budget format. Six of the most common operating budget formats are presented in this chapter. They are representative of formats found in most sport, tourism, and leisure service organizations.

## Object Classification and Line Item Budgets

The object classification and line item budgets are the most common of all budget formats used to by sport, tourism, and leisure service organizations. Both styles of budgets, for example, rely on a coding system for all revenue and expenditure items. In this section, primary emphasis is given to the object classification budget, although the same principles can be used for a line item budget. An object classification or a line item budget organizes budgets into predetermined categories. Each line in the budget reflects either an expenditure or a class of expenditures. For example, "personnel costs" becomes a class with sub-classifications. Sub-classifications might include types of personnel (program, maintenance, support, full-time, and part-time). "Benefit costs" is another class that can be subdivided into accounts, such as medical, retirement fund, and uniforms. The emphasis in the object classification budget is on input rather than measurement. Conformance and compliance with an established budget is paramount to understanding how the funds are being used or collected. Construction of an object classification budget involves four steps, but before initiating the budget construction, specific information must be gathered. The data to be gathered were addressed in Chapter 14 and are partially repeated here. In

an object classification budget, the organization commonly uses a fixed ceiling approach to allocation. Preparation items include: (1) budget letter with guidelines from the legislative authority; (2) approved budget growth (usually in percent of allowed growth of current budget); (3) list of classification codes (this can run to many pages); (4) personnel salary ranges and steps; (5) specific or unusual budget request issues; and (6) budget forms. Items 1, 2, 4, and 5 will be common to most budget formats.

### Step 1: Collect all budget data.

Begin by collecting all budget data from the organization's budget managers. The assignment of budget data collection should be delegated to the lowest possible level. Budget managers should complete as much of the budget process themselves for familiarity purposes. The budget preparation officer will ultimately check all information provided.

### Step 2: Identify appropriate classification codes for each budget item.

The classification codes and budget forms will be unique to the object classification budget. The list of lines or classification codes is given to the budget preparation officer and budget managers who must ensure that each item in the budget conforms to the existing codes. The list of codes can be many pages long and will have definitions to assist the budget manager as he or she attempts to determine which item fits within a particular code. Examples of expenditure classification codes and definitions appear in Table 15.1.

### Step 3: Place items in detailed sub-classifications (object codes).

Assignment of expenditure and revenue items to classification object codes, as depicted in Table 15.1, is followed by placing the same items into more detailed expenditure and revenue object codes (Table 15.2). Recall that the purpose of the object classification budget is to provide financial control. Placing each expenditure and revenue item into a detailed sub-classification allows the CEO and the budget preparation officer to have a clear and detailed understanding of the total budget and where the money is going to be spent. It allows multiyear tracking of revenues and expenditures for comparative and evaluative purposes. The advantage of this type of a budget format lies in the CEO's ability to be aware of subtle, as well as major, shifts in the budget.

The amount of detail desired determines how many object codes the organization will utilize. An organization that is not concerned about budget detail may have few object codes, while an organization that is trying to gain control of its expenditures may require very detailed coding. One park and recreation director noted that almost 50 percent of the department's expenditures were coded as "miscellaneous." Upon investigation, it became obvious that no one had previously shown a concern about tracking expenditures. When it was explained to the organization's members that the goal

### Table 15.1
### Example object classification codes and definitions

| | |
|---|---|
| 100 | **Personnel Services** – Expenditures for direct personnel services including wages, benefits, overtime, special benefits, and the like. Includes full-time, part-time, and seasonal employees. |
| 200 | **Contractual Services** – Services involving work performance by non-organization employees through a contract or agreement. The work may include the contractor to provide equipment and commodities. |
| 230 | **Printing Services** – Expenses related to printing, copying, reproduction, binding, publications, advertising, and the like. |
| 240 | **Utilities** – Charges for heat, water, electricity, telephone, cable or satellite television, network connections, 2-way radio, and so forth. |
| 250 | **Repairs** – All repairs for fixed structures. Includes building repair, but does not include repairs to vehicles, equipment, and expandable items. |
| 300 | **Commodities** |
| 310 | **Materials** – Items more permanent in nature that may be combined or converted for other uses. Includes lumber, concrete, concrete blocks, paint, and other building materials. |
| 320 | **Supplies** – A commodity consumed, impaired, or worn out in an expectedly short period of time. Includes such items as paper, crafts, supplies, food, clothing, fuel, oil, grass seed, fertilizer, and so forth. |
| 400 | **Encumbered Obligations** – Fixed expenses and/or binding contracts created from previous obligations of the legislative authority. Included in this category could be temporary loans, interest on a city's debt, grants and subsidiaries, court ordered payments, and the like. |
| 500 | **Existing Charges** – Provided at the option of legislative authority. It could include costs of insurance, licenses, rent, leases, and the like. |
| 600 | **Debt Payment** – Includes the amount of annual payment for reduction on debt incurred by the legislative authority. |

**Table 15.2**
**Example classification codes by object (partial listing)**

| | |
|---|---|
| 100 - **Personnel** | 252 - Repairs to Buildings/Structures |
| 110 - Salaries, Regular | 253 - Repairs to Playgrounds, Equipment and |
| 120 - Salaries, Temporary | Services |
| 130 - Salaries, Seasonal | 300 - **Commodities** |
| 140 - Salaries, Permanent Part Time | 310 - *Materials* |
| 200 - **Services, Contractual** | 311 - Masonry |
| 210 - *Communications* | 312 - Road Materials |
| 211 - Postage | 313 - Lumber |
| 212 - Telephone | 314 - Paint |
| 213 - FedEx, UPS, Freight | 315 - Sand |
| 214 - Internet Communications | 316 - Other Materials |
| 215 - In State Travel | 320 - *Supplies* |
| 216 - Out of State Travel | 321 - Office Supplies |
| 220 - *Subsistence, Care & Support* | 322 - Program Supplies |
| 221 - Storage & Care of Vehicles | 323 - Sport Supplies |
| 222 - Per Diem - In State | 324 - Craft Supplies |
| 230 - **Printing Services** | 325 - Aquatic Supplies |
| 231 - Printing | 326 - Food Supplies |
| 232 - Photocopying | 327 - Clothing & Dry Goods |
| 233 - Wordprocessing | 328 - Chemicals, All Kinds |
| 234 - Photography | 400 - **Encumbered Obligations** |
| 236 - Marketing/Advertising | 410 - *Rent* |
| 237 - Publication of Notices | 411 - Buildings & Spaces |
| 238 - Blueprints/Plans/RFPs | 412 - Equipment & Vehicles |
| 240 - **Utilities** | 420 - Insurance |
| 241 - Natural Gas Utilities | 500 - **Existing Charges** |
| 242 - Propane | 510 - Interest of Debt |
| 243 - Electrical Utilities, Outdoor | 520 - Pensions & Retirement |
| 244 - Electrical Utilities, Indoor | 530 - Grants & Subsidies |
| 245 - Water Utilities | 540 - Taxes |
| 246 - Sewer Service | 600 - **Debt Payment** |
| 247 - Telephone Service | 610 - Serial Bonds |
| 248 - Network Connections | 620 - General Obligation Bonds |
| 250 - **Repairs** | 630 - Revenue Bonds |
| 251 - Repairs to Equipment | 640 - Sinking Fund Installments |
| | 650 - Other Debt Payment |

was to gain a better understanding of expenditures, the director refused to accept miscellaneous classifications, and expenditure control and knowledge of expenditures increased significantly. The object classification codes shown in Tables 15.1 and 15.2 are illustrative extracts from much larger documents.

Figure 15.1 illustrates how an object classification code is used. In this case, the first two numbers represent the department, such as the parks and recreation or the convention center. The middle four numbers represent the expenditure

classification code (Table 15.2), which describes where the money was spent. This can also be a revenue object code. The last four digits represent the program area (e.g., sports, recreation centers, office administration) and specific programs. This might include the sport program area and its programs of softball, volleyball, and flag football. Codes can allow highly detailed analyses of budgets.

The code in Figure 15.1 could be interpreted to represent the Parks and Recreation Department [24] purchasing art

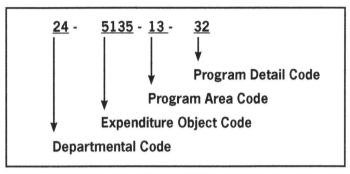

**Figure 15.1**
**Object classification code**

supplies [5135] for the arts program [13] pottery classes [32]. Expenditures identified down to the program detail provide budget managers with a clear picture of costs of programs and allow managers to make fiscal decisions based on relevant information. The object classification budget can function simultaneously with other budget formats.

*Step 4: Organize the budget information.*

Work at this stage involves collating the collected budget information, checking and verifying budget requests, organizing data for a budget review, making recommendations regarding budget allocations, and presenting the budget to the legislative body for approval.

Table 15.3 illustrates a traditional object classification budget for an aquatics program. The budget is combined with all other activity budgets in the agency to provide a total budget picture for the legislative body. The budget provided to the legislative body would provide the level of detail seen in Table 15.3, and a summary table representing all of the budget areas as depicted in Table 15.4.

The budget request is presented showing: (1) the previous fiscal year actual; (2) the current fiscal year approved,; and (3) the proposed fiscal year request (Tables 15.3 and 15.4). The terms used to present each fiscal year are important. In the case of Tables 15.3 and 15.4, the "last year actual" represents the expenditures for that fiscal year. The fiscal year is complete, and all of the expenditures have been reported and recorded. The current fiscal year approved indicates the budget that is in process and is called "this year projected." The legislative body has approved the budget, but because the fiscal year is not complete, there is only an estimate of what the actual budget will look like at the conclusion of the fiscal year. This picture of the budget is incomplete, but has been reported on the basis of anticipated revenues and expenditures. The proposed fiscal year is called "next year requested." At this point, the legislative body has not approved the proposed budget. Until it is approved, it remains a requested budget.

The object classification budget is the most common of all budget types. It is malleable enough to be used with other budget formats. This flexibility allows the sport, tourism, or leisure service organization to maintain fiscal control and simultaneously administer the budget in other formats in order to accomplish other objectives.

Table 15.3
Partial object classification/line item budget

| Object Code | Description | Last Year Actual | This Year Projected | Next Year Requested |
|---|---|---|---|---|
| 100 | Personnel | | | |
| 110 | Salaries, Permanent Full-Time | $35,242 | $37,568 | $38,556 |
| 120 | Salaries, Temporary | $2,500 | $1,850 | $3,240 |
| 130 | Salaries, Part-time | $67,561 | $72,558 | $75,042 |
| 200 | Services: Contractual | | | |
| 220 | Subsistence & Support | | | |
| 221 | Storage & Care of Vehicles | $250 | $325 | $380 |
| 328 | Chemicals, Pool | $2,785 | $3,200 | $3,540 |
| 322 | Program Supplies | $986 | $1,100 | $1,250 |
| | *Concession Supplies* | | | |
| 326 | Snack Bar Supplies | $2,250 | $2,685 | $2,100 |
| 328 | Cleaning Supplies (Chemicals) | $250 | $250 | $285 |
| 252 | Repair Concession Counter | $0 | $0 | $2,500 |
| | *Other Supplies* | | | |
| 322 | First Aid Kits | $250 | $310 | $365 |
| 323 | Sports Awards - Patches | $185 | $200 | $225 |
| 235 | Flotation Devices | $450 | $250 | $520 |
| 240 | Utilities | | | |
| 241 | Natural Gas | $1,100 | $1,250 | $1,400 |
| 244 | Electricity | $1,150 | $1,500 | $1,850 |
| 247 | Telephone | $1,200 | $1,300 | $1,400 |
| 248 | Internet Connection | $75 | $100 | $115 |
| 420 | Insurance | | | |
| 421 | Fire & Comprehensive | $850 | $1,000 | $1,200 |
| 422 | Liability | $4,500 | $6,500 | $7,200 |
| 230 | Printing Services | | | |
| 236 | Marketing | $35,000 | $42,000 | $51,000 |
| 235 | Web Site Design | $2,500 | $1,500 | $3,200 |
| 231 | Printing, Brochures | $12,000 | $15,000 | $18,000 |
| | Total | $171,084 | $190,446 | $214,368 |

## Program Budget

Program budgeting is also called the program planning budgeting system (PPBS). Traditional budgeting formats focus on input (personnel, program, and capital costs), but program budgeting focuses on outputs (end results, goals, and objectives). The emphasis of program budgeting is upon effectiveness rather than efficiency or spending. This emphasis represents a major shift in the way budgets have historically been constructed. The major advantage of the program budget is its ability to cross departmental or divisional boundaries when budgeting for a program with expenditures from more than one department. Program budgeting has fallen into disfavor at the

Table 15.4
Summary budget data

| Object Code | Description | Last Year Actual | This Year Projected | Next Year Requested |
|---|---|---|---|---|
| 100 | Personnel | $102,893 | $110,126 | $114,314 |
| 200 | Servcies, Contractual | $1,072 | $4,100 | $4,500 |
|  | Utilities | $1,072 | $1,164 | $1,425 |
|  | Insurance | $3,625 | $3,871 | $4,125 |
|  | Marketing | $14,343 | $16,250 | $17,500 |
| 300 | Supplies & Equipment | $8,747 | $9,954 | $12,336 |
|  | Total | $131,752 | $145,465 | $154,200 |

federal level, but has flourished at the state, municipal, not-for-profit, and commercial levels. The emphasis on outcomes and measurement has been received positively by administrators and the consuming public alike. Recent initiatives and trends in output measurement through goals and objectives, public surveys, satisfaction determination, and benchmarking have all contributed to the acceptance of program budgeting.

A program budget takes expenditures and breaks them down into viewable units according to the service provided. For example, the object classification budget looks at the entire budget, but not at programs. It provides no understanding of how or why funds are to be expended. The program budget provides more information to the budget manager and others who have a desire to know how the allocated funds will be expended. The budget is subdivided into program areas, and each program area is reported as a separate part of the budget. For program managers, this separation provides greater authority and accountability. Their decisions are reflected in their management of their portion of the budget. Figure 15.2 depicts how a program budget format might be organized. A program budget is organized to provide details to the pro-

gram manager, the administrators, and the legislative/policy body.

The department represents the level of budget authority and responsibility. At this level, the department or division refines the organization's vision, mission, and major goals to fit programs. The program areas are aimed at specific goals, or in the example of many sport, tourism, and leisure service organizations, program-specific areas (or populations). Programs are designed to meet more specific population needs; they are also referred to as support activities. They emphasize the importance of focusing on who is to benefit from the service or program. Program elements represent the basis that budget units use to achieve the goals and objectives of the organization. Consistent with the budgeting process is the development of goals and objectives at each level of the structure. Examples of goals and objectives developed for the adult sports tennis program in Figure 15.2 are represented in Figure 15.3.

The development of program budgeting has necessitated the rethinking of how budgets are administered. Moving decision making and budget administration down to the lowest levels of the organization fostered a new set of concepts and terms, such as *cost centers*. Cost cen-

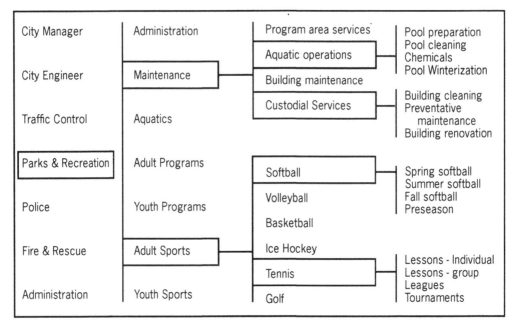

**Figure 15.2**
**Example program budget**

Department of Parks and Recreation
    Goal: To provide recreational services and opportunities for leisure experiences for all members
        of the community.

Program Area: Adult Sports
    Goal: To provide opportunities for adults to participate in life-time sport, promoting physical and
    mental well-being.

Program: Tennis
    Goal: To increase the opportunity for members of the community to be exposed to and to
        participate in tennis programs
    Objective:  Provide opportunities for individual lessons.
            Provide opportunities for group lessons.
            Provide leagues for individual and team participation.
            Provide tournaments for local, regional, and state level participation.

Program Element: Individual Lessons
    Goal: To provide opportunities for individuals to improve their tennis game through individualized
        instruction.
    Output Measures: Number of individuals participating in lessons.
            Number of individuals returning from previous sessions/years.
            Effectiveness of lessons as measured by participant satisfaction survey.
            Cost-effectiveness of program.

**Figure 15.3**
**Program budget goals and objectives for Figure 15.2**

ters comprise an independent entity embracing all of the costs of activities and items necessary to achieve a distinct and measurable outcome. Operating funds for the cost center may come from several divisions or departments. When expenditures are made, they are charged back to the parent budget authority, but the cost center identification remains consistent. Assuming softball is a cost center, the maintenance division will fund softball field maintenance and preparation and charge it back to adult sports. In an object classification budget, field maintenance and preparation would only appear as an expenditure that's not necessarily tied to a program area. In a program budget, with softball as a cost center, the cost of maintenance and preparation is linked to both the program area and the maintenance division. Maintenance knows how much it is spending overall and how much it is spending just for softball.

For the budget manager who may have previously budgeted only for staff and program supplies, he or she now has a clear picture of the total cost of the program, including salaries, supplies, maintenance, marketing, and administration.

The new concept of *responsibility centers* (also called budget decision points) has also been introduced. The term indicates a focus on budget analysis and decision making. A responsibility center manager knows each program budget's cross-functional boundaries within and between divisions and departments. Program managers with cost center responsibilities make decisions regarding budget allocations within the context of their authority and negotiate with other responsibility center managers for additional resources. For example, if the budget manager for softball determines that maintenance costs need to be in-

creased substantially, he or she cannot arbitrarily make that decision. Rather, the cost center budget manager must discuss the issue with the functional area budget manager. In this case, the adult sports supervisor will discuss the issue with the maintenance superintendent.

*Step 1: Goals and objectives.*

Step 1 assumes the organization is already organized around program areas of functions, as illustrated in Figure 15.3. This suggests that program managers and functional area budget managers are already talking to one another. The sport, tourism, or leisure service organization develops goals and objectives for the fiscal year that can be a continuation from previous years, updated, modified, or completely new for each fiscal year. Program managers develop goals and objectives for each level of the program budget, down to program detail. Desired outcomes are determined in advance, as well as decisions about methods of measurement.

*Step 2: Provide detailed narrative for each program.*

Program areas were identified in step 1. In step 2, the program manager will identify those features of the program that meet specific goals and objectives. The program manager further explains how and why each is important. The narrative relates to the program's goals and objectives.

*Step 3: Determine expenditures and revenue for the program.*

Using the processes discussed regarding the preparation of a simple activity budget (see Chapter 13), the budget is adjusted to a program budget format. In those areas where measurements are defined, the expenditures will be tied to specific objectives.

Table 15.5 illustrates a completed aquatics program budget. Presenting revenue plans is accomplished in the same way; however, revenues are not necessarily tied to objectives. The budget presented in Table 15.5 depicts a program budget with objectives, a narrative, measurement criteria, and income and expenditure expectations. Although each sport, tourism, and leisure service organization will have its own format for developing a program budget, each will follow a similar pattern. The components remain remarkably similar, with an emphasis on outcomes rather than inputs.

## Performance Budget

A performance budget is frequently referred to as a measurement of efficiency. It is most frequently used with recurring tasks, where measurements can be readily developed and applied. Performance budgeting became popular with municipal governments in the early 1950s and remains in use today. It fits well into operations where repetition and measurement can be made easily, such as certain repetitive maintenance functions (e.g., mowing, grounds maintenance, and custodial work). One of the benefits of a performance budget is its ability to provide managers with performance-cost data. Although the development of measurement data is beyond the scope of this book, it requires an assessment of what work needs to be accomplished, what equipment is available to do the work, and capabilities of employees to accomplish the task. It requires a constant assessment and monitoring of the measurement performance standards by managers.

*Step 1: Identify those components of the budget that fit a performance format.*
The budget preparation officer must

determine which of the organization's operations are most conducive to a performance budget format. These operations should meet the following criteria: (1) It should be possible for the work to be quantified into measurable work units; (2) it should be possible for the quality of the provided service or activity to be measured; and (3) the performance should be able to hold constant. Examples of work that can be easily quantified include mowing, tree planting, fertilizing, ball diamond preparation, and most grounds maintenance activities, construction activities, and some custodial work.

*Step 2: Establish work units.*
For each activity that will be measured, work units must be established. This is accomplished by measuring current work levels, benchmarking work activities against the same work accomplished by similar organizations, and looking at standards established by various measurement organizations. In the early stages of establishing standards, flexibility is important until an achievable and acceptable standard is determined. Work units are normally measured in performance per hour, although they can be established in other ways. Examples of measurements include square feet per item, cubic yards, acres, sales per advertising campaign, revenue per available room (RevPAR), etc. A grass-mowing crew using hand mowers may have a work unit established as .75 acres per hour. The same crew using gang mowers may have a standard of 4.5 acres per hour.

*Step 3: Determine the cost per work unit to be measured.*
The cost per work unit is based on a number of variables, which include the task to be completed, the capabilities of the employees, the cost of expendable

**Table 15.5**
**Example program budget**

| Program: Aquatics |
| --- |
| *Program Description:* The aquatics program is designed to provide recreational opportunities, competitive opportunities, and learn-to-swim lessons to residents. |
| *Performance Objectives:*<br>1. Provide open swim opportunities for all members of the community.<br>2. Increase the number of program offerings by 5% over the previous year.<br>3. Achieve a 90% positive satisfaction rating from participants in all programs. |

| Measurement | Program | Objective | 2007 Actual | 2008 Projected | 2009 Proposed |
| --- | --- | --- | --- | --- | --- |
| *Demand* | | | | | |
| Estimated Participants | Open Swim | 1 | 38,146 | 45,000 | 47,600 |
| | Other Swim | 1 | 9,877 | 10,000 | 10,500 |
| | Learn-to-Swim | 1 | 2,300 | 2,600 | 2,800 |
| Estimated Programs | | 2 | 30 | 45 | 47 |
| *Workload* | | | | | |
| Actual Registrations | Open Swim | 1 | 38,166 | 45,000 | 47,600 |
| | Other Swim | 1 | 9,877 | 10,000 | 10,500 |
| | Learn-to-Swim | 1 | 2,300 | 2,600 | 2,800 |
| Actual Programs | | 2 | 30 | 45 | 47 |
| Actual Participation | | 2 | 50,353 | 57,645 | 60,947 |
| Total Community Population | | | 110,000 | 110,000 | 110,000 |
| *Productivity* | | | | | |
| Average cost per participant | | | $2.67 | $2.51 | $2.52 |
| Average cost per participation | | | $2.67 | $2.51 | $2.52 |
| *Effectiveness* | | | | | |
| Program participation increase/decrease over previous year | | | 0.00% | 14.48% | 5.73% |
| Program offerings increase/decrease over previous year | | | 0.00% | 50.0% | 4.44% |
| Participant percentage positive rating | | | 88.00% | 88.00% | 90.00% |
| Percent Total Population Served | | | 45.78% | 52.40% | 55.41% |
| *Narrative* | | | | | |
| The aquatics program serves a variety of populations in the community, including people with disabilities, adults, seniors, and pre-school and school-age youth. | | | | | |
| *Resources* | | | | | |
| Expenditure categories | Personnel | | $102,893 | $110,126 | $115,200 |
| | Operations/Maintenance and Supplies | | $13,590 | $15,038 | $16,800 |
| | Insurance | | $3,488 | $3,600 | $3,800 |
| | Marketing | | $14,354 | $16,200 | $18,000 |
| | SUBTOTAL | | $134,325 | $144,964 | $153,800 |
| Revenues | General | | $15,600 | $15,000 | $16,000 |
| | Fees & Charges | | $105,314 | $109,964 | $115,000 |
| | Donations & Grants | | $13,368 | $20,000 | $25,000 |
| | SUBTOTAL | | $134,282 | $144,964 | $156,000 |

supplies and special equipment, the depreciation of equipment, and travel time and distance. The budget preparation officer looks at all of the variables that affect the work unit and establishes a cost standard. For a mowing crew that travels throughout the city, the cost standard would include travel time between sites, salaries of the mowing crew, cost of gasoline for travel and mowing equipment, maintenance costs of equipment, actual time spent on site mowing, and other associated costs of the task. Assume an 18-acre park has 10 acres of open area suitable for a gang mower; four acres that require hand mowing with a 42-inch mower; and two acres that call for 22-inch hand mowers. Two acres are not mowed. The mowing crew takes an average of 2.5 hours to accomplish the task. The cost of personnel is $26.00 an hour and other costs are figured at $10.00 per hour, with an additional 30 minutes assigned for travel. Three people work on the mowing crew. After a period of assessment and evaluation, the following standards are established:

- Gang mowing at 8 acres per hour.
- 42-inch hand mowing at 2.2 acres per hour.
- 22-inch hand mowing at .75 acres per hour.

Sufficient time is available to accomplish all of the tasks, except the 22-inch hand mowing. Either the standard, the time available for the work, or the equipment must be modified.

*Step 4: Determine the frequency with which work must be completed.*

Determining costs is, in part, a decision on how frequently particular work needs to be completed. Frequency of recurring tasks and of annual tasks is based on need and the level of quality assigned to a particular task. Using the mowing example, the standard for cutting is that the grass will be cut when it reaches six inches in height. In a normal year, that would be every ten days from late April through mid-October. If, however, it rains more than normal, the grass will grow more quickly, and mowing may occur every eight days instead of every ten. This alteration will require a budget adjustment. It will also require a workload adjustment, as the mowing crew will not be able to accomplish other tasks that may have been assigned to them. Just the opposite would occur in a low-rain year, when mowing might only occur on demand, maybe as infrequently as every three weeks. More than likely, the mowing crew's responsibilities would change, and they might have to water new trees and turf areas to preserve them through a drought. At best, the budget manager must work on what he or she believes will occur. In those activities not affected by weather, the budget planning can be more accurate, but nonetheless, the budget manager must recognize that things will not always go as planned.

*Step 5: Organize budget.*

When all of the performance budget steps are completed, the budget manager or budget preparation officer compiles the budget. Table 15.6 depicts a sample format for a performance budget.

## New Directions in Performance Budgets

In recent years, public agencies have made major advances in quantifying outcomes. While performance budgeting follows the same process previously described, it is also linked to strategic planning. One of the key elements of a performance budget is its collection of adequate

**Table 15.6**
**Performance budget format**

| Activity | Work Unit | Cost per Work Unit | Number of Work Units | Frequency | Number of Times | Total Cost |
|---|---|---|---|---|---|---|
| Softball diamond preparation | per diamond | $9.45 | 18 | daily | 98 | $16,669.90 |
| Gang mowing | per acre | $4.45 | 800 | 10 days | 12 | $42,720.00 |
| Hand mowing | per acre | $7.25 | 120 | 10 days | 12 | $10,440.00 |
| Tree planting | per tree | $12.85 | 1200 | once a year | 1 | $15,420.00 |
| Pool cleaning | per pool | $32.50 | 3 | 7 days | 18 | $1,755.00 |
| Trash pickup | per day | $26.50 | 2 | daily | 275 | $14,575.00 |
| Sign installation | per sign | $21.50 | 40 | as required | 1 | $860.00 |
| Total | | | | | | $102,439.80 |

performance data, and while this collection is routinely done in the private sector, it is an approach that is relatively new to the public sector. Results have been less than convincing to many budget managers, but processes continue to be refined. The key difference in performance-based budgeting is the asking of a different set of questions. In traditional object classification budgeting, budget managers ask what it will take to complete a particular task. In performance budgeting, the first question asked is, "What is the outcome to be achieved?" The outcomes become the basis for performance measures. For example, the question might be, "How many softball teams will play in the summer?" The outcomes are defined through a modified strategic planning process that considers the critical issues facing the agency, along with the organization's capabilities and input from stakeholders.

Minnesota's state government reported that it had been involved in performance budgets off and on for 25 years, but only recently has the system been reintroduced and begun to show success. Even with the performance mandate for recent budgets, the state determined that many agencies reported existing data in new ways to emphasize performance, although agencies usually did not provide outcome-based rationales when making proposals for new spending initiatives. It was expected that "It will likely take time for agencies to develop a consensus on appropriate measures of performance and collect reliable supporting data" (Minnesota Report on Performance Budgeting). Most public administrators agree that performance budgeting is a growing trend in public and private agencies and that measurement techniques will be refined.

### Running Budget

A running budget has become more common among not-for-profit organizations and businesses, as they attempt to adjust budgets to changing revenue streams. The running budget reflects more of a way of managing expenditures than it does constructing a budget. The budget can be constructed in any format, but decisions about expenditures are made on a scheduled basis throughout the fiscal year. If revenues exceed expectations, the budget can be adjusted to reflect the increased revenue. If revenues decline, the budget can be reduced to accommodate the decreased income.

There are some distinct disadvantages to this type of budget. First, budget managers never know from day to day exactly what their budget will be. Second, good decision making is hampered when the focus of decisions appears to be on revenue rather than on needs. Third, budget managers may be encouraged to make big purchases early to ensure that their major items are secured. This can lead to a mind-set in the organization that is not conducive to stability or growth.

On the positive side, a running budget allows an organization that experiences negative financial growth to be responsive to that situation by appropriately reducing costs. In addition, the organization does not extend itself beyond its capabilities and also recognizes a responsibility to its legislative body and to its constituents by not incurring debt. This type of budget is most often seen in organizations experiencing or anticipating significant declines in funds available for the operating budget.

*Step 1: Construct the operating budget.*

Any budget format can be used, whether it is an object classification, line item, program, or performance budget. The principles for construction are similar to those for any of the other budget formats. As just noted, the change comes in the administration of the budget. When the budget preparation is complete, it is submitted to the legislative body for review, modification, and ultimate adoption.

*Step 2: Determine frequency of budget reporting.*

The essence of the running budget is that it helps the organization to always know the status of its expenditures and revenues and to make adjustments in authorized expenditures. Adjusting expenditures at multiple times during the fiscal year allows the organization to adjust its budget when revenues are uncertain. Adjustments can occur on a daily, weekly, biweekly, monthly, or quarterly basis. The decision of frequency will be determined in great part by the anticipated variance in revenues and how often revenues are received. A historical analysis provides a great deal of information for making this decision. If it is a membership-based organization, and membership dues are received on a scheduled basis, anticipated revenues might be predetermined. If, for example, dues statements are sent out quarterly, then the organization can project on a quarterly basis its progress toward achieving its revenue goals. Under these circumstances, it may only be necessary to do a budget adjustment on a quarterly basis.

*Step 3: Establish spending limits.*

Establishing spending limits is a common practice of budget preparation officers as they attempt to lighten the impact of concentrated spending by the organization. In a running budget, it is particularly important. Each part of the organization will need to negotiate levels of spending in any given time period. For example, arbitrarily allowing the different parts of the organization to spend only one-fourth of their budget per quarter does not take into account the special needs of the different parts of the organization. The administrative branch might easily spend one-fourth of its budget each quarter, but the convention division might spend 60 percent of its budget in the second quarter and the other 40 percent over the next three quarters due to normal seasonal fluctuations. Creating an acceptable balance of spending across the different parts of the organization requires a thorough understanding of the budget process. Of necessity, it must be negotiated with the budget managers throughout the organization.

*Step 4: Determine how often the budget will be adjusted.*

Making budget adjustments based on actual revenue and expenditures is the heart of the running budget process. Applying the same criteria discussed in step 2, the legislative/policy body must determine how often the budget will be adjusted. Typically, budget adjustments will be made in both the revenue and expenditure portions of the operating budget. A fiscal quarter (three months) is the most frequently accepted adjustment period; however, in a highly volatile budget situation, adjustments can be made more often. Historical and current information must be provided to the legislative body, along with recommendations for adjustment. A clear rationale should be made for the adjustment, along with a discussion of how the adjustments will affect programs, services, and outcomes.

### Zero-Based Budgeting

A zero-based budget is so named because it assumes that the organization starts each fiscal year as if it doesn't have an existing budget. While this isn't entirely true, its purpose is to allow the sport, tourism, or leisure service organization to look at everything it does and value each activity's importance to the organization and its stakeholders. It allows the organization to look at all of its operations, activities, and functions and to justify each one. In doing so, it promotes the re-allocation of funds from lower priorities to higher priorities. The zero-based budget is an effort to be responsive to changing needs of the organization and of those it serves. This budget format is designed to facilitate competition among units and functions.

### Assumptions of Zero-Based Budgeting

Several assumptions are made about an organization's capability to implement zero-based budgeting. First, it is assumed that the organization can clearly define

*Boards and commissions deliberate over budget recommendations made by the professional staff.*

goals and objectives for the entire organization. This is a sometimes daunting task that requires considerable attention at each level of the organization. Second, it is assumed there is adequate budget preparation time. Zero-based budgeting is a time-consuming task. If the organization's members do not have time to contribute, then it should not be used. Third, it is assumed there is a healthy relationship between units of the organization. There will be an impact upon the morale of the organization, due mostly to increased competition for available budget funds. Fourth, it is assumed that the budget can appropriately be based on internal needs. Zero-based budgeting is internally focused and does not always take into account external needs or requirements. Fifth, zero-based budgeting assumes a significant cost in terms of time, money, and effort as the initial transition is made. There will be ongoing costs for time and effort as the process progresses.

*Step 1: Defining goals and objectives and decision units.*

Program and budget goals and objectives are established and decision units are defined at the program/service level. The development of measurable goals and objectives is based on outcomes and user/customer-defined expectations. Great care must be taken in developing these goals so that effective measurement can occur. Goals are developed at multiple levels and assumed to be part of a top-down process. The organization's goals are developed at the CEO level jointly with the legislative or policy body. These goals become the guiding or overarching goals of the organization. All other goals and objectives developed need to be consistent with these goals. Ultimate measurement of the effectiveness and appropriateness of programs and services will

be based on these goals. At each descending level, goals are developed to provide direction and to ensure consistency.

A decision unit is a point at which budget and programming decisions are made—ideally, at the lowest reasonable level in the organization. In aquatics, for instance, the decision unit may not be the whole aquatics program, but rather, could be divided into learn-to-swim, swim club, adult lessons, and youth lessons. At a later analysis level, these could be combined or remain separate. Budget requests should be based on previously experienced levels of expenditures. To do so reduces the effectiveness and purpose of zero-based budgeting.

Table 15.7 depicts an example decision unit worksheet without the fiscal information. The decision units do not need to be consistent with the organizational structure, but frequently are. In a YMCA, the initial decision unit would likely be at the program manager level. If a program manager has responsibility for multiple program areas, however, the decision unit could be modified. It would seem logical that, wherever possible, the decision unit and organizational structure would be consistent.

*Step 2: Decision assessment and analysis.*

Step 2 involves analyzing and assessing each decision unit within the framework as a *decision package*. The decision package becomes the building block of zero-based budgeting. The decision package is a cluster of decision units related to the accomplishment of the unit's goals and objectives. As the budget process moves up the organization, decision packages can be grouped according to commonality of objectives. This grouping could result in decision units not remaining within the structure of the organiza-

### Table 15.7
### Decision unit worksheet example

| Program Area: Learn-to-Swim | Division: Aquatics | Fiscal Year 2009 |
|---|---|---|
| Level of services currently provided | Justification for current/expanded level of service | Funding Recommendations |
| • Lessons offered throughout the year with an emphasis on summer months<br>• Lessons offered for beginners through advanced swimmers<br>• Lessons offered to pre-school through seniors and people with disabilities<br>• Summer services offered at 11 community pools 3 times a week and 4 times each day<br>• Other seasons offered at 3 indoor pools after school for youth, during the day for seniors and people with disabilities, and evening for adults<br>• Currently meet Red Cross learn-to-swim guidelines | The learn-to-swim program has been offered for over 40 years by the department. Each year more than 5,000 youth and adults are served by the program. It represents the only community-wide program provided. The school district does not provide a program and the YMCA caters to a smaller number of individuals, all members. The program has consistently been revenue positive (paid for itself and generated a profit) in the aquatics division. | It is recommended funding be retained at the current levels. Any reduction in funding would result in a degradation of the program and it has high community support and visibility. It has consistently received high marks from those who participate. In some cases families are in their 3rd generation of participation in swim programs. Revenue levels could be increased if fees are increased. A study to determine the impact of a fee increase is recommended. |

tion. Managers at the program delivery level must look at alternative means of achieving objectives, as well as determining appropriate levels of service and use of resources. The notion of zero-based budgeting is meant to encourage managers to focus their energies on those activities that are perceived as most critical to the organization's mission and vision. Activities that do not directly contribute to the vision and mission are either eliminated or receive reduced levels of funding. Such decisions encourage managers to set up levels of service and to seek alternative funding.

Included in the decision process are variables such as workload, performance measures, cost-benefit associated with each level of service, revenue, and expenditures. Each decision package can receive one of four actions: (1) increased resources, (2) maintenance of current resources, (3) reduced resources, or (4) elimination of resources. Additionally,

decision makers are afforded alternatives to accomplish each decision unit. The alternatives allow decision makers to determine the most appropriate approaches for the delivery and level of services.

*Step 3: Ranking decision packages.*

Once all of the data have been generated, the ranking of decision packages occurs at predetermined levels. Decisions are based on consistency with the organization's goals and objectives, determined cost-effectiveness, how well each decision package meets the needs of the users, availability of funds, and any predetermined policy guidelines. Rankings of decision units are made and funds are allocated to the decision units. Once funds are allocated to decision units, they are returned to the appropriate organizational level for budget action. If a decision unit does not receive the level of funding necessary for sustaining it, the program manager will already have created alternatives for funding at reduced or increased levels, either for different delivery approaches, or for no funding at all. The decision process will put such alternative approaches into action.

*Step 4: Budget request formulated.*

The budget format may be any of the budget formats previously discussed. It is submitted through normal processes to the budget preparation officer and the CEO for final submission to the policy or legislative body.

## Advantages and Disadvantages of Zero-Based Budgeting

There are several advantages to using a zero-based budgeting format. First, in zero-based budgeting, all programs start out on equal footing at the beginning of the process—no single program is favored over another. Programs, services, and functions all have the same opportunity to receive funding. Second, budget decision makers will find that more detailed information is generated than it is with other budget formats. When implemented properly, there is a systematic and well-conceived allocation process. Third, the goals of the organization and its individual and collective activities are under constant review and prioritization. As such, individuals who work in this format are more actively engaged in goal setting, goal attainment, and goal negotiation. Fourth, this budget format provides service level options where none may have existed before. It requires that program managers look at alternative program and service delivery methods and at what level each program or service should be delivered. Finally, it has been suggested that zero-based budgeting eliminates waste in the organization by eliminating or reducing funding for programs that are not meeting the needs

of the organization or its clientele.

A number of disadvantages have been suggested for zero-based budgeting. Most significant among the reported disadvantages is that it has not lived up to its promises. In instance after instance, there were high levels of budget pre-activity as individuals and groups attempted to influence the decision making (sometimes with high levels of influence in the outcomes). The results provided outcomes similar to the pre-zero-based budgeting format and also what appeared to be no perceptible change in the decision making. The second major disadvantage of zero-based budgeting concerns information overload. Decision making is ultimately top-down in zero-based budgeting, and everything generated at the lower levels is designed to aid the decision maker. One governor found himself with 11,000 decision packages, far more than any management expert would recommend and more than can be effectively dealt with by any one individual.

## Modified Zero-Based Budgeting

While zero-based budgeting as a single budget format for an organization has fallen out of favor, it remains in use in a modified form as a supplemental format in many organizations. For example, in Phoenix, Arizona, city departments submit an estimate (called the base) of the costs associated with providing their current levels of service for the following year. City budget and research staff review the base budget submissions to ensure that only that funding necessary for current service levels is included in the department's base. The review is called a "technical review" because of its non-programmatic line-item-by-item review of a department's budget. A department's base funding may differ from its current-year funding for a variety of reasons. For example, an increase or a decrease in utilities would be reflected in the base.

In addition to base budget submissions, departments submit five percent to 10 percent of their following year's base budget for potential elimination. These submissions are called "base reductions," and they represent the department's lowest-priority activities. At the same time, departments are also asked to submit any requests for new, restored, or expanded programs, which are called "supplemental budget requests." The base reductions and supplemental requests include all costs associated with a specific program or service, such as the cost of operating a new swimming pool. Costs for pool operation would include those associated with personnel, chemicals, building maintenance, supplies, and utilities.

When the base reductions and supplemental requests are submitted, they are ranked together according to the department's priorities. The department's ranking indicates whether it would be possible to make a base reduction in order to add a new program. The ranking also indicates which supplemental programs and base reductions are most critical to the department.

## Summary

Budget formats allow sport, tourism, and leisure service organization managers and administrators to view a budget from a particular perspective. These formats may be combined for differing purposes. The object classification budget is the most common of all budget formats for sport, tourism, and leisure service organizations. Other common and effective budget formats include the program budget, the performance budget, the running budget, and the zero-based budget.

## References

Minnesota Report on Performance Budgeting. (1995.) In *Money Matters,* Volume 10, Number 1. Minnesota House Ways and Means on Government Finance Staff.

## NOTES

# CHAPTER 16

# Capital Budgeting

## Introduction

Capital budgeting addresses a sport, tourism, and leisure service organization's major expenditures for equipment, buildings, and land. For the most part, sport, tourism, and leisure service organizations manage two budgets—one for operations and another for capital expenditures. Capital budgeting is not directly concerned with the costs of daily activities and functions. It concerns the management of debt and investments in capital resources. Capital budgets are generally approved annually at the same time as the operating budget, but annual capital budgets are just a part of a larger Capital Improvement Program (CIP) that may represent a five- to ten-year period of time. The CIP pulls together all of the identified major asset desires and needs of the organization over a predetermined period of time. Although the CIP extends over a period of years, it is reviewed and updated annually. Capital budgeting is conducted in similar ways in the public, private not-for-profit, and commercial sectors. In the public and commercial sectors, sport, tourism, and leisure service organizations may issue bonds for short- or long-term debt, while not-for-profit sport, tourism, and leisure service organizations would more likely use a capital campaign, which is an extension of the fundraising processes discussed in Chapter 11.

## Benefits of Capital Budgeting

The use of capital improvement programs and budgets provides some important advantages to organizations. Several of the most important reasons for adopting a capital budget are described below.

High-cost items could have a negative effect on operating budgets if they are included in an operating budget.

Organizations desire a level of stability in their operating budgets that shows minimal fluctuation from year to year and responsiveness to public demand. Removing capital items eliminates major fluctuations in the operating budget and presents a more accurate projection of actual operating costs. For example, a public parks and recreation department has an annual operating budget of $2 million, and it constructs a new band shell in a city park at a cost of $450,000. The construction of the band shell is financed through a five-year loan. If this capital expenditure was included in the operating budget, it would increase that annual budget significantly and give a false picture of the organization's financial health. Placing the same $450,000 in a separate capital budget allows the observer and budget manager to readily see how money is being used for operations and for capital development. Capital projects are normally funded from separate capital improvement funds rather than from the operating budget. Some funds and sources may be similar, but other funds, such as general obligation bonds, revenue bonds, and special assessments, are specifically designed for capital projects.

Capital budgeting allows for planned growth and spending. It strives to anticipate specific needs of the organization and to budget for those in advance. If land is to be purchased in the future, current planning can anticipate that and set the stage for securing funds and planning for short- and long-term debt.

Capital budgeting provides focus. It allows the organization to put its energy into a few well-conceived capital proj-

*Sport, tourism, and recreation facilities are capital projects that require special funding.*

ects and purchases rather than be distracted through an inefficient "shotgun" approach.

## The Capital Budgeting Process

Capital budgeting allows for planning of expenditures that may have a significant impact on the sport, tourism, and leisure service organization's budget. Capital budgeting is a four-step planning process that involves inventory of capital assets, needs analysis, cost analysis, and financing.

An *inventory of capital assets* is an essential first step in any capital improvement program. An inventory should include, at least, the following: (1) a description of the type of facility, land, or equipment; (2) the purchase price; (3) any improvements that were made; (4) its current condition; (5) the projected replacement cost for equipment; (6) the depreciated value; and (7) the projected end of the useful life.

The inventory allows the sport, tourism, and leisure service organization to know, at any given point, the status of its capital assets. For example, if vehicles are purchased on a five-year cycle, the inventory can show what year each vehicle was purchased, how many will have to be purchased in the next five years, and any unanticipated need to purchase in advance of the five-year cycle. For a building, the inventory can show the date it was built, the dates and types of renovations made, its current condition, and its current use.

A *needs analysis* looks at the future needs of the organization and attempts to identify how those needs will be met and what capital investments will be required. For example, if a fitness club owner determined she needed to expand her facilities in the next five years, the needs analysis

would be a part of the process of determining the type and size of the expansion. A needs analysis also looks at replacement needs. Most organizations assume a certain life span for the equipment that they purchase and use that consideration as they plan for the eventual replacement of that equipment.

The *strategic plan* should be a key element in the needs-assessment process. The strategic plan looks three to five years into the future, providing vision, purpose, goals, and objectives. It provides direction to the capital budgeting process. There are a number of factors that influence the outcome of the needs-analysis process. They include: demographics; cultural changes; the local, regional, and national economy; legislation that has an impact (such as the Americans with Disabilities Act); community growth or lack thereof; technological obsolescence; disaster planning; and replacement schedules. Each must be taken into account in the needs assessment.

*Cost analysis* is a decision-making process that helps to pinpoint where to spend available funds for capital improvements. It is not very different from most decision-making processes. The crux of the cost analysis is the determination of where to allocate limited resources in response to seemingly unlimited demands. The inventory and needs analysis set the stage for cost analysis.

Cost analysis provides key information for the prioritization of projects. There is no single method for establishing priorities. Organizations must take into account a number of variables and weigh each of them accordingly. Some of the variables to consider in the prioritization process include the following:

- relationship of the project to future needs;

- legal mandates;
- capital costs versus operating costs;
- costs relative to the benefits of competing costs;
- political costs and benefits;
- external funding potential;
- impact on improved effectiveness and/or efficiency;
- spin-off benefits;
- costs relative to competing costs;
- financial impact on defined stakeholders; and
- relationship of the proposed asset to defined beneficiaries.

A four-part approach to cost analysis is suggested. *Part 1* involves determining the turnkey cost of the project. For a new facility, such as a family aquatic center, the turnkey costs would include costs for services, construction, and fees as identified in Figure 16.1.

While those represented activities may not account for all of the costs, they represent a major share of the anticipated costs. Table 16.1 depicts the projected costs, as presented in a capital budget, for a proposed water playground. The budget includes all of the expected costs of the project.

*Part 2* involves estimating the annual operating costs of the project. Operational costs occur after the purchase or after the project is completed and are typically funded from the operating budget. They include the cost of utilities, staffing, insurance, maintenance, equipment repairs, etc. While construction is a major cost to the organization, operating the facility requires a long-term commitment. The operating budget can begin as a "rough estimate" and then be formalized into a more detailed analysis later. Table 16.2 presents sample data collected from four comparable facilities/sites that can be used in estimating operational costs and revenues for a new family aquatic center.

Always remember that after building a facility, there will be an ongoing additional cost of operating it. Failure to take the added operational requirements into account could result in serious budget problems. One midwestern community constructed a 50-meter indoor aquatic

---

The proposed Family Aquatic Center will have a capacity of 4,200 people (4% of the population) and be open from Memorial Day through Labor Day (99 days). The facility will include a wave action pool, zero-depth leisure pool, activity/water play pool, lazy river with zero-depth entry, flume slide, water-play apparatus, and a flo rider. In addition, the 16-acre facility will have parking for 1,000 cars, internal and external landscaping, support facilities, concession operations, a bath house, wet sand play, sand volleyball, and other amenities. The projected cost of the facility, less administration costs, utility hookups, and access is $14,700,000.

| | | |
|---|---|---|
| Land acquisition | Platting fees | Furniture and equipment |
| Architectural fees | Bringing utilities | Attorney's fees to the site |
| Engineering fees | Cleaning | Interim construction interest |
| Debt financing | Construction costs | Landscaping |
| Contingency fees | Project management fees | Insurance |

**Figure 16.1**
**Cost items associated with a capital development project**

## Table 16.1
### Projected capital budget costs for a water playground

| Item | Size | Estimated Amount | Total |
|---|---|---|---|
| **Pre-construction work** | | | **3,500** |
| 1. Topographic survey | Allowance | 2,000 | |
| 2. Soils Investigation | Allowance | 1,500 | |
| **Demolition** | | | **40,000** |
| 1. Demolition of existing bath house and pool | L.S. | 40,000 | |
| **Earthwork** | | | **4,500** |
| 1. Cut and fill on site (approx.) | 350 cu. yd. | 4,500 | |
| **Water playground** | | | **40,000** |
| Water play equipment | 40,000 | | |
| Tea cup (1) | | | |
| Tumble buckets (1) | | | |
| Rain drop (1) | | | |
| **Pool Construction** | | | **50,000** |
| 1. Concrete zero-edge pool | | 50,000 | |
| Water depth 0-18" | | | |
| Gals., 28,500 | | | |
| Bathers, 250-300 | | | |
| **Support Elements** | | | **231,635** |
| 1. Perimeter decks | 2,804 sq. ft. | 16,824 | |
| 2. Admission/Mech./Restrooms | 1,296 sq. ft. | 142,560 | |
| 3. Landscape and restoration | 8,360 sq. ft. | 25,080 | |
| 4. Perimeter fence 6' high, vinyl | 356 lin. ft. | 7,170 | |
| 5. Pool mechanical | L.S. | 40,000 | |
| **Utilities and Infrastructure** | | | **75,000** |
| **Construction Subtotal** | | | **444,635** |
| **Contingency and Fees** | | | **102,265** |
| **Estimated Project Budget** | | | **$546,900** |

complex. When it was completed, the leisure service organization discovered that it had not adequately prepared itself to meet the new operating costs. In order to cover those operating costs, two full-time positions were eliminated.

*Part 3* of the cost analysis is a review of the qualitative and quantitative benefits to be derived from the project. In some cases, projects offer a monetary return that may be estimated and compared with their cost. In commercial enterprises, the cost of capital projects is frequently compared to their payback period. In public projects, this may be only one of several considerations. As part of this step, a cash-flow analysis should be conducted (see sample depicted in Table 16.3). Because the proposed project has not incurred costs or received income, the cash-flow analysis uses projections that are based on communities or facilities of comparable size and with similar services (such as in Table 16.2).

Public organizations also consider the *social benefits* derived from projects. This is less a concern for commercial sports, tourism, and leisure service enterprises. That is why, for example, there are no commercial fire stations in most commu-

## Table 16.2
**Comparative data to help in estimating costs of and revenue from a family aquatic center**

| Comp. Site | Capacity | Avg. Daily Attendance | Total Season Attendance | Cost Per User | Total Operational Costs | Revenue Per User | Total Revenue |
|---|---|---|---|---|---|---|---|
| A | 4,200 | 2,115 (50%) | 209,385 | 9.80 | 2,051,973 | 10.50 | 2,198,542 |
| B | 3,800 | 2,020 (52.9%) | 198,990 | 2.30 | 457,677 | 4.00 | 795,960 |
| C | 4,400 | 1,985 (45.1%) | 196,515 | 7.40 | 1,454,211 | 8.50 | 1,670,378 |
| D | 4,000 | 2,300 (57.5%) | 227,700 | 8.00 | 1,821,600 | 10.00 | 2,277,000 |
| Mean | 4,100 | 2,103 (51.3%) | 208,148 | 6,88 | 1,430,997 | 8.25 | 1,717,221 |

nities. They simply are not profitable, but their social benefit warrants their public cost. Assessment of the qualitative benefits of a capital project should include consideration of the following:

- Congruence with the vision and mission of the organization.
- Long-range impact on the organization's strategic plan.
- Effect on the organization's image.
- Influence on stakeholders, including primary customers.
- Compliance with mandatory requirements or policy.

*Part 4* of the cost analysis requires an evaluation of the project and should be conducted when both the project's costs and the detailed operational and revenue budgets are available. There are two analyses that can be conducted that will help in evaluating the project. The first analysis addresses the need to earn back, in a reasonable amount of time, the original money invested in the capital project. This method of evaluation tells the organization how long it will take for the project's newly generated cash flow to pay for the cost of the capital development

## Table 16.3
**Basic cash flow analysis**

| Month | Jan | Feb | Mar | Apr | ... | Dec |
|---|---|---|---|---|---|---|
| Projected Revenue | 280,000 | 300,000 | 370,000 | 350,000 | ... | 200,000 |
| Projected Expenses | 360,000 | 320,000 | 250,000 | 240,000 | ... | 235,000 |
| Cash Flow | (80,000) | (20,000) | 120,000 | 110,000 | ... | (35,000) |
| Net Cash Flow | (80,000) | (100,000) | 20,000 | 130,000 | ... | 266,000 |

that generates the increased cash flows. If a new indoor tennis complex adds a fitness center at a cost of $1.6 million, and it generates revenue of $200,000 per year (after paying operating expenses), then the payback period is eight years. The payback period is calculated by dividing the capital cost by the annual net operating revenue. Note that the payback period assumes a constant value of the dollar throughout the payback period. Is a payback period of eight years good or bad? That is for the investor to decide. Whether it is good or bad depends on how long the organization wants to wait to recover its capital development investment.

Evaluation of the project can also be facilitated by calculation of the *internal rate of return* (IRR). This provides another way of describing the investment opportunity cost of the project. The IRR is calculated by equating the initial investment with the present value of the returns and solving for interest rate that validates the equation.

Initial Investment = Annual returns x $((1-(1+i)^{-n})/i)$

Where: i = the interest rate (IRR), and n = the number of years of receiving the return.

Table C at the end of the book provides values for $((1-(1+i)^{-n})/i)$. Therefore, the formula can be rewritten as:

Initial Investment = Annual returns x $T_c$

A $1.6 million fitness center addition with a projected life of 10 years that generates a net revenue of $200,000 per year would have an IRR of approximately 4%. This is calculated as shown below:

$1,600,000 = $200,000 $T_c$
$T_c$ = 8.00

From Table C, when $n=10$ years and the tabulated value is 8.00, $i$=approximately .04 (or 4%).

Once the calculations of the two methods are made, projects can be ranked. The payback method is the more common approach in this early judgment phase. If the IRR is calculated, then that figure should be compared to the organization's cost of borrowing. If the IRR is lower than the cost of borrowing, then the project may not be advisable. If, for example, the cost of borrowing the $1.6 million was 7%, then the tennis complex in the above example would not be built (they are paying 7% to borrow money that pays back 4%). However, a 3.0% interest rate for borrowing capital funds would greatly improve the chances of the tennis center project being approved (they are paying 3% to borrow money that earns 4%).

There are two major approaches to financing any capital project in the public sector. They are referred to as *pay-as-you-go* and *pay-as-you-use*. The pay-as-you-go approach is the most conservative. It requires all the money needed for the project to be available before it is started. The advantage of this method is the avoidance of debt (and the costs of debt servicing). With the entire cost of the project being paid for in advance, there is no concern for the payback period. A disadvantage to pay-as-you-go is, however, that many of those in a mobile and aging population who contributed to building up the cash fund for the project may not ever benefit from its use. Additionally, the time that it takes to save up the needed cash may, because of inflation, erode its purchasing power (see Chapter 7).

The pay-as-you-use approach requires getting into debt for the capital project. Pay-as-you-use allows for the cost of the project to be paid while it is being used. Payments are made from revenues generated by the project or from funds generated through taxes, special levies, fees and charges for services, fund raisers, investors, etc. The argument in support of the pay-as-you-use approach is that those who benefit from the capital asset will be the ones who pay for it. The contrary argument focuses on the increased cost of the project due to debt servicing.

## Capital Improvement Revenue Sources

Capital improvements usually require different sources of income than what is used for general operations. Table 15.3 illustrates some of the sources of income used for public capital improvement funding. While some public agencies may use the general fund to provide the necessary revenue for capital improvements, the nature and size of many capital improvements frequently make it inadvisable to rely on this fund. Most capital improvements involve taking on short-term debt and, in some cases, long-term debt. One of the reasons for taking on debt is that taxpayers and others who will contribute to the cost will not have to suffer a significant financial burden over a short period of time. A $10 million recreation center paid for over 15 years places considerably less annual burden on taxpayers than does the same recreation center paid for in three years. It places the debt into a longer payback period, allowing the agency to structure the debt so it has minimal impact on those who will assist in retiring it. While Table 16.4 demonstrates

most of the commonly accepted ways of financing debt, it is not all-inclusive.

## Bonds

The traditional source of capital improvement revenue for governments is bonding. In 1997 there were $1.3 trillion in municipal bonds outstanding and, at the same time, $2.5 billion in bonds had been issued for state parks across the United States. Bonding allows organizations to borrow large sums of money without a significant impact upon the community's taxing ability. Bonding provides immediate funding to a state, county, or community at a level it could not achieve in any other way. A bond comes in many forms, but there are two ways of classifying bonds. The first is according to the sources of revenue for repayment by the government, and the second is according to the method of retirement of the bond. They are named, respectively, *serial bonds* and *term bonds*.

*Serial bonds* allow public sport, tourism, and leisure service organizations to make regular payments, usually annually, on both principal and interest for the life of the bond. A serial bond is similar to installment buying; however, governments typically pay a much smaller interest rate because their bonds are guaranteed by the taxing power of the legislative body. *Straight serial bonds* make annual equal payments of principal until the bond maturity is paid. Since the principal payments are made equal, the interest paid is much higher at the beginning of the period and much lower toward the end. This approach to bond payment suggests that the highest payments are made when the facility is new and has the greatest opportunity for revenue generation. The overall value of the payments by the government

**Table 16.4**
**Revenue sources used by public agencies**
**(adapted from the Urban Park Institute and Trust for Public Land)**

| Financing Source | Provides Funds | Re-payment | Advantages | Disadvantages |
|---|---|---|---|---|
| General Obligation Bond (GOB) | Immediately | All taxpayers over a 5-30 year term | • Funds available immediately<br>• Payments tied to benefits received<br>• Potentially lowers interest costs | • Increased property taxes<br>• Competes with local services for limited resources<br>• Separates payment from benefit |
| Revenue Bonds | Immediately | By users over 5-30 years | • Funds available immediately<br>• Payment linked to benefits<br>• Payment may be linked to users | • Increases rates or fees<br>• Interest costs potentially higher than GOB |
| Tax Increment Financing Bonds | Immediately | By all taxpayers within defined boundaries | • Ties benefit to specific geographic area<br>• Reduces impact on overall capital budget<br>• Reduces competition for limited resources | • Revenues dependent upon willingness and ability of individuals in area to make payments<br>• Revenues dependent upon growth in assessed values |
| Bond Banks | Varies | By all taxpayers over 5-30 year period | • Particularly helpful for small communities<br>• Lowers cost of insurance | • Bond issuance may be delayed until enough communities apply |
| Certificates of Participation | Immediate use of land area | By all taxpayers over a defined period of time | • Allows land purchase over a period of time<br>• Payments made annually<br>• Not recommended as formal debt<br>• Does not impact community's debt limit | • Hides debt of community from bond appraisers<br>• Less public control, no vote required |
| Lease Purchase and Certificates | Immediate use of facility or equipment | By all taxpayers over a 5-10 year period | • Provides a way to purchase without issuing debt | • High interest rates<br>• Payments may not be related to benefits |
| Real Estate Transfer Tax | Immediately | By individuals transferring or purchasing real property | • Provides income every time property is sold<br>• Places burden for development and renovation on real estate purchases | • Unfairly taxes purchasing and selling home-owners for benefits received by entire community |
| Impact or Dedication Fees | Immediately | By those purchasing property sold for first time, or by developer | • Allows for new residents in fast growing areas to pay for improvements, rather than the whole community<br>• Easy to administer and collect<br>• Promotes growth management | • One time tax only—does not provide for ongoing maintenance<br>• Unfairly taxes developer and new owner for benefits received by entire community |

## Table 16.4
### Revenue sources used by public agencies - continued
### (adapted from the Urban Park Institute and Trust for Public Land)

| Financing Source | Provides Funds | Re-payment | Advantages | Disadvantages |
|---|---|---|---|---|
| Mitigation Financing | Immedi- ately | By those developing property | • Places burden on developer to provide open space in new development<br>• Takes burden off tax- payer for infrastructure development<br>• Provides local govern- ment with flexibility in land acquisition | • Places unfair burden on developer<br>• Allows developer to pro- vide land within develop- ment or another location |
| Revolving Loans | Immedi- ately | By ratepayers over 12-20 years | • Makes funds available immediately<br>• Ties payment to benefit received<br>• Could lower interest costs | • Increased rates or fees and charges<br>• Reporting and administra- tion may be cumbersome<br>• May not be consistent with agency priorities |

gradually diminishes over the life of the bond, even though the principal payment remains the same. Tables 16.5 and 16.6 depict the difference between payments on a serial and straight serial bond when interest is set at 4% and the amount received from the bond is $8 million.

*Serial annuity bonds* provide for an equal payment each year until the debt is paid. In the early years of a bond, the bulk of the payment is to cover interest charges. In the later years, the bulk of the payment is to reduce the principal.

*A term bond* is paid off with a single payment at the end of the loan period. The public agency must establish a *sinking fund* where funds are deposited over the life of the bond. The interest generated from the funds received from the bond and the annual deposits guarantees payment at the end of the borrowing period. This is a situation where the future value of a sum must be calculated in order to determine how much to allocate to the sinking fund each year. The term bond has fallen into disfavor because of the difficulty of managing the fund and attempting to project interest payments. Most state governments have legislatively abandoned the use of sinking fund bonds.

The second major method of classifying bonds is by the sources of revenue that will be used to repay the debt. Public sport, tourism, and leisure service agencies have undertaken a variety of approaches to bonding.

The most common bonding method used by public agencies is the *General Obligation Bond* (GOB). GOBs are issued by a public agency with the expectation of providing benefits to the entire community. Almost every community, has issued some type of GOB. Because the benefits of GOBs are to the entire community the retirement of the debt is also spread across the entire community. Retirement of debt is most frequently accomplished through increases in real property taxes. General obligation bonds are particularly

#### Table 16.5
#### Cost of an $8 million serial bond on interest rate of 4.0% (numbers in $)

| Year | Principal Paid | Interest Paid | Total Paid | Principal Balance |
|------|----------------|---------------|------------|-------------------|
| 1 | 666,328 | 320,000 | 986,328 | 7,333,672 |
| 2 | 692,981 | 293,347 | 986,328 | 6,640,692 |
| 3 | 720,700 | 265,628 | 986,328 | 5,919,992 |
| 4 | 749,528 | 236,800 | 986,328 | 5,170,464 |
| 5 | 779,509 | 206,819 | 986,328 | 4,390,955 |
| 6 | 810,689 | 175, 638 | 986,328 | 3,580,266 |
| 7 | 843,117 | 143,211 | 986,328 | 2,737,149 |
| 8 | 876,842 | 109,486 | 986,328 | 1,860,307 |
| 9 | 911,915 | 74,412 | 986,328 | 948,392 |
| 10 | 948,392 | 37,936 | 986,328 | 0 |
| Total | 8,000,000 | 1,863,280 | 9,863,280 | |

attractive to investors because they are exempt from federal income tax. In some instances they may be exempt from state and local taxes. Furthermore, GOBs are insured by the full faith and credit of the city, county, or state. This makes them a very secure source of income for an investor, even if the interest rates are not high. The major opposition to GOBs is the increase of property taxes. In public parks and recreation, this has been a particular challenge over the years. However, more recently the level of bonding has increased significantly, as well as a general public acceptance of the value of parks and recreation. The National Trust for Public Land reported that between 1987 and 1997, bond sales increased

#### Table 16.6
#### Cost of an $8 million straight serial bond on interest rate of 4.0% (numbers in $)

| Year | Principal Paid | Interest Paid | Total Paid | Principal Balance |
|------|----------------|---------------|------------|-------------------|
| 1 | 800,000 | 320,000 | 1,120,000 | 7,200,000 |
| 2 | 800,000 | 288,000 | 1,088,000 | 6,400,000 |
| 3 | 800,000 | 256,000 | 1,056,000 | 5,600,000 |
| 4 | 800,000 | 224,000 | 1,024,000 | 4,800,000 |
| 5 | 800,000 | 192,000 | 992,000 | 4,000,000 |
| 6 | 800,000 | 160,000 | 960,000 | 3,200,000 |
| 7 | 800,000 | 128,000 | 928,000 | 2,400,000 |
| 8 | 800,000 | 96,000 | 896,000 | 1,600,000 |
| 9 | 800,000 | 64,000 | 864,000 | 800,000 |
| 10 | 800,000 | 32,000 | 832,000 | 0 |
| Total | 8,000,000 | 176,000 | 9,760,000 | |

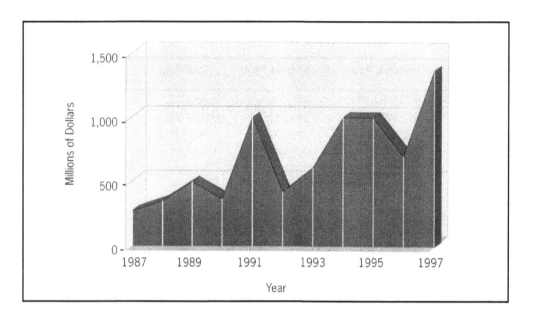

**Figure 16.2**
**Parks and recreation bonds, 1987-1997**

from $270 million to $1.37 billion. Figure 16.2 depicts the growth over that 10-year period.

*Revenue bonds* have received increased attention and emphasis over the last 25 years. Revenue bonds are used to finance a revenue-producing facility with the anticipation that revenues from the facility will wholly retire the bond. Increasingly, facilities such as aquatic parks, golf courses, artificial ice arenas, and recreation centers have been financed through this method. A major challenge of the use of revenue bonds is to ensure that there is sufficient revenue to both retire the debt and also to operate and maintain the facility. In some cases, subsidization has been used to finance operations and capital improvements. In most cases, however, the emphasis has been upon the facility generating sufficient revenue to cover both operating and debt retirement expenses.

*Certificates of participation* are authorized in about 25 states and allow public entities to purchase land and pay for it over a period of time. When a willing seller and a public agency enter into a certificate of participation, the public agency agrees to pay a specific price for the land and to make annual payments for a designated period. A certificate of participation does not require a public referendum and, most importantly, is not counted against the organization's debt limit.

*Tax increment financing bonds* (TIFs) allow public organizations to secure financing for projects that are enclosed within a political boundary. Commonly used to finance public improvements in development areas (sometimes called redevelopment districts), TIFs have been used to support sport, tourism, and recreation developments. They are most common in urban areas, but have been used in some rural areas. Implementation of a TIF plan freezes the assessed valuation of real property within the designated area. It does not freeze the tax rate. Taxes are collected on the property at the base level while investments are made by public agencies, and new businesses are attracted and property values thereby increase. Project costs or bond costs are paid for from additional sales tax revenues, personal income tax revenues, and the increased assessed value of the property. Bonds issued from TIF districts are paid for only on the projected increase of the value of the property, not on the full faith and credit of the city. TIF districts are common throughout the United States and may provide opportunities for the purchase and development of new park land, as well as renovation of existing parks.

*Bond banks* are usually organized at the state level for the purpose of allowing government entities that might not have sufficient borrowing power or debt rating to secure an acceptable interest rate. Bond banks allow multiple governmental entities to pool their bond requests into a single bond sale. By pooling their resources, smaller governmental agencies can issue a larger bond and secure a more advantageous interest rate. The public entities desiring the bonds are not purchasing them directly from the bond market, but from a bond bank typically established by a state. The Maine Bond Bank, for example, was established by the legislature in 1972 to provide a unique financing program allowing Maine towns, cities, counties, school systems, water districts, sewer districts, or other governmental entities access to national money markets for their public-purpose borrowing needs. The Maine Bond Bank retains a high investment rating and is able to secure bonds at a low interest rate and then purchase bonds from public agencies. Local agen-

cies submit an application to the bond bank, and it is evaluated on the purpose of the bond, estimated cost, construction schedule, state and local valuation, tax levy or user charges, demographic trends, recent financial and debt history, and economic stability. The local agency is able to sell bonds to the bond banks at their lower interest rates.

## Other Capital Improvement Revenue Sources

*Lease purchases and certificates* are becoming more common among public sport, tourism, and leisure service organizations as a method of financing projects. This alternative allows a public agency to join with private sources to finance major projects. In most cases, a not-for-profit holding corporation is created. This not-for-profit holding corporation can purchase, develop, and operate the property. Usually, however, the not-for-profit organization will purchase and develop the property and lease it to the public entity that will operate it. The lease is an annual or multiyear lease with an automatic renewal and an option for the public agency to purchase the developed land at any time. The leasing organization makes the lease payments from revenue generated from use of the property. Then the not-for-profit holding corporation uses the lease payment to retire the principal and interest. When the debt for the property is paid, it can then be given to the public agency, and the not-for-profit holding corporation can be dissolved. The not-for-profit corporation has no taxing power, but it can help the public agency to avoid a risky and expensive requirement to hold a public referendum on the capital project. In many ways, a lease purchase and certificate program is similar to issuing revenue bonds.

*Real estate transfer tax* is levied on the sale of certain classes of property, such as residential, commercial, and industrial. The tax generally increases with the size and value of the property being transferred (sold). Tax rates are controlled by state legislatures, but the revenues from this source of income are generally collected at the county level. It has become a particularly acceptable form of income for public agencies to accommodate the needs that urban growth places upon community services. The allocation of these taxes for natural resources development has become more commonplace. Florida and Maryland were pioneers in requiring that a portion of these taxes be used for park and recreation acquisition and development. Real estate transfer taxes are a fairly reliable source of income, since they are imposed each time property is transferred.

*Impact or dedication fees* are assessed by local governments in connection with new housing and commercial developments. Their purpose is to defray the cost of providing new or expanded public facilities that are necessary to serve the development. The fees typically require cash payments in advance of the completion of development, are based on a methodology and calculation derived from the cost of the facility and the nature and size of the development, and are used to finance improvements away from, but of benefit to, the development. Local governments throughout the country are increasingly using impact fees to shift more of the costs of financing public facilities from the general taxpayer to the beneficiaries of those new facilities.

The impact or dedication fees supplement local government resources that otherwise have decreased because of di-

minished state and federal transfers of funds. Local governments have also used impact fees to delay or serve as a substitute for general property tax increases. Impact fees, when based on a comprehensive plan and used in conjunction with a sound capital improvement plan, can be an effective tool for ensuring adequate infrastructure to accommodate growth where and when it is anticipated. In Noblesville, Indiana, for example, the Parks and Recreation Department receives an average of $100 for every new home built. During the late 1990s, this contributed about $100,000 annually to the department's budget.

*Revolving loans* allow an organization to secure a specified amount of money for a specified period of time. A line of credit is authorized, and the sport, tourism, and leisure service organization can then draw off of the line of credit to finance specific projects or equipment purchases. Revolving loans usually carry a higher interest rate than other financial resources. Their value lies in the ability of the organization to have immediate access to a level of funds without requiring an extensive approval process. Revolving funds have been successfully used with smaller, short-term projects, where debt retirement payments will be made from a secure source. It is not generally considered an effective method for financing major projects.

*The mitigation land bank* has long been a source of development resources for public leisure service organizations. The bank allows developers to either dedicate land in a development for open space preservation or to identify off-site locations they will dedicate. The administering public agency and the developer work together to identify suitable land. The governmental entity may have the authority to create a land bank where developers can substitute money or land in another area of the community for land they are developing. In one Iowa community, the parks and recreation department worked with local developers to acquire a greenbelt along a stream in the community, preserving it for future generations. The use of the land bank is particularly useful when the developer has failed to meet the requirements of land dedication during the development phase of the project.

*Special taxes*, such as the transient occupancy tax (also called a bed tax or lodging tax) and the meal tax, can also be used as revenue sources for tourism capital projects. While these funds are typically used to operate destination marketing organizations, they can be and are used to endow grant programs that support local capital projects designed to create a well balanced tourist destination.

## Capital Budgeting in the Commercial Sector

Capital budgeting in the commercial sector is a little different from that in the public or private not-for-profit sectors. There are some key differences that need to be highlighted here. Commercial sport and leisure service organizations bond for one of four reasons:

- *Replacement projects.* Investments in new equipment to replace old, worn out, or damaged equipment.
- *Cost reduction projects.* Replacing existing equipment with new equipment that may operate more efficiently, be more state of the art, or be required to keep up with customer expectations.
- *Safety/environmental projects.* Investments required to comply with safety

and/or environmental regulations.
- *Expansion projects.* The expansion of existing services and resources.

All sport, tourism, and leisure service organizations should have a long-range plan or a capital project that corresponds with their corporate vision. Essential components of a capital project proposal include market forecasts, revenue projections, acquisition and construction cost estimates, anticipated operating expenses, and expected profit. The information collected for the capital project proposal helps the organization to have a better understanding of the long-term financial implications of the proposed capital expenditure. Although public and not-for-profit sport, tourism, and leisure service organizations may emphasize the merit approach to a capital project, a commercial sport, tourism, and leisure service organization must emphasize the profit approach. The capital budgeting process involves project evaluation and decision making. These are typically approached from an accounting perspective, with emphasis on the net present value, cash flow, and payback period.

### Decision Processes

Several different decision tools are used by commercial sport and leisure service organizations to determine the potential contribution of a capital project to the financial health of the organization. One common method is to determine the present value of the returns generated by the project and compare that value to the investment amount. The *net present value* (NPV) is the difference between the present value of returns and the initial investment. In the decision-making process for a capital project, the investor wants to know if additional value is created by undertaking the project. If the

NPV is positive, it means that the present value of the investment, and therefore, the project, will add value to the firm and also increase the wealth of the owners. Therefore, the Net Present Value Decision Rule is:

If NPV > 0, then the project meets the standard for approval.

To determine NPV, the organization must anticipate the future cash flow. Cash flow represents earnings before depreciation, amortization, and non-cash charges. For example, a fitness center invests $100,000 in new fitness equipment, supplementing what it already has. It is estimated that, as a result of the investment, an additional cash flow of $22,000 will be realized each year for the next five years. The expected market interest rate (i.e., the interest rate that could be reasonably expected by any other investment carrying the same degree of risk) during those five years is eight percent. If returns are equal (i.e., the same amount each year), the NPV can be calculated by applying the formula:

$$NPV = RT_c - C$$
Where: R = annual returns
C = the initial investment, and $T_c$
$= (1 - (1 + i)^{-n}/i)$ or the corresponding

value found in Table C at the end of this chapter.

In this example,

$$NPV = \$22,000\ T_c - \$100,000$$
$$= \$22,000\ (3.993) - \$100,000$$
$$= -\$12,154$$

The NPV is negative; therefore, the investment is not advisable.

If the annual returns are unequal (which is a more likely scenario), a different way of calculating NPV must be used. If, for example, the $100,000 five-year investment in a market where eight percent interest is expected yields cash flows of $30,000 in year 1, $29,000 in year 2, $26,000 in year 3, $25,000 in year 4, and $18,000 in year 5, then the present values can be calculated by multiplying each year's returns by an appropriate interest factor to determine the present values. The present values are then summed, and the initial investment is subtracted from the total present value of the returns. This results in a calculated NPV. The interest factor to be used is found in Table B at the end of this book. Table 16.7 shows present values for the preceding example.

The cash flows described above and shown in Table 16.7 have a combined present value that is greater than the initial investment. According to the NPV decision rule, this is a good investment.

Table 16.7
Sample data for NPV decision using unequal returns (8% interest)

| Year | Cash Flow | TB | Present Value |
| --- | --- | --- | --- |
| 1 | 30,000 | .926 | 27,780 |
| 2 | 29,000 | .857 | 24,853 |
| 3 | 26,000 | .794 | 20,644 |
| 4 | 25,000 | .735 | 18,375 |
| 5 | 18,000 | .681 | 12,258 |
| Total | | | 103,910 |

Figure 16.3 illustrates how NPV is calculated using a timeline. The timeline illustrates the increased revenue at the end of each year, beginning with the $100,000 investment and a market interest rate of 10 percent. In this example, returns during each of the five years are $38,000, $47,000, $58,000, $70,000, and $79,000.

NPV takes into account the time value of money. The time value of money suggests that a dollar invested today is worth more than a dollar in the future, because the dollar received today can earn interest up until the time the future dollar is received. To account for the time value of money, the interest factor from Table B is used to determine the present value.

Another approach to decision making is to determine the *payback period* (discussed earlier). The payback period is the length of time it takes to recover the initial cost of a project. Payback is usually measured in years. The shorter the payback period, the better the investment. The formula for determining the payback period is illustrated below. This formula is used when the return on the project is expected to be consistent from year to year. If a project cost $100,000, and it expected a $22,000 return each year, it would take 4.5 years to pay for the project.

Cost of Project/Annual Cash Flow = Payback Period

$100,000/$22,000 = 4.5 years

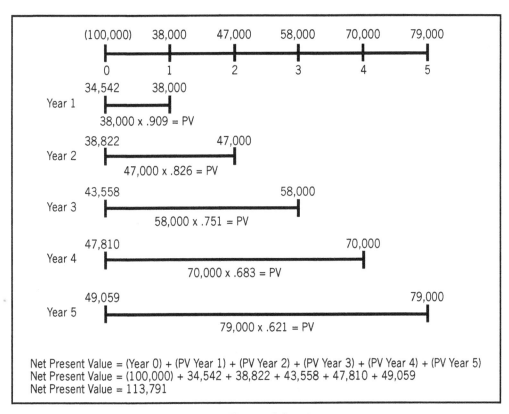

Net Present Value = (Year 0) + (PV Year 1) + (PV Year 2) + (PV Year 3) + (PV Year 4) + (PV Year 5)
Net Present Value = (100,000) + 34,542 + 38,822 + 43,558 + 47,810 + 49,059
Net Present Value = 113,791

**Figure 16.3**
**Net present value timeline**

When the return varies each year, as in Table 16.7, simply add up the expected returns for each succeeding year, until the total cost of the project is equaled. In this case, the payback period would be achieved early in the fifth year. There are some disadvantages to the payback period approach to evaluating capital projects. A payback period approach assumes that cash inflows (or revenue) will exceed cash outflows (or expenses). Second, a payback calculation does not usually consider the time value of money. In a payback model, the interest the money could achieve is not considered.

### Income Sources of Commercial Capital Projects

The same two approaches to financing capital projects in the public sector are also used in the commercial and nonprofit sectors. They are referred to as pay-as-you-go and pay-as-you-use. It was noted earlier in this chapter that the pay-as-you-go approach assumes the availability of all the money needed for the project before it is started. The pay-as-you-use approach incurs debt for the capital investment that is paid off during the use of the asset.

Corporate bonds are another common method of securing funds for capital projects. A corporate bond involves lending money to a public corporation. In return, the lender is promised a fixed rate of return on the investment, with the loan to be repaid in full at a future date. Corporate bonds are usually issued in multiples of $1,000 or $5,000. Bonds are sold with different maturity dates. Maturity tells the investors when they can expect to get their principal back and how long they will receive interest payments. Corporate bonds are divided into three groups: short-term notes, which ma-

ture in one to two years; medium-term bonds, which mature in five to 12 years; and long-term bonds, which extend beyond 12 years before maturing.

There are three types of corporate bonds. *Mortgage bonds* issue bonds backed by real estate and/or other physical assets. Just as with a home that is mortgaged, if the corporation defaults on the bond, the real estate and/or physical assets are sold to pay the mortgage bond. *Equipment trust certificates* are similar to automobile loans. Traditionally, the corporation provides 20 percent of the cost of the capital project. The balance is then paid off over the next 15 years. When it is paid off, the trustee provides the corporation with a clear title. The final type of corporate bond is an *income bond*. Income bonds only pay interest if earned, and to the extent it was earned. There is no set time when the bonds must be paid off. Usually, such bonds are issued by firms in bankruptcy. Additionally, the bond holders are frequently the creditors of the bankrupt firm.

### Summary

Capital budgeting is an essential process for most organizations; it stands alone, in planning purposes, from the operating budget. Its focus is on long-term purchases of equipment, land, or facilities. Capital budgeting allows an organization to systematically address long-term needs and to plan financially for those needs.

### References

Aronson, J. R., & Schwartz, E. (1996.) *Management policies in local government finance.* Washington, D.C.: International City/County Management Association. *221 Managing Financial Resources in Sport and Leisure Service Organizations*

Kelsey, C. W., Gray, H. R., & McLean, D. D. (1993.) *The budget process in parks and recreation: A case study manual.* Reston, VA: American Alliance for Health, Physical Education, Recreation and Dance.

Listro, J. P., (1991). *Nonprofit organizations account and reporting (2nd ed.).* Dubuque, IA: Kendall/ Hunt Publishing Company.

Rabin, Jack (Ed.). (1992.) *Handbook of public budgeting.* New York: Marcel Dekker, Inc.

Reed, B. J., & Swain, J. W. (1997). *Public finance administration.* Thousand Oaks, CA: SAGE Publications.

## NOTES

# CHAPTER 17

# Budget Presentations

## Introduction

Budget preparation essentially ends with required presentations to key decision makers. Decision makers are policy or legislative bodies that may include board members, city council members, the owner of the company, key stakeholders, or members of the organization. All agencies must, at some point, make budget presentations. There is no standardized format for creating a budget presentation and each organization may approach budget presentations differently. It could include a simple overview of proposed revenues and expenditures or a more complex description of program areas, projected revenues and expenditures, and a linkage with the organizational goals and vision.

## Purposes of Budget Presentations

Budget presentations have many purposes, but ultimately, the primary purpose of the presentation is to inform decision makers and facilitate a discussion and decision for the proposed operating and capital budgets. Beyond an informative role, budget presentations serve several additional purposes. A budget presentation is the culmination of the budget preparation period and suggests to those receiving it a completion. Secondly, the presentation provides an overview of the proposed budget with sufficient detail to determine sources and amounts of revenue and projected expenditures. It allows for a historical perspective when the budget presentation includes comparisons with previous years' budgets.

The budget presentation is seen as an introduction to the detailed budget. In public and not-for-profit organizations, as well as in commercial business enterprises, the budget presentation is frequently made in conjunction with the delivery of the budget document. Most organizations operate with goals and objectives, and effective budget presentations link financial plans to organizational goals and objectives. Budgets are a reflection of trends that impact an organization's need to deliver products and services in a specific area. Elmhurst (IL) Park District states in their budget document,

> *"The District's vision for the future of park and recreation services in Elmhurst is articulated in the Strategic Plan. This vision provides a direction for the Board and staff to ensure that the needs of the Elmhurst community are met. Staff has followed that direction by including specific funding for objectives within the strategic priorities approved by the Board and articulated in the 2007 Strategic Plan Action Plan. The total investment included in the 2007 proposed budget is $4,962,152."*

Budgets are tools used by organizations to create new or expanded resources in communities and organizations. In the Elmhurst Park District budget, seven areas were identified in the strategic action plan for capital investment:

* Redevelopment of the 1860s Wilder Mansion ($1,750,000)
* Continued redevelopment of East End Pool and Bathhouse ($1,500,000)
* Installation of two synthetic turf athletic fields ($950,000)
* Construction of the Salt Creek Greenway Trail ($397,940)
* Installation of the Wagner Community Center Sprinkler System ($175,000)
* Completion of the Sugar Creek Golf Course driving range lighting ($37,500).
* Transfer of funds from the Enterprise Services Fund to the Capital

Improvement Fund for capital projects ($151,712). (Elmhurst Park District, 2007, Long Range Capital Plan. http://www.epd.org/budget)

In the preceding example, the seven emphasis areas involved capital improvement funds (Chapter 16). Elmhurst Park District's use of a strategic plan is typical of many organizations. Reference to strategic plans, master plans, and long-range budget plans are all part of the budget presentation and strengthen decision makers' understanding of relationships between the operating and capital budgets, as well as intended agency outcomes.

## The Written Budget Document

The core of a budget presentation is the budget document. It contains the complete operating and capital budget for the organization. The two documents can be separated and are sometimes discussed during separate presentations. Budget documents, for mid-size and large communities, may be hundreds of pages in length. For a separate agency, such as a park district, professional sports team, or an event management agency, their budget document may be considerably smaller. The larger and more complex the organization, the larger the budget document. Almost all organizations utilize a standardized budget format, and this standardization allows for consistency in reporting processes and for comparison between budgets.

The budget document is organized around the operating and capital budget, including front matter that provides direction for document preparers. Typically the document has an introductory letter from the chief executive officer (CEO) presenting the budget and providing a transmittal letter or an executive summary style letter. It is written to the governing body, such as a city council, park board, board of trustees, or owner. The next items in the budget document are included at the discretion of the CEO. These can include, but are not limited to:

- Vision, mission, and goals—provide the core direction setting documents and measures for the organization. Most agencies link their budgets to these documents. Stakeholders are demanding increased budget accountability, and so alignment with the vision, mission, and goals are essential.
- Budget philosophy—provides the decision maker with the fundamental commitments associated with the budgeting process. For example, the Arlington Heights, IL Park District identified among their budget philosophies the commitment to (1) maintain high-quality programs and facilities, (2) provide excellent customer service, (3) maintain a stable tax rate, (4) reward good staff, and (5) "take care of what we have."
- Current challenges—represent issues or concerns with which the organization is presently dealing. In most instances these are major issues, areas of focus, or new initiatives that were introduced with the previous year's budget.
- Significant or proposed changes—identify shifts in the organization's funding priorities. The section alerts readers to changes that impact the overall budget. In some instances the changes may signal a major realignment of expenditure or income priorities. More often new projects, expansion or contraction of existing

projects, shifting funding from one project or program to another, elimination of programs, and the like are included in this area. The changes are presented separately for the operating and capital budget.

- Future issues and concerns and trend analysis—demonstrate an awareness of potential new funding commitments or reduction in funding sources. Trend analysis allows the organization to identify future issues and concerns that will positively or negatively impact the organization. Budget presentations focus on these issues and alert decision makers to potential changes.
- Organizational chart—provides the decision maker with an overview of the organization of the agency. It allows decision makers to view the organization and understand where funding is being allocated. Knowledge of organizational structure allows decision makers to make better judgments.
- Revenue summary - provides a written description of the revenue sources, the level of revenue anticipated from each, shifts in the revenue, historical presentation of revenue services, and projections for the next fiscal year. The revenue summary provides an overview for decision makers and helps the CEO focus discussion on key issues.
- Expenditure summary—does the same thing as the revenue summary, except for expenditures.
- Budget detail—is usually the last item in the budget document and includes the entire budget. It is the largest section of the budget. The budget detail gives the particulars of each component in the organization. For example, a sport facility might have its

operating budget divided into personnel, multiple program operations (such as special events, sport specific events, rentals), maintenance operations to include specific and general, and so forth.

## Presenting the Budget

The budget presentation will be crafted by the CEO or chief finance officer (CFO). It follows the structure of the written budget document but emphasizes more global elements. A budget presentation can take 10 minutes or several hours, based on organizational traditions, complexity and size of the budget, expectations of the board, or the desire of the CEO. In more complex organizations the CEO may require each division or department to provide a budget presentation. The presentation is designed for delivery to the governing body.

There are no standardized formats for budget presentations. Orange County, Florida's Parks and Recreation Division budget presentation focused on three areas: overview, accomplishments, and budget summary. Their proposed operating budget of $27.7 million was presented using 18 visual aids (PowerPoint slides). The overview included statistical facts about the parks and recreation system, progress toward meeting performance measures, programs, and planned and completed capital projects. The overview section focused on orienting decision makers to the organization and to what the CEO perceived to be consistent with the vision and mission. The second section, accomplishments, included data about youth initiatives and senior programs and included only one slide. The budget summary included the operating budget, capital budgeting, and funding sources. Orange County Parks and Recreation is a division of the county government organized under the Department of Community and Environmental Services and their budget presentation was a component of a larger budget presentation comprising many divisions and departments.

Arlington Heights, Illinois Park District is an independent governmental agency with separate taxing power. Its $21 million budget took 29 slides to present and included budget philosophy, major goals, focus points, budget capability, a five-year financial forecast, the proposed budget, fund balances, and department presentations. The parks and planning department's budget presentation provided detail on capital projects such as playground replacements, paving and parking lots, athletic field establishment and renovation, and vehicle and equipment replacement. The recreation and facilities department focused on the delivery of programs and services and divided the budget presentation into delivery areas including recreation programs, indoor swim center, museum, racquet and fitness club, tennis club, and golf operations for three golf courses. For each area the presentation included, at a minimum, user statistics, program participation, revenues, evaluations, and expenditures.

### Principles of Effective Presentations

The budget presentation is typically accomplished with standard presentation software, such as Microsoft's popular PowerPoint application. Below are some guidelines to assist CEOs and program managers when utilizing such visual aids in presenting budget information.

First, know the audience. Most individuals, including board members and stakeholders, will not readily understand some of the terminology used by the staff. When making assumptions about what listeners know, it is better to provide more rather than less explanation. For example the term CIP, meaning capital improvement program, can also mean catalog in production, classification of instructional programs, center for international policy, center for instructional performance, center for institutional planning, and so forth. It is not necessary to provide a description of the terminology on the presentation screen, but it is always safest to avoid the use of acronyms.

Second, ask "What do I want the final product to look like?" Begin with the end in mind and look at the presentation as a set of blocks that, when organized, create a broad level of understanding. In other words, the whole is more powerful than the parts, but the whole cannot exist without the parts. Presentations should be outlined in advance of putting them into a presentation software. Too often budget presentations are organized in sections that are independent of one another and the final product looks disjointed and fails to flow. When a presentation is poorly organized, the decision makers are left at a disadvantage, trying to determine what is more important and what is less important. Smoothly guiding the viewers to suggested alternatives or solutions allows for better decision making.

The font size and type should be easy to read from a distance. As a general rule, the font size should not be smaller than 30 point. There are two primary styles of typography. Serif fonts are considered to be more readable on the printed page while sans-serif fonts are considered to be more legible on monitors or projection screens. A sans-serif typography is depicted in Figure 17.1. Common sans-

serif fonts used for presentations include arial, trebuchet, tahoma, gill sans, and verdana.

It is effective and useful to utilize graphics and photographs. Research suggests retention is improved by 50 percent when graphics are used and only 10 percent when bullet points are exclusively used. The principle of keeping it simple should be maintained in the use of graphics. The graphic should support the text. A good rule of thumb is to see if the graphic can stand without the text. If so, then consider either eliminating the text or reducing it considerably. Too many presentations include whole paragraphs of information with the presenter reading the information to the listener. Figure 17.2 provides an example of a slide that focuses on simplicity. Presenters should avoid using busy backgrounds. The use of photos as a background to the text is difficult to achieve and too often the background overrides the text (Figure 17.3). If the text is difficult for the listeners to read, then they won't read it. They may even disengage from the presentation.

Avoid putting too much information on a single slide. Information overload reduces the attentiveness of the listener. It is better to spend two or three slides on

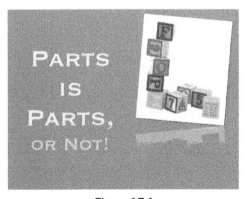

**Figure 17.1**
**Illustration of a well-organized slide using minimal text and supporting graphics**

**Figure 17.2**
**Principles of simplicity focusing on the background, text, and graphic all in support of each other**

a topic than to cram it into a single slide. Figure 17.4 shows a slide that is guilty of information overload. The text is informative and deemed important by the organization, but the viewer is drawn to conflicting important points. The result is disassociation with the slide and loss of communication.

Using background sounds and audio clips to highlight slides, a variety of different slide transitions, and multiple builds of text is tempting, but it is distracting to your audience. The slide transition and text builds should remain consistent and simple throughout the presentation. Individual letters flying all over the screen only confuse the viewer. Remember the focus of any presentation is the delivery and understanding of a budget, not a demonstration of the presentation software's flexibility.

The presentation of graphs and tables should be done carefully with the viewer in mind. Most individuals cannot process multiple sources of conflicting data. For example, a chart that shows many crossing lines is much more difficult to follow than a bar chart depicting data more simply. It is difficult for the brain to conceptualize more than three or four data points simultaneously. Figure 17.5 shows a slide with seven data points. The scale

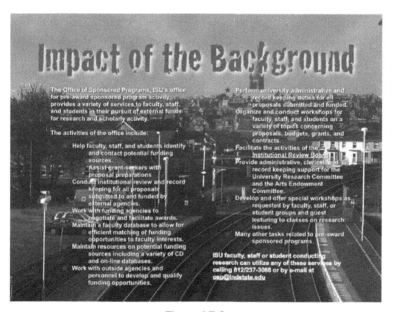

**Figure 17.3**
**Use of a background with large or small text detracts from the readability and understandability of the presentation.**

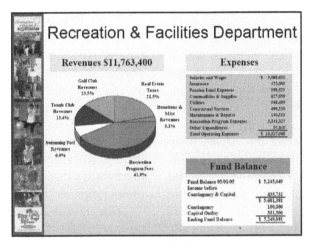

**Figure 17.4**
**Information overload makes it difficult for viewers to comprehend content.**

is too small to show differences between the data. It leaves the viewer confused about the data because they cannot make sense of them. The presenter would need to spend considerable time explaining the data and likely they would still not be understood.

Figure 17.6 is a historical treatment of the city's share of property tax over a 23-year period. The line graph depicts a data point for each year supplemented by a corresponding value label that reports the actual percentage. The graph is

simple, the title is reflective of the content, and the reader can visually track the decline in the city's share of property tax. The graph is both descriptive and expressive. The only problem with this representation is the size of the font. The text is so small that it would be difficult to read from a distance.

The use of tables and pie charts is very common, as is the use of colors and legends that show what the colors depict. Resist the use of colors (some readers are colorblind and most photocopiers do not

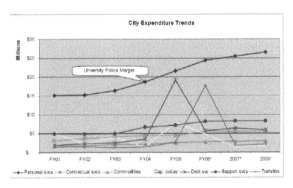

**Figure 17.5**
**An example of a poorly designed data set, resulting in confusion for the viewer.**

adequately differentiate between converted grayscales). Label tables and charts and, where appropriate, elements within the graphs. Creativity is generally a valued attribute, but it is best to stay away from 3-D charts and tables. They are like having too many transitions in presentation slides and can distract the viewer. Keep the tables and charts simple, as demonstrated in Figures 17.6 and 17.7. Figure 17.7 shows two effective ways that the same data can be displayed; a bar chart and a pie chart. Pie charts are graphically pleasing, but individuals have more difficulty determining value differences in pie charts than in bar charts.

Note the use of within-graphic text rather than a legend, and the actual percentages are presented on the pie chart so that viewers do not need to guess.

## Presentation Tips

Here are some final tips for presentations. The first is practice, practice, practice. Rehearse the presentation in the presence of individuals who will challenge the presentation. Rehearse it in front of a mirror and look at the performance. Record it and critique the recording. Be critical and watch for personal idiosyncrasies that might detract from the presentation.

During a presentation it may be important to have the audience focus on the speaker rather than on the screen. Punctuate the visual presentation with dark screens, then return to the graphic or text slide when appropriate. In some software packages, the dark screen feature is referred to as the "B" key.

Do not present in the dark. Keep the

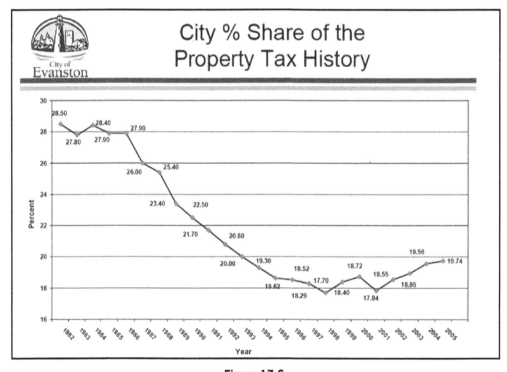

**Figure 17.6**
**Property Tax History represented by a line chart showing two data points:**
**percentage and year.**

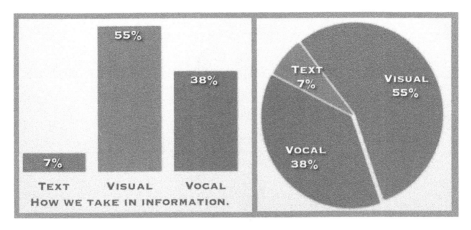

**Figure 17.7**
**The same data represented two different ways: a bar chart and a pie chart.**

lights on. Today's projectors have sufficient power to project in a well-lit room. Don't use a podium unless mandated. Most individuals do not perform their best when trapped behind a podium. Know the material well enough to walk away from the podium and remove the barrier between the speaker and the audience. Make eye contact. Listeners want to know that the speaker is interested in them. Eye contact gives the speaker hints about audience attention, questions, concerns, and acknowledgment. Finally, don't be afraid to show passion for the cause that is being promoted.

## Summary

The budget document may be a simple overview of proposed revenues and expenditures or a more complex description of program areas, projected revenues and expenditures, and a linkage with the organizational goals and vision. Budget presentations may have many purposes, but ultimately, the primary purpose of the presentation is to inform decision makers and facilitate a discussion and decision for the proposed operating and capital budgets. The use of best practices in presentations will enhance the delivery and reception of a budget presentation.

## NOTES

# CHAPTER 18

# Accounting and Reporting

## Introduction

One of the most important factors that from a financial management perspective separates successful sport, tourism, and leisure service enterprises from those that fail is the system of keeping records and reporting financial activity. The system of keeping financial records is called accounting, and its purpose is to allow the sport, tourism, and leisure service manager to find and easily understand information about the history of transactions and about the current financial condition of the organization. This chapter presents the basic principles of accounting and explores its use in reporting important findings to the financial manager. There could be as many ways in which financial information is recorded and organized, records are managed, and reports are summarized and interpreted as there are people who need the information. Highly customized accounting systems might meet the very specific needs of financial managers and decision makers, as well as help to keep confidential information as cryptic as possible, but therein lies their weakness. If a highly customized accounting system is so unique that it is understood only by the user, others who may need specific financial information in order to regulate or cooperate with the organization may find it difficult or impossible to do so. This may result in penalties and/or loss of opportunity. For example, imagine a taxpayer tossing out the tax department's forms and submitting her annual tax return using a different method of reporting that she developed to match her shoebox filing system. Not a good idea! Imagine asking the bank for a business loan and providing a financial report that uses budget classifications, record systems, and report formats that are completely incompatible with those of the potential lending institution. Also not a good idea!

There is a need for order in business, and that need is probably nowhere greater than in the area of financial management. The established order for recording and reporting financial information in sport and leisure service organizations is referred to as Generally Accepted Accounting Principles (GAAP). These principles are described in publications by such recognized organizations as the Financial Accounting Standards Board or are derived from familiarity with the professional body of knowledge and prevalent practices. It is important to note that the principles and practices discussed in this chapter are "generally accepted," not "universally applied."

## Stock and Flow

In developing an understanding of and appreciation for accounting, it is important to differentiate between the concepts of stock and flow. *Stock* refers to the financial resources available to the sport and leisure service organization at a given point in time. It is a measure of what the organization owns and what it owes. Stock information is used by financial managers to report on and to make decisions based on the current financial condition of the organization. To use a sports analogy, stock information is the score at a particular point in an athletic contest. At the beginning of the game, both teams have 0 points of stock. At the end of the game, the home team may have 45 points and the triumphant visiting team may have 52 points. Obviously, coaches' decisions made when the stock (score) is 0-0 at the start of the contest will be very different from those made when the clock is about to run out and the stock (score) is 50-43.

*Flow* refers to the movement (increase or decrease) of financial resources during a certain period of time. Reports of flow focus on the net change (loss or gain) in resources, but also provide information about the nature and extent of financial activity that brought about the eventual loss or gain. In the sports analogy, flow is the activity between the start of the game and the final buzzer. The official score sheet, coaches' comments, and newspaper articles describing the game are forms of flow reports. They describe how the game moved from a score of 0-0 to a score of 45-52. Measuring and reporting flow helps managers to know how the organization moved from one stock position to another. Financial managers use balance sheets to report point-in-time (stock) conditions, while the income statement (also called a profit and loss statement or

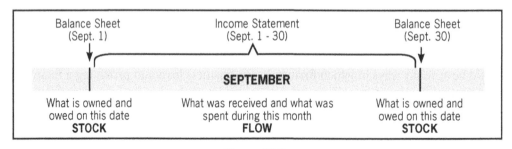

**Figure 18.1**
**The relationship of balance sheets and the income statement in detailing stock and flow**

an operating statement) is used to report on financial activity (flow) between two points in time.

## The Balance Sheet

What the organization owns and what it owes at a given point in time are recorded on the balance sheet (see Figure 18.2). Things that are owned are referred to as assets and are detailed on the left side of the balance sheet. Assets may be tangible items or properties, such as cash, equipment, inventories, buildings, land, etc., or they may be valuable intangible items, such as trademarks, names, or patents. Furthermore, assets may be classified as "current" (i.e., something that is or can be converted into cash within one year) or "fixed" (i.e., something that cannot readily be converted into cash). Assets are economic resources that are owned or controlled by the organization and which may benefit future operations. What the organization owes are called liabilities and are recorded on the right side of the balance sheet. Liabilities include short-term (current) and long-term financial obligations or commitments to staff, contractors, lenders, suppliers, etc.

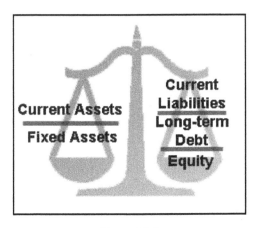

**Figure 18.2**
**Placement of information on the balance sheet**

The current value of investment made by the owner(s) is also a liability in the sense that it is a financial resource that is owed to the owner(s). The value of the owners' investment in the organization is more commonly termed equity. Both liabilities and equity appear on the right side of the balance sheet and are equal in combined value to that of the assets. Remember, the left side of the balance sheet is equal to (i.e., balances) the right side.

The simple equation that describes the balance sheet is:

Assets = Liabilities + Equity.

Figures 18.3 and 18.5 are sample balance sheets for Natalie's Quilting Center. One describes the financial condition of the quilting center on February 1, and the other describes the conditions on February 29.

Figure 18.4 is a sample income statement covering operation of the quilting center between February 1 and February 29. Notice in Figure 18.3 the current asset item called "accounts receivable." This item includes all amounts that the organization expects to receive in the near future due to services actually rendered or goods actually sold to customers. For example, the quilting center may have issued an invoice to a customer and is waiting for a $250 check as compensation for tutoring services recently provided. The accounts receivable category differs from cash in that the former represents money due but not yet received; and it differs from inventory in that the latter is the value of goods or service-related goods that the organization holds but has not yet exchanged for currency.

On the right side of the balance sheet shown in Figure 18.3 there is a liability category identified as "accounts payable." This short-term liability item presents the

## Natalie's Quilting Center

### Balance Sheet
As of February 1, 2008

| Assets | | Liabilities | |
|---|---|---|---|
| Current Assets | | Current Liabilities | |
| Cash | $4,000 | Accts. Payable | $8,550 |
| Accts. Receivable | 250 | | |
| Inventory/Supplies | 7,000 | Long-Term Debt | |
| Fixed Assets | | Mortgage | 48,000 |
| Building | 90,000 | | |
| | | Equity | 44,700 |
| Total Assets | $101,250 | Total Liability and Equity | $101,250 |

**Figure 18.3**
**Sample balance sheet (February 1, 2007)**

value of all goods or services received by the organization and for which payment is imminently due. For example, the pile of utility bills on the director's desk represents some of the ongoing or regular payable accounts.

### The Income Statement (a.k.a. Profit/Loss Statement)

Financial transactions that occur during a specified period of time (a fiscal period) are summarized in a document called the income statement. A typical income statement (illustrated in Figure 18.4) reports all expenditures and all income during the business period and identifies the difference between the two totals as either a profit or a loss. Revenue and expenditure categories used in the income statement mirror the income and expenditure categories used in the orga-

nization's formal budget document.

It is natural to expect that the net revenue or net loss shown on the income statement would be evident in the difference between the balance statements prepared for the first and last days of the period of financial activity. That is, it seems that the $44,700 equity shown on February 1 (Figure 18.3) should increase by the $1,320 profit realized in the following 29 days (Figure 18.4). While it may occasionally be so, such a clear relationship is rarely this discernable. The reason it is not is that the balance sheet contains some information that reflects future financial activity. Note that the balance sheet in Figure 18.3 lists accounts receivable and accounts payable. Each of these items, respectively, indicates expected in-flows and out-flows of cash during the period covered by the next income state-

# Natalie's Quilting Center

## Income Statement
As of February 1 - 29, 2008

| Revenue | | Expenditures | |
|---|---|---|---|
| Tuition | $5,378 | Wages | $6,500 |
| Consulting | 3,075 | Fabric Supplies | 1,200 |
| Sale of Materials | 1,450 | Utilities | 375 |
| Royalties | 1,367 | Advertising | 125 |
| | | Mortgage | 1,400 |
| | | Auto Lease | 350 |
| Total Revenue | $11,270 | Total Expenditures | $9,950 |
| Net Revenue (Loss) $1,320 | | | |

**Figure 18.4**
**Sample income statement (February 1–29, 2008)**

ment (Figure 18.4). The balance sheet for the end of the reporting period, however, may have different asset, liability, and equity amounts, simply because those amounts will include expected receivables and payables for the period immediately after (see Figure 18.5). The February 28 balance sheet is based on the stock described on the February 1 balance sheet, the flow described in the February 1–28 income statement, and additional economic activity for which there are new accounts receivable and payable.

## Internal Control

Most large sport, tourism, or leisure service organizations employ trained accountants and bookkeepers to control financial operations, accounting, and reporting. These people will record transactions, pay bills, deposit funds, and maintain accounts. They will also help the sport, tourism, or leisure service administrator to establish a petty cash fund and thereby reduce some potential organizational barriers to efficient program management.

### Petty Cash

Most expenses of the sport, tourism, and leisure service organization are paid by check, but sometimes it is impossible or inefficient to draw a check to make a payment. For example, on-street parking or postage stamps may cost so little that the expense of writing the check would exceed the cost of the item. Furthermore, it would be very difficult to find a parking meter that accepts checks! To help the organization deal with small expenses, a

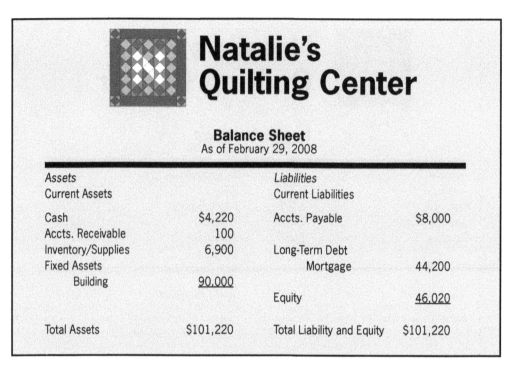

**Figure 18.5**
**Sample balance sheet (February 29, 2008)**

*petty cash fund* may be established.

In establishing the petty cash fund, clear guidelines or rules regarding its use must be articulated. One guideline might be a limit on the amount of expenses to be paid from this fund. Expenses in excess of $20 are usually paid by check. Another guideline might describe the types of expenses that may be paid with petty cash funds. Petty cash funds are not typically used to pay recurring expenses, such as utilities or subscriptions, regardless of the size of the expense. Yet another guideline or rule concerning the petty cash fund might concern management of the fund, someone should be appointed as custodian of the fund and held responsible for its proper management.

The petty cash fund is created by the treasurer upon writing a check to the custodian or manager of the fund for a fairly small amount of money, usually $50–$100. The check is recorded. The fund manager cashes the check and places the cash in a petty cash secured envelope or cash box. Authorized persons within the organization may then claim funds in advance or as reimbursement for minor (petty) expenditures. Petty cash funds are issued after the claimant submits a petty cash voucher (with attached receipts where possible). Pads of blank petty cash vouchers like the one shown in Figure 18.6 can be purchased at most stationery or office supply stores. After the claimant has been paid, the petty cash voucher is kept in the petty cash box. The money in the box and the face value of all the vouchers in the box should always add up to the original amount of cash issued to establish the fund. When the money in the petty cash box is almost spent, the

```
┌─────────────────────────────────────────────────────────────┐
│                   PETTY CASH VOUCHER                        │
│                                                             │
│   Date: _____    │
│   Amount: $ _____    │
│   For: _____    │
│                                                             │
│                                                             │
│   Account #: _____    │
│   Received by: _____    │
│                                                             │
│        Attach receipts immediately following purchase.      │
└─────────────────────────────────────────────────────────────┘
```

**Figure 18.6**
**Example of a petty cash voucher**

vouchers and receipts are submitted like any other invoice, and a check for the total value of the vouchers is issued to the fund manager. The check is cashed and the money returned to the petty cash box in order to bring its total back to the level of funds originally established.

It is important to note that petty cash is not a budget line. It is a means of payment only. Any expense that is paid using petty cash is charged to the appropriate budget account. Periodically, the fund manager should prepare a *petty cash reconciliation statement*. This simple form (shown in Figure 18.7) helps the manager to monitor the fund and anticipate cash replenishment needs. The petty cash fund offers convenience, but because of that convenience, it also has the potential to be abused. Great care should be taken

```
┌─────────────────────────────────────────────────────────────┐
│           Petty Cash Reconciliation Statement               │
│   Date:                                                     │
│                                                             │
│   Opening cash on hand                       $  _____   │
│                                                             │
│   ADD                                                       │
│   Payments to petty cash fund                $  _____   │
│                                                             │
│   SUBTRACT                                                  │
│   Total amount of vouchers paid              $  _____   │
│                                                             │
│   Cash on Hand (this should be the same as the  $  _____  │
│   amount of cash in the cash box)                           │
└─────────────────────────────────────────────────────────────┘
```

**Figure 18.7**
**Sample petty cash reconciliation statement**

to manage the petty cash fund according to established principles and practices of accounting.

## Reporting

There are many kinds of reports that can be generated by accountants and bookkeepers. Three of the most useful for financial managers in sport, tourism, and leisure service organizations are described below. They are *budget statements*, the *project report*, and the *RevPAR report*.

### The Budget Statement

The sport, tourism, or leisure service organization budget is a revenue and spending plan for a period of time, usually a year. The goal of the financial manager is to ensure that revenues reach the expected level and that expenses do not exceed the projected amounts. This two-pronged goal is referred to as "staying within the budget," and the realization of this goal must be a priority for the financial manager. The budget statement is a useful tool that allows the manager to review the financial activity of the organization with respect to the budget. The sample budget statement shown in Figure 18.8 lists key budget classes and the amount of money projected as revenue or expenditure for that class. As of the date listed at the top of the budget statement, the actual receipts and expenditures are reported, along with any commitments for revenue or expenditure that have been made. The budget statement also shows

**PINE CREEK RESORT**
Recreation Services Department
Budget Statement

June 30, 2007 (50% of budget period)

|  | Budget | Actual | Committed | % | Balance |
|---|---|---|---|---|---|
| REVENUE |  |  |  |  |  |
| Guest Service Assessment | 120,000 | 60,000 | 0 | 50.0 | 60,000 |
| Bike Rentals | 18,000 | 5,920 | 0 | 32.9 | 12,080 |
| Supply Fees | 2,000 | 831 | 0 | 41.6 | 1,169 |
| Total Revenue | 140,000 | 66,751 | 0 | 47.7 | 73,249 |
| EXPENSES |  |  |  |  |  |
| Personnel | 108,000 | 42,000 | 2,000 | 40.7 | 64,000 |
| Equipment Maintenance | 9,000 | 6,850 | 0 | 76.1 | 2,150 |
| Program Supplies | 1,500 | 988 | 0 | 65.9 | 512 |
| Transportation | 4,500 | 2,123 | 1,200 | 73.8 | 1,177 |
| Promotion | 2,000 | 1,112 | 400 | 75.6 | 488 |
| Administration | 12,000 | 5857 | 0 | 48.8 | 6,143 |
| Contingency/Enterprise | 3,000 | 800 | 500 | 43.3 | 1,700 |
| Total Expenses | 140,000 | 59,730 | 4,100 | 45.6 | 76,170 |

**Figure 18.8**
**Sample budget statement**

the portion (percentage) of each budget item that has been received or spent and reports the remaining balance.

In the preceding example, 50 percent of the budget period has elapsed, but less than 50 percent of the revenues have been received and less than 50 percent of the expenditures have been made. Noticeably, several expenditure items are at or near 75 percent, and a major revenue category is at 33 percent. Is this disparity an early warning of budget problems? Not necessarily. The budget statement only tells the manager how much of the budget has been received or spent at a particular point in the fiscal period. It does not indicate how much of the revenue should be received or how much of the expenses should have been paid at that time. The manager must use his or her knowledge of seasonal and other fluctuations in demand and cost in interpreting the budget statement and making judgments about how well the organization's finances are being managed.

## Project/Event Report

In addition to the budget statement, many sport, tourism, and leisure service managers find the project report to be particularly useful. This report compares projected and actual revenues and expenditures for specific programs or events and includes commentary that helps future organizers of the program/event to understand what contributed to the financial success or failure of the project. A sample project report is shown in Figure 18.9. The project report is a document that helps organizers of future events. It is rarely used in financial audit situations or for legal or highly technical documentation. For these reasons, the project report should be accurate and, more importantly, easily read and understood.

## RevPAR
## (Revenue Per Available Room)

Managers in the tourism industry, particularly those with hotel or resort management responsibilities, rely on the RevPAR report an important measure of performance. The RevPAR report provides a single metric, which is a function of both room rates and occupancy. RevPAR is calculated by multiplying the average daily room rate times the occupancy rate.

For example, if the Cummorah Resort and Lodge has 300 rooms that sell for an average of $210 per night, and an average occupancy rate of 74%, then RevPAR is calculated as follows:

RevPAR = Average Daily Rate x Occupancy Rate

RevPAR = $210 x .74 = $155.40

RevPAR is usually expressed and discussed as an annual average, but it can also be calculated and used to measure performance over a shorter period of time, such as a season, a month, or even a week. The period to which the RevPAR value pertains should be clearly stated on the report.

Financial managers look for changes in RevPAR. A rising RevPAR indicates that either occupancy is increasing, or average room rates are up (or a combination of both). RevPAR is also used as a ratio for comparisons with other properties. Finally, it is important to remember that RevPAR is not the only measure of financial health in the hospitality sector. It evaluates the strength of only one revenue stream, and should be used in conjunction with other budget statements and activity reports for profit centers such as restaurants, golf courses, casinos, spas, meeting services, etc.

## FROSTY ❄ FROLIC
### WINTER FESTIVAL ASSOCIATION

**Project Report**

Project/Event: Snow-Pitch Softball Tournament
Date: Feb. 11 - 13, 2007

|  | Project Budget | Actual |
|---|---|---|
| REVENUE |  |  |
| Community grant | 1,000 | 1,000 |
| Corporate sponsorships | 500 | 600 |
| Registration fees | 800 | 800 |
| Concession sales | 1,100 | 1,400 |
| Total Revenue | 3,400 | 3,800 |
| EXPENSES |  |  |
| Publicity/Administration | 400 | 380 |
| Referee honoraria | 900 | 900 |
| Equipment purchase | 400 | 450 |
| Awards | 150 | 150 |
| Facility fees | 50 | 60 |
| Kick-off reception | 850 | 980 |
| Insurance | 610 | 670 |
| Total expenses | 3,360 | 3,590 |
| Net Income (Loss) | 40 | 210 |

Submitted by:  Zo Bell

Comments:    Reception overage due to requirement use caterer.
Colder weather necessitated charge in menu.

**Figure 18.9**
**Sample project report**

### Daily Operations Report

In hospitality settings such as hotels or resorts, a frequently used report is the Daily Operations Report. Similar reports may also be used in other sport, tourism, and leisure service enterprises. This report is usually prepared at the end of the business day by the hotel's night auditor and includes a summary of the business conducted that day. The Daily Operations Report is used by the general manager and by other department heads as they review revenues, receivables, disbursements, operating statistics, and cash exchanges at the front desk.

### Summary

In order to effectively and efficiently manage the financial resources of a sport, tourism, or leisure service organization, the manager must have a basic understanding of accounting principles and practices. By following generally accepted accounting principles, reports that are meaningful, timely, and accurate can be prepared for use in executive decision making. The report or financial statement that indicates the single-point-in-time condition of the organization is the balance sheet. The income statement (also called the profit and loss statement, statement of receipts and disbursement, or operating statement) details financial activity between two dates for which balance sheets are prepared. Where available, trained accountants and bookkeepers help to prepare financial reports. Sport, tourism, and leisure service administrators may, however, be respon-

sible for maintaining and being accountable for a petty cash fund. Rules governing the use of the petty cash fund should be understood and followed by all users. A particularly useful report that helps the sport, tourism, or leisure service manager to be aware of the state of the budget is the budget statement. This report shows how much of each budget category has been received or spent at a particular point in the fiscal period. For specific programs, projects, or events, the project report is a common form of reporting on the financial outcomes of the project. RevPAR is the important efficiency monitoring report used by the tourism industry for measuring the success of crucial hotel and resort operations.

# NOTES

# SECTION F

# Planning

The final section of this book on financial management for sport, tourism, and leisure service organizations addresses the need for financial managers to be able to plan for new enterprises and/or expand existing activities. The business plan is an important long-term planning document that can be instrumental in generating sufficient funds to implement its design. Chapter 19 describes each element of the business plan and explains how the information contained therein is used by the plan developer, suppliers, investors, and creditors. The business plan provides essential support for and documentation of claims and analyses that are used in generating resources needed for capital development.

# CHAPTER 19

# Business Planning

## Introduction

The oft-repeated advice to sport, tourism, and leisure service managers to develop and follow business plans is too commonly relegated to the "nice concept, but not for me" file. For some managers, this ignorance (the act of ignoring the advice) is based on ignorance (a lack of understanding or knowledge). Business plans, it is erroneously believed, are for high-risk, high-volume production companies that depend on major investments and have a high degree of accountability to investors. Just as erroneously, some sport, tourism, and leisure service managers believe that business plans are master planning documents that establish general directions only for the entire organization and are of little direct relevance to specific programs or events. The business plan is an effective tool for the management of sport, tourism, and leisure service organizations. Failure to develop and follow business plans at a variety of levels of operation is a serious management flaw, which this chapter is designed to help overcome.

A business plan is a written document that describes all aspects of an enterprise. An enterprise could be a program, service, event, or activity. The business plan differs from a program plan in its inclusion of detailed analyses of resource opportunities, requirements, and management functions. It is especially concerned with (but not limited to) the financial elements of the sport, tourism, or leisure enterprise. It is, in effect, the management "game plan." The business plan is a proven and effective tool for facilitating an internal evaluation of existing or proposed programs or services. It helps those who have dreams and aspirations to objectively determine the desirability and feasibility of their ideas. It helps to identify and consider all conditions that relate to the potential success of an enterprise. Business planning, like other types of planning, forces a manager to seriously consider everything that is necessary for the success of the enterprise. It identifies foreseeable problems and expresses specific commitments to the resolution of those problems. It also identifies available resources and articulates the intended application of those resources to the achievement of stated objectives.

Beyond serving this internal evaluation function, the business plan also helps to meet the information and documentation requirements of external providers of required operational resources. The plan states the objectives to be met by the enterprise and then outlines the chosen approach to meeting those objectives. In so doing, it allows investors, lenders, donors, regulators, suppliers, employees, and customers to develop confidence in the enterprise and, thereby, justify extending credit, permission, patronage, or other support that is needed for success. Readers of the business plan will view it from different perspectives and focus on those elements that are relevant to their interests. Bankers, for example, will read business plans and pay particular attention to descriptions of fixed assets and available collateral. This information helps to determine how well their loans are protected and how ably the borrower can repay loans on schedule and at the agreed-upon rate of interest. Suppliers, such as the owner of a sports stadium, will focus on market and competitive analyses and expect the business plan to demonstrate a reasonable expectation of corporate viability and longevity before entering into a long-term lease agreement with, for example, a minor league baseball team. Furthermore, prospective major charitable donors will study the management and product/service elements of the business plan of a not-for-profit youth-serving agency to learn about how their philanthropic support would be used. In the tourism industry, investors will look carefully at the financial projections in the business plan before deciding about investing in a resort or attraction.

## Format of the Business Plan

The following paragraphs describe the essential elements of and a commonly used format for effective business plans. Note that such documents do provide for the demonstration of creativity in presentation, and there is a wide variety of styles used in business plans for sport, tourism, and leisure enterprises.

### Title Page

The title page or cover page is used to identify the plan at a glance. Obviously, the name of the enterprise should be boldly displayed. Also, the name, address, and telephone number of the plan's author (or corporate agent for whom the plan was prepared) should be included on the title page. The aesthetic aspects of the cover page do deserve attention, but inordinate energy and resources should not be dedicated to this part of what is really a rather technical document. The entire business plan should be professional in its presentation, both visually and substantively, and the cover page is a good place to demonstrate this standard.

Inasmuch as business plans articulate ideas that may provide a competitive advantage or should more appropriately be unveiled in a controlled setting, the title page should, where applicable, include a clear notice of the confidential nature of the document. If the business plan is

GUILDFORD
SQUASH CLUB

# BUSINESS PLAN

Prepared by:
Mission College Consulting
Ste 017 - 4208 Sheffield. Dr.
Pleasantview, NY 55409

(631) 555-7890

**Figure 19.1**
**Sample business plan cover page**

a confidential or restricted-distribution document, then the restrictions should be clearly stated either on the cover or very early on in the document.

## Front Matter

Included in the front matter are all those parts of the plan that are organized for ease of reading. Following the title page, a transmittal letter or preface officially introduces the plan to the reader. This brief section (usually less than one page of text) can also be used to "hook" the reader by highlighting some major points of the plan that would be of particular interest. The preface is followed by a table of contents, which offers the reader an outline of the plan by listing all the headings and subheadings. In addition to its value as an overview of the contents of the plan, this table provides references to the locations of various sections in the plan. The front matter might also include

a table of tables or a table of figures to further assist the reader in finding key information within the body of the business plan.

## Executive Summary

The executive summary is a concise review of plan highlights that enables the reader to quickly get a sense of the nature of the sport, tourism, or leisure enterprise and the resource needs of its management team. It must be brief enough (two to three pages) that even the busiest person could find time to read it, and it should be crafted in such a way as to capture the reader's interest and motivate further exploration and consideration of the plan. Although the executive summary is positioned at the beginning of the business-plan document, its writing should be done after the main body of the plan has been completed. Some business managers have also appended to the Executive Summary a "Fact Sheet," which states, in number form, the following:

1. The name of the sport, tourism, or leisure organization and the program or enterprise covered by the plan.

2. The address and telephone number of the organization representative responsible for the program or enterprise.

3. The type of industry (Standard Industrial Classification) in which the organization operates.

4. The form of agency organization (government agency, proprietorship, partnership, or corporation).

5. The principal product(s) or service line(s) included in the plan.

6. Any registered patents, trademarks, or service marks affected by the plan.

7. The number and names of founders, partners, corporate commissioners,

and shareholders.

8. The length of time the enterprise and the organization have been operating as such.
9. The current and/or projected market share.
10. The funds invested in the enterprise to date and their source.
11. Any additional financing required.
12. Proposed terms and payback period for required financing.
13. The total value or net worth of the organization.
14. The names of business advisors (legal counsel, accountant, others).

## The Enterprise

The first section of the body of the business plan is designed to provide the reader with a context in which to consider all the information that follows. This important part of the business plan effectively familiarizes the reader with the history of the enterprise and the organization, provides insight into the current situation, and speculates about the future of the enterprise. Historical information is presented in the form of a narrative about how, when, and why the enterprise was or will be started, as well as an identification of the key individuals directing the activity and a description of the principal products or services to be offered. If the business plan has been developed for an existing activity, a discussion of the success experienced thus far should be included. The description of current conditions is limited to relevant circumstances, such as market opportunities, production capabilities, and competition, while speculation about the future takes the form of vision statements and articulated goals, objectives, and strategies.

## The Industry

The preparation of this second section of the body of the document provides an opportunity for careful examination and description of the nature and scope of the industry in which the enterprise will operate. Since it is likely that at least one of the readers of the business plan has little familiarity with the industry or field, this part of the business plan is important because it brings all readers up to the same high level of understanding and awareness that the plan's author has of the environment in which the plan will be implemented. Other readers who are in the industry may already have that understanding, but nonetheless will welcome the author's demonstration of environmental consciousness. The principal characteristics of the industry to be described in the business plan include its size, sales/participation levels, and performance standards. For example, the business plan of a public learn-to-swim program would include a description of the number of such programs offered in the community, region, state, and country. In addition, the total number of program participants, the time of year that courses are typically offered, and the number of badges awarded at each level of instruction would be useful information to offer.

This analysis of the industry will also identify the major participants in the industry and describe their market niches, market shares, strengths and advantages, and weaknesses or disadvantages. The manager of the public swimming program might, for example, explain that aquatic instructional programs in the area are offered by several agencies, including the YMCA, the Boys and Girls Club, and the Community School Corporation. She would then point out that the Boys and Girls Club and the schools do not offer summer programs, and the YMCA has a recreational orientation for its family-based membership. The public agency is targeting young adolescents in the summer season for a highly structured program of aquatic safety training. It will compete with the YMCA to some degree, but it has a competitive advantage through pricing and location.

Further understanding of the industry is promoted by a discussion of industry trends. This requires a careful study of past performances in light of past conditions, as well as speculation about future successes based on an educated guess as to how the relevant operating environment will be. Fortunately, many elements of the sport, tourism, and leisure service industry are closely monitored, and trend analyses are readily available. For example, the trends in aquatic programming are discussed in a variety of publications, such as the regular *Parks and Recreation* magazine special issues on aquatics. The business plan for the learn-to-swim program might emphasize and detail an industry-wide observation that interest in such programs is increasing.

### Product/Service Offering

In describing the product or service that will be delivered to consumers, the business plan should focus on its unique features and emphasize its particular advantages. If a novel concept is being introduced, more detail will be required in its description than would be in the description of a product or service with which the reader is already very familiar. In this section of the business plan document, it may be sufficient to describe a proposed three-on-three basketball tournament with just a scant reference to the rules of play and play-down structure and a slightly more descriptive account of the scheduling, setting, and game format to be applied. Conversely, a proposed ice-sculpting competition and winter festival would warrant extensive explanation of the purpose of the event, nature of the activity, schedule of events, qualifications for participation, warm weather alternatives, theme guidelines, site selection, security measures, etc. This is the section of the business plan that is used to ensure that its readers know exactly what the program, service, good, or event is that they are to consider while examining the other important information presented later in the plan.

If the sport, tourism, or leisure product is not in the public domain and is protected by copyright, patent, or other proprietary rights, the nature of that protection should be described in this section. Any contract releases received or awarded should also be identified. It is important for sport, tourism, and leisure service managers to assure the readers of their business plan that the products they "sell" are rightfully theirs to produce or distribute. For example, a sports merchandiser's business plan should state that his invention, the portable heat-generating arena cushion, is patented. If the cushion is to be adorned with the logo of a professional hockey team, the merchandiser will also need to articulate the rights he has to use the logo, as stated in the copyright permission or license agreement.

This part of the business plan also provides an opportunity to discuss the ways in which the product or service under consideration contributes to the realization of organizational objectives. It should include an estimate of the potential for this enterprise to grow, or, if it is a program within a larger set of programs and services, its contribution to the effectiveness, stability, profitability, and growth of the sport, tourism, and leisure organization should be described.

## Market Analysis

In the previous section of the business plan, the product was described. Of course, a well-defined product is of little value to the sport, tourism, and leisure service organization if there are no consumers of that product. Potential consumers constitute the market, and understanding the market is vital to the success of the sport, tourism, or leisure enterprise.

The business plan describes the relatively homogenous group(s) of individuals that might be customers, clients, program participants, or service recipients. This description should clearly establish that the target market is (1) large enough to warrant the offering of a program or service; (2) sufficiently distinct to guide product development, distribution, pricing, and promotion decisions; and (3) accessible to the sport, tourism, or leisure service organization. It may be that the target market is made up of several meaningful market segments; if so, each segment should be described separately. Readers of the business plan will be interested in knowing who and where the market is, what makes individuals in the target market good customer/client candidates, and how successful the organization has been in the past in serving their needs.

It is likely that there will be some form of competition for the attention and resources of the target market. Significant forms of competition include the following:

- Other sport, tourism, and leisure services offered by the organization.
- Services and products offered by other sport, tourism, and leisure organizations with access to the same market(s).
- Other discretionary activities avail-

able to the target market.
- Market inertia.

The market analysis includes an assessment of the strengths, weaknesses, advantages, and disadvantages of all major competitors, along with a statement of how the sport, tourism, and leisure service organization plans to address the competitive challenge. Based on the organization's understanding of the market's needs, constraints, and opportunities, as well as an awareness of the competition it faces in the marketplace, it is also expected that this section of the business plan will include a realistic and defensible estimate of the share of the market that can be attracted at different stages of the enterprise's development. It is understood that estimates are nothing more than educated guesses based on relevant information and certain assumptions. The assumptions, therefore, should also be stated.

## Marketing Plan

Marketing plans are usually separate, extensive documents that relate market conditions to strategic decisions about product development, sales and distribution, pricing, and promotion. The business plan incorporates a synopsis of the marketing plan and provides the reader with a clear sense of how the organization will manage the marketing of its sport, tourism, or leisure product throughout that product's lifetime. Since some elements of a full marketing plan are addressed in the preceding sections of the business plan, this section will focus on pricing, distribution, and promotion matters:

*Pricing.* The business plan should discuss the price that will be set for the sport, tourism, and leisure service products of the organization. In addition, the following questions (among others) should be answered:

- How are these prices determined?
- What cost-recovery ratio(s) do these prices reflect?
- How do they compare to those charged by competitors?
- How will these prices contribute to achievement of the organization's financial goals?
- What will be the impact of price changes on consumer responsiveness?

*Distribution.* How, when, and where the sports, tourism, or leisure service will be delivered to the consumer is also of great interest to the reader of the business plan. This section would normally include descriptions of the service area, season(s) of operation, schedule of marketable events, sales force, and locations of service delivery.

*Promotion.* The promotions mix (which might include advertising, publicity, personal selling, public relations, and/or sales promotions) should be described in order for the reader to judge the likelihood of the sport, tourism, or leisure service organization reaching its target market and effectively facilitating a desired exchange. The promotions budget should be outlined, along with a process for assessing the impact of the various strategies employed in the promotional plan. Financially oriented readers would be interested in seeing an estimate of the conversion ratio. The conversion ratio is simply an estimate of the consumption (sales revenue or participation) directly resulting from promotion activities in relation to the costs of implementing those promotional activities. For example, the conversion ratio for a $2,500 advertising campaign that increased sales of karate lessons by $12,500 is a respectable 5:1.

## Development Plan

If the product around which the enterprise is being established is not fully developed at the time of the business plan's preparation, then this section may be used to report on the status of the product's development. All costs associated with getting the product into a marketable form should be identified, along with development schedules. The improvement, refinement, or expansion of existing or market-ready products may also be considered in this section. Again, development schedules and associated costs should be identified.

## Production/Operations Plan

In the production of sport, tourism, and leisure services, there are certain aspects of operation that contribute significantly to the success of the enterprise. They include location, facilities and equipment, and labor. For most businesses, including sport, tourism, and leisure service enterprises, the three most important details are said to be "location, location, location." Consider, for example, the obvious folly of establishing an alpine ski shop in the plains of west Texas, or a mountaineering school in Saskatchewan. A less obvious but equally disastrous mistake might occur in offering a public recreation program at a neighborhood park which, unbeknownst to the recreation agency, has become a place of clandestine drug distribution. Such mistakes do sometimes occur quite innocently, but the opportunity exists in this section of the business plan to show that every reasonable care was exercised in selecting a location that will contribute to the realization of business goals.

Any facilities and/or major equipment that is required to operate the sport, tourism, or leisure service should be described in the business plan. Sometimes sample floor plans or photographs of buildings and rooms are included to help the reader visualize those physical needs. Recognizing that not all buildings or equipment must be owned by the organization in order for them to be used in production or service delivery, a listing of leased and purchased items should be presented, along with the costs of such properties.

In general terms, the labor requirements should be described. Especially in the delivery of sport, tourism, and leisure services, personnel are key to the success of the enterprise, and the labor needs of the organization deserve careful scrutiny. In this section of the business plan, the number of employees and their general job duties should be discussed. Sometimes, business plans also describe the qualification requirements of employees, their availability (i.e., the number of qualified people in the area that could be hired), compensation and benefits programs, and union affiliations.

### Management Team

Even with a good product and a meaningful, identifiable, and accessible target market, a sport, tourism, or leisure service or program can experience limited success because of managers who are not well suited to the enterprise. The business plan provides an opportunity to identify the management team and expound on that team's qualifications for directing the program or service. For many readers of the business plan, this information is as important, or even more important, than the details of the program, market, or financial structure. They believe that the right person managing the enterprise will make sure that the product is good and the financial aspects of the activity are sound.

An organizational chart focusing on the management structure could be used to illustrate hierarchies and functional responsibilities. Whether in chart form or as a narrative, the names of each member of the management team or program leadership staff should be listed, along with brief résumés and annotated job descriptions for each person. More complete résumés and job descriptions can be appended to the business plan if necessary or desirable. The purpose of providing this information is to help readers develop confidence in the management and operation of the enterprise.

It is also customary to discuss the compensation package (salaries, benefits, other contract terms, etc.) that each manager will receive, although such disclosure is often unnecessary when the business plan is used as a planning and evaluation tool for programs and services that are just one part of a larger set of activities conducted by the sport, tourism, or leisure service organization. It should be noted that, if the manager is already on staff and is compensated in a manner consistent with his previous position, declaring the manager's compensation for this enterprise may be a contractual violation, or in some other respect, considered to be inappropriate. If the manager is also the owner, a partner, or a shareholder in the organization, the level of ownership needs to be reported, as do any incentive stock options that may be offered.

In concluding this section, it is appropriate and desirable to list other individuals who are not a direct part of the management team, but may influence it significantly. This list includes consultants, professional mentors, advisors, accountants, bankers, and lawyers. This listing should also indicate the amount of compensation (retainers, consulting fees, stipends, honoraria, etc.) received by these influential advisors for their professional service to the sport, tourism, or leisure service organization.

### Financial Plan

One of the main reasons for going through all the work to develop a business plan is to demonstrate the advisability of investment in the particular sport, tourism, or leisure service enterprise. Therefore, it is essential that the plan clearly indicates the level of financial investment that is required. Not only must the business plan state how much money or credit is needed, but it should also describe the type of funding that is needed. For example, the proponent of a new guide fishing enterprise may need $450,000 to acquire equipment, licenses, advertising, etc., but would like to have only $150,000 as debt (i.e., borrowed money) and the remaining $300,000 as equity (i.e., shared ownership). In order to justify the confidence of a lender or an equity investor, the author of the business plan should discuss and include (either in this section or as an appendix) the following financial documents (see Chapter 17 for examples):

### 1. Current Financial Statements (if the enterprise is already in operation)

Profit and loss statements and balance sheets for the current and preceding two years should be provided.

### 2. Financial Projections (for new enterprises)

Profit and loss forecasts, pro forma balance sheets, projected cash flow statements, and a break-even analysis for the sport or leisure event (or first three years of an ongoing operation) should be provided. Since these are projections and, as

such are subject to the limitations of current knowledge and optimistic expectations of future conditions, effort should be exercised in protecting decision makers from the enthusiasm of the enterprise proponent. It is generally considered wise to be as realistic as possible in making financial projections and then temper that realism with conservatism when estimating income. Conversely, realistic expenditure projections should be tempered with liberalism. In other words, estimate low for revenue and high for expenses.

### 3. Ratio Analysis

Ratios are quantitative indicators of financial strength and operating success. The figures used in calculating ratios come from financial statements (or projections) like the balance sheet and income statement. Different readers of the business plan will focus on the ratios that interest them most. For example, lenders will be most concerned with ratios that indicate the degree of risk associated with extending credit to the sports, tourism, or leisure service organization, and potential equity investors will be more concerned with return-on-investment indicators. Not surprisingly, there are many ratios that could be calculated and reported in this section of the business plan. Those that are of greatest utility in the development of a business plan for a sports, tourism, and leisure service enterprise are briefly described here. Ratios of four general types are discussed. *Liquidity ratios* (also called solvency ratios) indicate the ability of a sports, tourism, or leisure business to meet its short-term obligations. *Activity ratios* (also called efficiency ratios) are quantitative indicators of the ability of the business to expediently and efficiently exchange its products for financial resources. *Profitability ratios* show how successful the business has been during a certain period of time (usually a year) in terms of investment returns. *Debt/Coverage/Leverage ratios* measure the long-term solvency of the business. Examples of the commonly used ratios are as follows:

a. Liquidity Ratios
*Quick Ratio:* Used to estimate the ability of a business to meet its short-term financial obligations without selling off its inventory.

Quick = (Current Assets-Inventories)/ Current Liabilities

*Current Ratio:* Used to estimate the ability of a business to meet its short-term financial obligations (assuming ability to dispose of inventory at full value). It is sometimes called the *banker's ratio.*

Current = Current Assets/Current Liabilities

*Debt-to-Net Worth Ratio:* Used to compare the total financial obligations of the business to the investment of its owners. This is used by lenders as a measure of risk involved in extending credit to the business.

Debt-to-Net Worth = Current and Long-Term Liabilities/Net Worth

*Current Liability-to-Net Worth Ratio:* Another measure of the short-term risk associated with lending to the business.

Current Liability-to-Net Worth = Current Liabilities/Net Worth

*Current Liability to Inventory Ratio:* Used to estimate the ability of a business to meet its short-term financial obligations without disposing of its assets (other than inventory).

Current Liability to Inventory = Current Liability/Inventory

b. Activity Ratios
*Average Collection Period:* This is not a ratio, but is often included in the ratio analysis. It shows the average time (in days) to receive payment for products delivered.

Avg. Coll. Period = (Accounts Receivables/Sales) x 365 days

*Sales-to-Inventory Ratio:* Used to indicate the inventory turnover rate. Low numbers may indicate an overstock situation.

Sales-to-Inventory = Cost of Goods Sold/Average Inventory

*Assets-to-Sales Ratio:* This ratio is used in determinations of how well the assets are being utilized.

Assets-to-Sales = Total Assets/Total Sales

c. Profitability Ratios
*Return on Sales:* This ratio is used only when comparing with similar businesses or with performance over a period of time. It indicates ability to generate profits from sales.

Return on Sales = Net Income/Net Sales

*Return on Assets:* Sometimes called the productive ratio, this index is useful for comparisons with other enterprises and with gauging the effectiveness of asset utilization.
Return on Assets = Net Profit after Taxes/Total Assets

*Return on Net Worth:* This ratio measures the ultimate profitability of the enterprise from the perspective of stockholders/owners. It indicates ability to earn adequate profits and should be higher than conservative (safe) investment rates.

Return on Net Worth = Net Profits after Taxes/Equity

### d. Debt/Coverage/Leverage Ratios

*Equity Ratio:* This ratio indicates the extent of the owner's investment in the enterprise.

Equity Ratio = Equity/Total Assets

*Debt-to-Total Asset Ratio:* This ratio indicates the extent of the enterprise's borrowing.

Debt-to-Total Asset Ratio = Total Liabilities/Total Assets

The ratios that are calculated are instructive in themselves, but they also provide very specific information that allows the readers of the business plan to compare the current or expected financial condition of the enterprise with others in a similar class of ventures. In *ratio analysis,* comparisons are made between the enterprise in question and the class of businesses represented by an appropriate Standard Industrial Code (SIC). Unfortunately, but understandably, not all sport, tourism, and leisure enterprises fit neatly into existing SICs. This means that ratio analysis can only provide a comparison between the proposed enterprise and others in an industrial classification that is judged to most closely resemble it.

Table 19.1 lists most of the sport, tourism, and leisure service–related SICs used in the United States since 1997.

In reviewing the list presented in Table 19.1, the difficulty in classifying an enterprise such as a resort-based recreation program becomes readily apparent. Should it be included in SIC#7011 (Hotels and Motels), where lodging and other major business activities strongly influence ratios, or might it more appropriately be included in SIC#7997 (Membership Clubs) because being a guest at the resort is, in fact, like having membership privileges in the exclusive resort recreation club setting? Perhaps the fitness orientation of the program makes it best suited to SIC#7991 (Fitness Facilities), or SIC#7999 (Miscellaneous Amusement and Recreation).

This system of classification has been used in the United States, Canada, and Mexico since 1997, and is called the North American Industrial Classification System (NAICS).

Once the appropriate comparative industrial classification has been selected, a variety of publications can be referred to in order to find the industry standard for each ratio. The most popular publications of this type are the following:

- Robert Morris and Associates' Annual Statement Studies.
- Dun and Bradstreet's Industry Norms and Key Business Ratios.
- Leo Troy's Almanac of Business and Industrial Financial Ratios.
- The Financial Survey of Canadian Business Performance.

Ratios reported in these publications are often given for businesses that differ in sales output, asset value, or place within the range of reported ratio values. These reports recognize that, although they may reside in the same industrial classification, businesses vary greatly in their productivity, efficiency, and profitability.

**Table 19.1**
**Sample enterprises from selected North American Industrial Classifications**
**(U.S. Census Bureau, 1998)**

| | | |
|---|---|---|
| **4511  Sporting Goods, Hobby and Music Instr** sport goods stores, hobby, toy, game stores, music instruction, sewing and needlework stores **4512 Book, Periodical, and Music Stores** book stores, recorded music stores **4811  Sched. Air Transport.** Passenger transport by air **4821  Rail Transport.** **4871-9  Scenic and Sight-seeing Transport** land, water, and other transport **5121  Motion Picture and Video Industries** production, distribution, and exhibition **5141  Information Services** libraries **5322  Consumer Goods - Rental** video tape and discs | **5615  Travel Arrange.** Travel agencies, tour operators, convention and visitor bureaus **7111  Performing Arts** dance companies, musical groups, theater companies **7112  Spectator Sports** sports teams and clubs, racetracks **7113  Arts, Sports Promoters** with facilities and without **7114  Agents and Managers** for artists and for athletes **7115  Independent Artists** writers and performers **7121  Museums, Historical Sites, and Similar Inst.** Museums, historical sites, zoos, nature parks, etc. | **7131  Amusement Parks and Arcades** theme parks and amusement arcades **7132  Gambling** casinos **7139  Other Amusement and Recreation** golf/country clubs, skiing facilities, marinas, fitness/ rec. sports, bowling centers, other recreation **7211  Traveler Accommodation** hotels, motels, and casino hotels **7212  RV Parks/Camps** RV campgrounds and RV camps **7213  Rooming and Boarding Houses** **7221  Full Service Restaurants** **7222  Limited Service Restaurants** **7223  Special Food Services** **7224  Drinking Places (alcoholic beverages)** |

Fortunately, some publications list ratios and other important financial data for similar enterprises across a wide range of sizes (as measured by sales volume or by value of assets). For example, Troy (2006) identifies operating costs (including salaries, advertising, interest, taxes, etc.) and income (including sales, interest, rent, and royalties) SIC#7131 - Amusement, Gambling and Recreation Industries, as well as ratios for businesses with less than $500,00 in assets, $500,00-$1,000,000 in assets, and so on. In SIC#7131, the current and quick ratios for businesses with less than $500,000 in assets are 1.1 and 0.7 respectively. For larger businesses in the same SIC, the comparable ratios are 1.6 and 1.2. This emphasizes the need to conduct a ratio analysis using the industry norms for the type and size of business that most closely matches the one being proposed in the business plan.

Reporting the results of the ratio analysis is simply a matter of tabulating the calculated ratios for the enterprise and for the comparative industrial class, as well as providing commentary to explain major differences between those ratio figures. For example, consider the following: In reviewing the industry standards, it may seem that the statistics given are an indication of "what should be." In fact, they are merely measures of "what is." They reflect the current conditions of the entire industrial class and are therefore very useful benchmarks. However, a particular enterprise at a particular stage of its development may have quite different ratios, and what is most important is that the manager of that en-

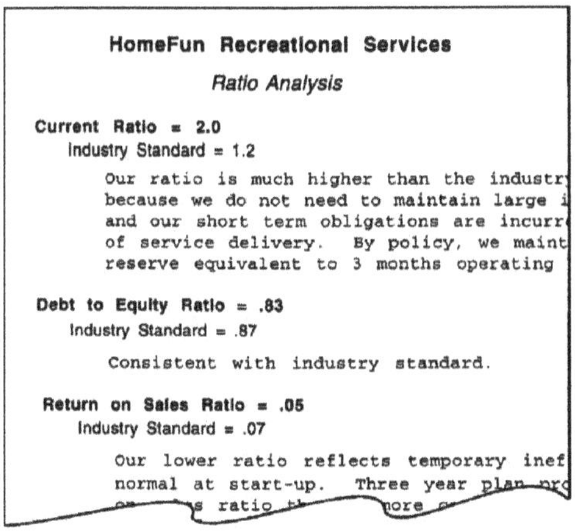

Table 19.2 displays selected ratios for three SIC classes of sport, tourism, and leisure service business in 2006. Again, these are indicators of how things were, not necessarily how things should have been.

## Appendices

Relevant material may be appended to the business plan. In deciding what to include as an appendix, the information needs of the reader must be the primary consideration. Material should not be included for the purpose of making the document thicker. Appended items should be referred to in the body of the plan and may include the following:

- Full résumés of members of the management team.
- Management team job descriptions.
- Product specifications.
- Relevant photographs.

---

**HomeFun Recreational Services**

*Ratio Analysis*

**Current Ratio = 2.0**
Industry Standard = 1.2

Our ratio is much higher than the industr[y] because we do not need to maintain large [] and our short term obligations are incurr[] of service delivery. By policy, we maint[] reserve equivalent to 3 months operating

**Debt to Equity Ratio = .83**
Industry Standard = .87

Consistent with industry standard.

**Return on Sales Ratio = .05**
Industry Standard = .07

Our lower ratio reflects temporary inef[] normal at start-up. Three year plan pro[] [] ratio [] []ore []

**Figure 19.2**
**Sample format for reporting results of ratio analysis**

terprise understands what the ratios and the comparisons are saying to the readers of the business plan.

---

**Table 19.2**
**Comparison of selected ratios reported for three types of sport, tourism, and leisure industries (Dun & Bradstreet, 2006)**

|  | SIC#7991 Physical Fitness Facilities | SIC#7011 Hotels, Motels | SIC#7992 Public Golf Courses |
|---|---|---|---|
| Liquidity (solvency) | | | |
| Quick (times) | 0.9 | 0.7 | 0.4 |
| Current (times) | 1.0 | 1.0 | 1.0 |
| Total Liability to Net Worth (%) | 562.5 | 162.3 | 110.7 |
| Current Liability to Net Worth (%) | 17.5 | 32.1 | 33.9 |
| Activity (efficiency) | | | |
| Average Collection Period (days) | 12.1 | 9.5 | 1.8 |
| Sales to Inventory (times) | 129.2 | 82.1 | 35.4 |
| Assets to Sales (%) | 112.2 | 158.7 | 116.6 |
| Profitability: | | | |
| Return on Sales (%) | 5.2 | 4.6 | 1.1 |
| Return on Assets (%) | 5.2 | 2.7 | 1.7 |
| Return on Net Worth (%) | 12.5 | 8.1 | 2.9 |

- List of prospective customers or sources of customers.
- List of possible suppliers.
- Consulting reports and market surveys.
- Copies of legal documents.
- Letters of reference.

## Summary

The business plan reflects both the dreams and the careful consideration of the sport, tourism, and leisure service organization. It can cover the entire range of services offered by that organization, or just one program or event. Business plans are just as valuable in public and private not-for-profit organizations as they are in the commercial sector because they describe how the resources of the organization will be utilized to achieve its corporate objectives. Such an informative guiding document will naturally be of great interest and is, almost without exception, required by potential investors, suppliers, and creditors. Business plans typically include descriptions of the enterprise and its products and production capabilities. Also included are market descriptions and detailed statements disclosing the financial aspects of the enterprise.

## References

Dun and Bradstreet. (Annual). *Industry norms and key business ratios.* Parsippany, NJ: Dun and Bradstreet.

Robert Morris Associates. (Annual). Annual statement studies. Philadelphia: RMA.

Troy, Leo. (Annual). *Almanac of business and industrial financial ratios.* Chicago, IL: CCH.

# NOTES

# APPENDIX

# Interest Tables

**Interest Table A: $(1+i)^n$**

| n\ | 2% | 3% | 4% | 5% | 6% | 7% | 8% | 9% | 10% | 12% | 15% |
|---|---|---|---|---|---|---|---|---|---|---|---|
| 1 | 1.020 | 1.030 | 1.040 | 1.050 | 1.060 | 1.070 | 1.080 | 1.090 | 1.100 | 1.120 | 1.150 |
| 2 | 1.040 | 1.061 | 1.082 | 1.103 | 1.124 | 1.145 | 1.166 | 1.188 | 1.210 | 1.254 | 1.323 |
| 3 | 1.061 | 1.093 | 1.125 | 1.158 | 1.191 | 1.225 | 1.260 | 1.295 | 1.331 | 1.405 | 1.521 |
| 4 | 1.082 | 1.126 | 1.170 | 1.216 | 1.262 | 1.311 | 1.360 | 1.412 | 1.464 | 1.574 | 1.749 |
| 5 | 1.104 | 1.159 | 1.217 | 1.276 | 1.338 | 1.403 | 1.469 | 1.539 | 1.611 | 1.762 | 2.011 |
| 6 | 1.126 | 1.194 | 1.265 | 1.340 | 1.419 | 1.501 | 1.587 | 1.677 | 1.772 | 1.974 | 2.313 |
| 7 | 1.149 | 1.230 | 1.316 | 1.407 | 1.504 | 1.606 | 1.714 | 1.828 | 1.949 | 2.211 | 2.660 |
| 8 | 1.172 | 1.267 | 1.369 | 1.477 | 1.594 | 1.718 | 1.851 | 1.993 | 2.144 | 2.476 | 3.059 |
| 9 | 1.195 | 1.305 | 1.423 | 1.551 | 1.689 | 1.838 | 1.999 | 2.172 | 2.358 | 2.773 | 3.518 |
| 10 | 1.219 | 1.344 | 1.480 | 1.629 | 1.791 | 1.967 | 2.159 | 2.367 | 2.594 | 3.106 | 4.046 |
| 11 | 1.243 | 1.384 | 1.539 | 1.710 | 1.898 | 2.105 | 2.332 | 2.580 | 2.853 | 3.479 | 4.652 |
| 12 | 1.268 | 1.426 | 1.601 | 1.796 | 2.012 | 2.252 | 2.518 | 2.813 | 3.138 | 3.896 | 5.350 |
| 13 | 1.294 | 1.469 | 1.665 | 1.886 | 2.133 | 2.410 | 2.720 | 3.066 | 3.452 | 4.363 | 6.153 |
| 14 | 1.319 | 1.513 | 1.732 | 1.980 | 2.261 | 2.579 | 2.937 | 3.342 | 3.797 | 4.887 | 7.076 |
| 15 | 1.346 | 1.558 | 1.801 | 2.079 | 2.397 | 2.759 | 3.172 | 3.642 | 4.177 | 5.474 | 8.137 |
| 16 | 1.373 | 1.605 | 1.873 | 2.183 | 2.540 | 2.952 | 3.426 | 3.970 | 4.595 | 6.130 | 9.358 |
| 17 | 1.400 | 1.653 | 1.948 | 2.292 | 2.693 | 3.159 | 3.700 | 4.328 | 5.054 | 6.866 | 10.761 |
| 18 | 1.428 | 1.702 | 2.026 | 2.407 | 2.854 | 3.380 | 3.996 | 4.717 | 5.560 | 7.690 | 12.375 |
| 19 | 1.457 | 1.754 | 2.107 | 2.527 | 3.026 | 3.617 | 4.316 | 5.142 | 6.116 | 8.613 | 14.232 |
| 20 | 1.486 | 1.806 | 2.191 | 2.653 | 3.207 | 3.870 | 4.661 | 5.604 | 6.727 | 9.646 | 16.367 |
| 21 | 1.516 | 1.860 | 2.279 | 2.786 | 3.400 | 4.141 | 5.034 | 6.109 | 7.400 | 10.804 | 18.822 |
| 22 | 1.546 | 1.916 | 2.370 | 2.925 | 3.604 | 4.430 | 5.437 | 6.659 | 8.140 | 12.100 | 21.645 |
| 23 | 1.577 | 1.974 | 2.465 | 3.072 | 3.820 | 4.741 | 5.871 | 7.258 | 8.954 | 13.552 | 24.891 |
| 24 | 1.608 | 2.033 | 2.563 | 3.225 | 4.049 | 5.072 | 6.341 | 7.911 | 9.850 | 15.179 | 28.625 |
| 25 | 1.641 | 2.094 | 2.666 | 3.386 | 4.292 | 5.427 | 6.848 | 8.623 | 10.835 | 17.000 | 32.919 |

**Interest Table B**  $1/(1+i)^n$

| n\ | 2% | 3% | 4% | 5% | 6% | 7% | 8% | 9% | 10% | 12% | 15% |
|---|---|---|---|---|---|---|---|---|---|---|---|
| 1 | 0.980 | 0.971 | 0.962 | 0.952 | 0.943 | 0.935 | 0.926 | 0.917 | 0.909 | 0.893 | 0.870 |
| 2 | 0.961 | 0.943 | 0.925 | 0.907 | 0.890 | 0.873 | 0.857 | 0.842 | 0.826 | 0.797 | 0.756 |
| 3 | 0.942 | 0.915 | 0.889 | 0.864 | 0.840 | 0.816 | 0.794 | 0.772 | 0.751 | 0.712 | 0.658 |
| 4 | 0.924 | 0.888 | 0.855 | 0.823 | 0.792 | 0.763 | 0.735 | 0.708 | 0.683 | 0.636 | 0.572 |
| 5 | 0.906 | 0.863 | 0.822 | 0.784 | 0.747 | 0.713 | 0.681 | 0.650 | 0.621 | 0.567 | 0.497 |
| 6 | 0.888 | 0.837 | 0.790 | 0.746 | 0.705 | 0.666 | 0.630 | 0.596 | 0.564 | 0.507 | 0.432 |
| 7 | 0.871 | 0.813 | 0.760 | 0.711 | 0.665 | 0.623 | 0.583 | 0.547 | 0.513 | 0.452 | 0.376 |
| 8 | 0.853 | 0.789 | 0.731 | 0.677 | 0.627 | 0.582 | 0.540 | 0.502 | 0.467 | 0.404 | 0.327 |
| 9 | 0.837 | 0.766 | 0.703 | 0.645 | 0.592 | 0.544 | 0.500 | 0.460 | 0.424 | 0.361 | 0.284 |
| 10 | 0.820 | 0.744 | 0.676 | 0.614 | 0.558 | 0.508 | 0.463 | 0.422 | 0.386 | 0.322 | 0.247 |
| 11 | 0.804 | 0.722 | 0.650 | 0.585 | 0.527 | 0.475 | 0.429 | 0.388 | 0.350 | 0.287 | 0.215 |
| 12 | 0.788 | 0.701 | 0.625 | 0.557 | 0.497 | 0.444 | 0.397 | 0.356 | 0.319 | 0.257 | 0.187 |
| 13 | 0.773 | 0.681 | 0.601 | 0.530 | 0.469 | 0.415 | 0.368 | 0.326 | 0.290 | 0.229 | 0.163 |
| 14 | 0.758 | 0.661 | 0.577 | 0.505 | 0.442 | 0.388 | 0.340 | 0.299 | 0.263 | 0.205 | 0.141 |
| 15 | 0.743 | 0.642 | 0.555 | 0.481 | 0.417 | 0.362 | 0.315 | 0.275 | 0.239 | 0.183 | 0.123 |
| 16 | 0.728 | 0.623 | 0.534 | 0.458 | 0.394 | 0.339 | 0.292 | 0.252 | 0.218 | 0.163 | 0.107 |
| 17 | 0.714 | 0.605 | 0.513 | 0.436 | 0.371 | 0.317 | 0.270 | 0.231 | 0.198 | 0.146 | 0.093 |
| 18 | 0.700 | 0.587 | 0.494 | 0.416 | 0.350 | 0.296 | 0.250 | 0.212 | 0.180 | 0.130 | 0.081 |
| 19 | 0.686 | 0.570 | 0.475 | 0.396 | 0.331 | 0.277 | 0.232 | 0.194 | 0.164 | 0.116 | 0.070 |
| 20 | 0.673 | 0.554 | 0.456 | 0.377 | 0.312 | 0.258 | 0.215 | 0.178 | 0.149 | 0.104 | 0.061 |
| 21 | 0.660 | 0.538 | 0.439 | 0.359 | 0.294 | 0.242 | 0.199 | 0.164 | 0.135 | 0.093 | 0.053 |
| 22 | 0.647 | 0.522 | 0.422 | 0.342 | 0.278 | 0.226 | 0.184 | 0.150 | 0.123 | 0.083 | 0.046 |
| 23 | 0.634 | 0.507 | 0.406 | 0.326 | 0.262 | 0.211 | 0.170 | 0.138 | 0.112 | 0.074 | 0.040 |
| 24 | 0.622 | 0.492 | 0.390 | 0.310 | 0.247 | 0.197 | 0.158 | 0.126 | 0.102 | 0.066 | 0.035 |
| 25 | 0.610 | 0.478 | 0.375 | 0.295 | 0.233 | 0.184 | 0.146 | 0.116 | 0.092 | 0.059 | 0.030 |

Interest Table C:  $(1-(1+i)^{-n})/i$

| n\ | 2% | 3% | 4% | 5% | 6% | 7% | 8% | 9% | 10% | 12% | 15% |
|---|---|---|---|---|---|---|---|---|---|---|---|
| 1 | 0.980 | 0.971 | 0.962 | 0.952 | 0.943 | 0.935 | 0.926 | 0.917 | 0.909 | 0.893 | 0.870 |
| 2 | 1.942 | 1.913 | 1.886 | 1.859 | 1.833 | 1.808 | 1.783 | 1.759 | 1.736 | 1.690 | 1.626 |
| 3 | 2.884 | 2.829 | 2.775 | 2.723 | 2.673 | 2.624 | 2.577 | 2.531 | 2.487 | 2.402 | 2.283 |
| 4 | 3.808 | 3.717 | 3.630 | 3.546 | 3.465 | 3.387 | 3.312 | 3.204 | 3.170 | 3.037 | 2.855 |
| 5 | 4.713 | 4.580 | 4.452 | 4.329 | 4.212 | 4.100 | 3.993 | 3.890 | 3.791 | 3.605 | 3.352 |
| 6 | 5.601 | 5.417 | 5.242 | 5.076 | 4.917 | 4.767 | 4.623 | 4.486 | 4.355 | 4.111 | 3.784 |
| 7 | 6.472 | 6.230 | 6.002 | 5.786 | 5.582 | 5.389 | 5.206 | 5.033 | 4.868 | 4.564 | 4.160 |
| 8 | 7.325 | 7.020 | 6.733 | 6.463 | 6.210 | 5.971 | 5.747 | 5.535 | 5.335 | 4.968 | 4.487 |
| 9 | 8.162 | 7.786 | 7.435 | 7.108 | 6.802 | 6.515 | 6.247 | 5.995 | 5.759 | 5.328 | 4.772 |
| 10 | 8.983 | 8.530 | 8.111 | 7.722 | 7.360 | 7.024 | 6.710 | 6.418 | 6.145 | 5.650 | 5.019 |
| 11 | 9.787 | 9.253 | 8.760 | 8.306 | 7.887 | 7.499 | 7.139 | 6.805 | 6.495 | 5.938 | 5.234 |
| 12 | 10.575 | 9.954 | 9.385 | 8.863 | 8.384 | 7.943 | 7.536 | 7.161 | 6.814 | 6.194 | 5.421 |
| 13 | 11.348 | 10.635 | 9.986 | 9.394 | 8.853 | 8.358 | 7.904 | 7.487 | 7.103 | 6.424 | 5.583 |
| 14 | 12.106 | 11.296 | 10.563 | 9.899 | 9.295 | 8.745 | 8.244 | 7.786 | 7.367 | 6.628 | 5.724 |
| 15 | 12.849 | 11.938 | 11.118 | 10.380 | 9.712 | 9.108 | 8.559 | 8.061 | 7.606 | 6.811 | 5.847 |
| 16 | 13.578 | 12.561 | 11.652 | 10.838 | 10.106 | 9.447 | 8.851 | 8.313 | 7.824 | 6.974 | 5.954 |
| 17 | 14.292 | 13.166 | 12.166 | 11.274 | 10.477 | 9.763 | 9.122 | 8.544 | 8.022 | 7.120 | 6.047 |
| 18 | 14.992 | 13.754 | 12.659 | 11.690 | 10.828 | 10.059 | 9.372 | 8.756 | 8.201 | 7.250 | 6.128 |
| 19 | 15.679 | 14.324 | 13.134 | 12.085 | 11.158 | 10.336 | 9.604 | 8.950 | 8.365 | 7.366 | 6.198 |
| 20 | 16.351 | 14.978 | 13.590 | 12.462 | 11.470 | 10.594 | 9.818 | 9.129 | 8.514 | 7.469 | 6.259 |
| 21 | 17.011 | 15.415 | 14.029 | 12.821 | 11.764 | 10.836 | 10.017 | 9.292 | 8.649 | 7.562 | 6.312 |
| 22 | 17.658 | 15.937 | 14.451 | 13.163 | 12.042 | 11.061 | 10.201 | 9.442 | 8.772 | 7.645 | 6.359 |
| 23 | 18.292 | 16.444 | 14.857 | 13.489 | 12.303 | 11.272 | 10.371 | 9.580 | 8.883 | 7.718 | 6.399 |
| 24 | 18.914 | 16.936 | 15.247 | 13.799 | 12.550 | 11.469 | 10.529 | 9.707 | 8.985 | 7.784 | 6.434 |
| 25 | 19.524 | 17.413 | 15.622 | 14.094 | 12.783 | 11.654 | 10.675 | 9.823 | 9.077 | 7.843 | 6.464 |

# INDEX